POWERFUL
PROPOSALS

POWERFUL PROPOSALS

How to Give Your Business the Winning Edge

DAVID G. PUGH and **TERRY R. BACON**

HarperCollins
Leadership

An Imprint of HarperCollins

Powerful Proposals

© 2005 David G. Pugh and Terry R. Bacon

Published by HarperCollins Leadership, an imprint of HarperCollins Focus LLC.

Any internet addresses, phone numbers, or company or product information printed in this book are offered as a resource and are not intended in any way to be or to imply an endorsement by HarperCollins Leadership, nor does HarperCollins Leadership vouch for the existence, content, or services of these sites, phone numbers, companies, or products beyond the life of this book.

Bulk discounts available. For details visit:
www.harpercollinsleadership.com/bulkquotes
Email: customercare@harpercollins.com

ISBN 978-1-4002-4241-2 (TP)

*We dedicate this book to those hearty souls
everywhere who work against a relentless clock and
other mind-buckling pressures to develop proposals for
their companies, their customers, and the futures of both.*

Contents

Chapter 3:
Getting Your Message Across:
Technical Proposals for Every Reader

Chapter 4:
Selling the Benefits: Customer-Oriented Proposals

Chapter 5:
What It Takes to Win:
Credibility, Acceptability, and Preference

Chapter 6:
Winning Executive Summaries:
Your Most Powerful Selling Tool

Acknowledgments

So many people have "touched" this book as we reflected on our proposal experiences, gathered our thoughts, and wrote the words. We would like to thank them for their various contributions, without which this project would never have been completed. First, our colleagues at Lore International Institute whose cooperation, collaboration, ideas, moral support, and good humor have enriched the writing experience for us: Allison Anderson, Andrea Seid, Anna Pool, Barbara Singer, Ben McDonald, Bill Doherty, Bruce Spining, Chesney Frazier, Dan Osby, Darnell Place-Wise, David Gould, Debby Adjemian, Don Scott, Donna Williams, Eric Baker, Gale Roanoake, Greg Elkins, Gregor Gardner, Jana Freeburn, Jennifer Kwaitkowski, Jennifer Myers, Joey Maceyak, Kathy Uroda, Lat Epps, Laurie Voss, Linda Simmons, Mark Arnold, Martin Moller, Matthew Zick, Michael Hume, Nancy Atwood, Phyllis Lea, Sharon Hubbs, Sheri Ligtenberg, Sidney McDonald, Terryl Leroux, Tobi Wiseman, Torrey Tye, Trish Gyland, Val Evensen, and Wendy Ludgewait.

We are especially indebted to these fine people:

> Bruce Hogge, first a client and then a lifelong friend who collaborates freely across a wide variety of business and business development topics, doing so with a fine wit that adds even more value to the relationship.
> David Winton and Barry Fields with the Association of Proposal Management Professionals. Their belief in and genuine enthusiasm for our work always gives us a second wind just when we need it.
> John McCarthy, whose career path is testimony to the value of a liberal arts education, and who has become a first-class proposal manager and innovator in business development communication.

➤ Orlin "Chick" Davis, Mike Allred, and Filomena Leonardi of Heidrick & Struggles for their ongoing belief in our business development processes, models, and tools.

In many ways this book is grounded in our collaboration with business development professionals around the world, and we take tremendous pleasure in acknowledging them. There are, of course, far too many to cite here, but these people in particular will hear their voices in this work: Al Petrangeli, Al Potter, Al Troppman, Alison Carney, April Kinney, Bill Hardin, Bo Smith, Bob Moss, Bruce Adkins, Bruce Dell, Charles Emmerich, Cindy DePrater, Connie Oliver, David Birtwistle, David Meyers, David Preston, Dennis Norvett, Doug Jones, Eric Krueger, Erich Evered, Frank Henschke, Fred Brune, Fred Marsh, Gary Neff, Greg Meyer, Heidi Smith, Henry van Dyke, Jack Carr, Jan Spendrup, Janet Dodd, Jean-Pierre Jacks, Jim Becker, Jim Hamlin, Joanne Kincer, John Tarpey, Jonas Hogberg, Ken Bailey, Larry Casey, Martin Johansson, Michael Mahanes, Mike Healy, Pat Gallup, Pat Klein, Peter Beaupre, Peter Green, Rob Smith, Robert Van Cleave, Robin Young, Shari Krueger, Sioban Woods, Steve Morgan, Tom Crane, and Wayne O'Neill.

In addition to the Lore colleagues we've already cited, others truly went the distance in helping us to bring our book to completion, and we are grateful for them and their support. Sean Darnall—thought leader, gentle critic, and dogged fly fisherman—has for many years helped us sharpen our thinking and understand where it would lead us. His business acumen has had an impact on much more than this book. Stewart Hannay, who is such a powerful thinker he can enrich us all the way from Scotland even as he sends us a wee jab now and then about the funny way *we* talk. DeNeil Hogan Petersen, a thought partner for many years whose presence is especially felt in our discussions of executive summaries and postaward protocols for debriefing business development initiatives. Tom Fuhrmark, a fine graphic artist and devious snooker player, created the artwork under tough deadlines and sometimes less-than-explicit suggestions from us. Jan Maxedon did a wonderful job tracking the draft-review-revision cycles for each chapter, securing permissions, and implementing the edits.

We also want to give a special thanks to Marci Braddock, a longtime Lore editor, whose flashing red pen was tangible proof of her impressive copyediting skills. She also made countless stylistic suggestions to create a more reader-friendly text. Should a reader not find that to be a quality of our book, the fault is entirely ours, not hers.

Certainly we would be remiss if we failed to acknowledge Ellen Kadin, our AMACOM acquisition editor, for her guidance; her flexibility; and, most important of all, her warm and generous spirit. Her support for this project never faltered, and we are truly grateful.

We are grateful as well for the eleventh-hour contributions made by Ellen Coleman. A true professional, she not only did close editing; she worked wonders in addressing organizational issues both among the chapters and within them.

Then, at some point after the eleventh hour but before the final hour was struck, Niels Buessem stepped in to do some masterful editing, and we're truly thankful for his talents.

At another level entirely, we want to thank our families for their loving support over the years. Their presence has moved us through the inevitable dark hours of writing when nothing is coming, not even the dawn, and one of the few things we can state with bedrock certainty is that we could never be fulfilled without them.

In good proposal fashion, we completed this book late at night while the rest of our world slept. Yet even in our weary, disheveled state, we felt the first excitement from knowing that we were about to bring some of our proposal experiences and thoughts into the light of day. We can only hope that our readers will agree that it was worth the effort.

David G. Pugh
Terry R. Bacon

POWERFUL
PROPOSALS

Introduction

Clients, friends, and even strangers often ask why we named our company Lore International Institute. In particular, they ask, why *Lore*? Our answer to that question goes a long way toward explaining our approach to business development in general (and proposals in particular). One dictionary definition of *lore* is "knowledge gained through study and experience." As you will see, we learned a long time ago that researching past and current thought regarding proposal management and design will always be worthwhile, but the intellectual gain must be tested and validated, or modified or rejected, based on direct experience in the field. Perhaps more than any other business function, proposal expertise requires that practitioners learn by doing . . . and doing . . . and doing.

What's more, you can't go to a college or university, even those with world-class business schools, to learn about proposals for the simple reason that either such a curriculum doesn't exist, period, or doesn't exist in any form directly applicable to how companies create proposals for today's tough markets and the customers who define them. In a very real sense this means that although our book is certainly informed by our study of printed communication of all kinds, it is truly grounded in our hands-on, neckties-off work in the field with our clients. We have shared with them sleepless nights, too much cold pizza, and frazzled nerves—along with the pure joy of attending their victory parties after they've won the day and the deal.

It has often been said that there is nothing new under the sun, and although we could question that as a literal fact, we have to recognize that much of what is considered proposal state of the art and best practices has been around for a number of years. True, the ability to produce proposals electronically—with sophisticated software generating dazzling visuals, full color, and reader-friendly formats—all came about during the last twenty years. With the advent of the computer age, we also gained tremendous power in information discovery, storage, and retrieval to increase our proposal efficiencies, productivity, and richness. Yet with all of this and more at our fingertips, in our practice we still encounter company after company handing their customers proposals that appear to have been created twenty years ago.

Certainly, these companies are smart about many things, and, in most cases, they actually know that they need to invest in improving their proposal systems and tools. That's not their issue. Rather, it is the gap between knowing what to do and actually doing it that stumps many organizations, large and small.

Other companies, having taken the big step of investing in educational programs and consulting services to get their proposal managers and contributors up to snuff on how they're going to work going forward, discover that they're standing still before yet another gap that's more like a chasm: the skill–will–endurance gap. They now have the skill because they have gone through an intensive learning experience, but do they have the will to implement what they have learned? Or, if they have the will, do they have the final critical element—endurance? Can they stay the course? Suffer setbacks and fail forward? Not look for any excuse, during implementation, to return to business as usual?

Granted, creating a powerful proposal is hard work, but it isn't terribly complicated if you have the right tools, models, and processes, and use them effectively over time. Just think about how much work gets thrown at a lousy proposal in the form of false starts, endless revisions, last-minute changes, missing information, combing of boilerplate for hidden disasters, schedule slippages, executive proposal reviews that slash and burn, and so on. Unnecessary complexity is its own enemy and yours, and we haven't written this book to reveal exquisitely complicated, top-secret tips for improving proposals. Rather, we embrace simplicity (as distinct from anything simplistic), and revisiting the basics to write this book led us to new levels of creative thinking about how we develop proposals and what they need to accomplish.

This led us to consider the game of chess as our primary model for business development. (For a fully developed discussion of chess as a model for business development, see "Checkmate! How Business

Development Is Like Chess" in our earlier book *The Behavioral Advantage*.[1]) Figure I-1 shows the chess game of business development and what it accomplishes during opening game, middle game, and endgame.

One of the main reasons this model works so well is that it shows how all the activities either directly or indirectly related to winning contracts in B2B (business-to-business) markets are linked and lead to the award. In the case of proposal activity in endgame, business development is no different from chess. If you wait until endgame to try to win with whatever pieces you have left, you are doomed—unless, by chance, your opponent is equally inept. That happens occasionally in business development, too, and on a given deal you might just pluck victory from the jaws of defeat, but we wouldn't encourage any company to base their business future on that approach.

Instead, in business development, as in chess, you need a skillful opening game and a powerful middle game to become a consistent winner and defeat ever more capable competitors. What we are saying here in part is that our field experience tells us that the post-RFP (request-for-proposal) endgame is not a series of isolated events.

Figure I-1: **The chess game of business development.** Using chess as a way of understanding business development, we know that winning in endgame requires a strong opening game and a powerful middle game.

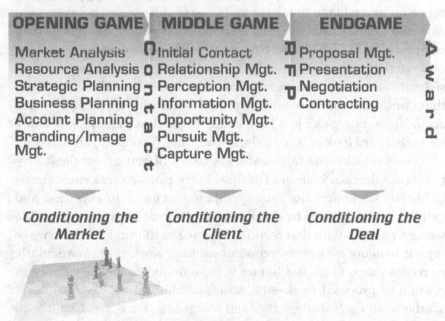

OPENING GAME	MIDDLE GAME	ENDGAME	
Market Analysis	Initial Contact	Proposal Mgt.	A
Resource Analysis	Relationship Mgt.	Presentation	w
Strategic Planning	Perception Mgt.	Negotiation	a
Business Planning	Information Mgt.	Contracting	r
Account Planning	Opportunity Mgt.		d
Branding/Image Mgt.	Pursuit Mgt.		
	Capture Mgt.		

Conditioning the Market   *Conditioning the Client*   *Conditioning the Deal*

Rather, the endgame is driven by all that came before it, and we have found that up to 90 percent of what drives major wins today occurs before the RFP. That's a lot of impact that needs to be accounted for in the proposal, but if it is, the endgame will provide your customer with powerful and compelling reasons to choose you, reasons they were fully aware of before issuing the RFP.

How to Use This Book

Chapter 1 establishes certain ideas and concepts that will reappear throughout the book. The first of these is a necessary discussion of how powerful proposals differ from cookie-cutter, mediocre proposals and why it's important for companies not just to understand the difference but to act on that understanding.

In Chapters 2 through 7 we discuss one of the central ideas of this book: Proposals are fundamentally sales documents, and nowhere does the knowing–doing gap show itself more clearly and more often than right here. Companies know beyond all doubt that their proposals must sell. That's about as basic as it gets. But knowing it and doing it are two very different things, and that is what Chapters 2, 3, and 4 are all about.

At the end of every day, a company needs to consider where, how, and why it is either winning or losing. In the succeeding chapters, we range far and wide to break the code on the differences between winners and losers. Certainly, each competitive procurement has its own peculiarities, but we've also been in the field on enough proposals to observe that certain drivers of wins and losses seem to show up consistently and pervasively year in and year out. One of those drivers is that consistent winners have identified those very drivers and acted accordingly, but losers just keep being driven. In Chapters 5, 6, and 7 we take a hard look at those drivers and what you can do about them.

Next, we tackle the nuts-and-bolts issues of getting excellent proposals out the door on time. That's seldom a pleasant task since across industries customers are reducing their procurement overhead and gaining earlier start-up by shrinking the proposal response period. We wrote Chapter 8 with that Sword of Damocles in mind, because we've seen it hanging over every proposal we have worked on, particularly in recent years. Then, in Chapter 9, we move on to the bare knuckles portion of proposal work—the actual creation of each section after all the analyzing, strategizing, and stargazing are done. Chapter 10 provides a simple, repeatable method for conducting this milestone activity with as much grace and as little pain as possible, while moving the proposal to a higher level of quality as a finished product.

Since a proposal is part of a business development continuum, once it has been submitted and the announcement of the winner and the losers has been made, companies can make huge gains when they have a process in place and effective tools for debriefing the entire effort to win the award. We've seen it happen, and therefore in Chapter 11 you will find both: a process and the tools. The value, both internally and with your customers, of deploying a systematic approach to analyzing each win and each loss cannot be overemphasized.

Appendix A offers a lighthearted retrospective of our experiences and lessons learned working with engineers and other technical professionals over the years.

As you read each chapter, you will notice that now and then our ideas will lap over from one to another—key among these are the metaphor of the chess game of business development and the Big Four questions that proposals must answer. This is not accidental. We repeat these ideas because we believe the reapplication or reconsideration of an idea in a different context serves not only to reinforce an idea but to strengthen both the idea and the context in which it is presented.

You will notice that throughout the book we've sprinkled what we call "Golden Rules." Some are lighthearted, some are straightforward, and some may surprise you. In any case, they crystallize some of the most essential concepts we've discovered while working on proposals large and small, around the world. We've shared these Golden Rules with our clients and others; here we share them with you and hope you enjoy them as markers on your tour through the world of proposals as we've enjoyed them in our daily work. Now, as you begin the journey, we hoist a slice of cold pizza and recommend it as your official proposal salute.

Note

1. Terry R. Bacon and David G. Pugh, *The Behavioral Advantage: What the Smartest, Most Successful Companies Do Differently to Win in the B2B Arena* (New York: AMACOM, 2004).

Chapter 1

THE POWER OF THE
A+ PROPOSAL

Art: The faculty of executing well what one has devised.
—MERRIAM-WEBSTER'S COLLEGIATE DICTIONARY

GOLDEN RULE:

In most cases, proposals do not win contracts, but
they can lose them in a heartbeat.

Every year thousands of companies compete for trillions of dollars in contract awards from other businesses or from local, state, or federal agencies. Except for such tangible and easily specifiable commodities as pencils, coffee mugs, and motor oil, most of these contracts are awarded based on competitive proposals.

In fact, the U.S. government has more than 60,000 federal and military specifications to buy goods and services through the IFB (invitation for bid) process. The specs are issued, any bidder that meets the specs is qualified, the bids are opened publicly, and the lowest-price bidder is declared the winner. The vast majority of contracts awarded by our national government are awarded through this IFB process. However, 85 percent of the money spent annually for goods and services is disbursed through the RFP (request for proposal) process precisely because whatever is being purchased cannot be specified down to a gnat's eyebrow. And often, what's being bought doesn't even exist yet. So, although most contracts go to low bidders who meet the specs, nothing more and nothing less, most of the dollars go to those companies that not only innovate in what they offer but communicate that offer in proposals that differentiate them from the competition. Indeed, the proposal has become so ubiquitous in business life as to warrant a special place in the way most companies organize and staff their business development operations.

The large, sophisticated aerospace and defense contractors have special proposal centers staffed by dedicated proposal managers, writers, editors, coordinators, graphic artists, and production specialists. Even smaller companies often have proposal specialists in departments that support the salespeople who write proposals. Companies also spend millions of dollars annually to educate their salespeople on how to write proposals and millions more hiring consultants to help them craft their "must-win" bids.

To say that much rides on the success of proposals would be a gross understatement. Companies and careers have literally been saved or lost due to the success or failure of a single proposal. Fortunes have been made and dreams dashed based on how favorably a customer viewed a proposal that may have taken its creators months to produce. In the twenty-five years we have been consulting on proposals and educating companies on proposal writing and management, we have seen scores of cases where big wins saved business units and jobs—or losses led to downsizing and outplacement. Proposals are among the most critical documents companies produce, yet they are often ill conceived; ill prepared; and, consequently, ill fated.

In *Powerful Proposals*, we introduce you to the high end of proposal accomplishment: what powerful proposals look like and how to create them. Before moving on, however, it's important to put proposals into perspective. They are critical, yes, but they are one of the final stages in a long business development process that begins well before customers request proposals and companies create them.

The Proposal: The Make or Break Move

Proposals are the critical endgame in a long process of business development. When they are executed with skill and finesse, they can bias customers toward you and act as the "icing on the cake" if you have successfully conducted your opening and middle games—that is, if you have positioned yourself well with the customer, built trust-based relationships, and presold your company and your solution. When proposals are not executed well, they can sour the customer's view of you, cause them to question their decision to award you the contract if they had been inclined to do so, and cost you the opportunity if the competition was close and one of your rivals submitted a superior proposal.

In today's highly competitive environment, proposals are too important to be left to chance. The opportunity costs are too great to risk creating and submitting the kind of uninspiring, lackluster, and nonresponsive proposals that often flood the marketplace. The old chestnut still holds: If it's worth doing, it's worth doing well. If you really want the business, then you should devote the requisite time and attention to mastering the creation of powerful proposals.

How to Put the "Power" into Your Proposals

Proposals are powerful (and ultimately successful) if they are fully responsive to the customer's needs; if they resonate with readers; if they are compelling, engaging, and enlightening; and if they demonstrate care, thoughtfulness, and artistry in their design and execution. Powerful proposals feel right to readers because they both demonstrate and stimulate insight, they make the right connections, they illuminate by exploring the implications of the customer's choices, and they educate. An artful proposal says, in effect, "I understand what you need. Moreover, I understand what you want to do, and of all the possible solutions that might work for you, I have the one that is most capable in its solution, most elegant in its simplicity, and most appropriate for your needs."

This was brought home to us several years ago when, after first working with a client on their proposal and then hearing that they had won the award, we joined them for a debrief with their customer's vice president for procurement. After a lengthy discussion on a variety of topics, we asked one last question: "Can you tell us in a sentence why you preferred our proposal over all the others?" The answer has stayed with us ever since. He said, "When I read your proposal, it was as though I was reading my own thoughts."

➤ *A powerful proposal doesn't just answer questions or list specifications; it tells a story.* Moreover, it tells its story in a compelling way—one that helps readers see the solution in a more insightful and interesting way than they had previously imagined. A powerful proposal builds trust and confidence. It reconfirms the positive perceptions created during the bidder's business development efforts prior to the RFP and proposal. It gives customers a formal basis for selecting the bidder even though, informally and intuitively, that decision might already have been made. A powerful proposal is one that allows the heads of evaluation teams to say to their decision makers, "We unanimously recommend this bidder, and this is why."

➤ *A powerful proposal gives the evaluators what they need to sell you when they go down the hall to make their recommendation.* The minute they do that, they become virtual members of your business development team. Therefore, your proposal must give them what they need to sell you and your solution to the people responsible for making the buying decision. If, in turn, the decision makers need to present their choice to the president or board of directors to get the funding approved, then a powerful proposal gives the decision makers what they need to sell you to the people with the money.

➤ *A powerful proposal requires no translation, no reformatting or repackaging.* It stands alone not only as the instrument of your own sales effort but also as the instrument for your customers to sell their decision internally. Finally, a powerful proposal "speaks" with one voice even though it was written and compiled by many people. You have taken the time and effort to refine the document so that in matters of style, tone, and voice it appears to have been composed by a single mind moving a single hand in a single sitting. It's the collective voice of your company speaking to your customer, and it's the voice that tells your story. How to tell that story in a powerful proposal is ultimately what this book addresses in a variety of ways.

Be Compliant: Powerful Proposals Give Customers What They Request

GOLDEN RULE:
In the early stages of evaluation, they aren't looking for the winner. They're looking for the losers.

To appreciate the difference between proposals that are successful and those that are not, we begin with the most fundamental requirement: *compliance*. This means that the proposal "answers the mail": It complies with the customer's request for information, meets the requirements, answers the questions, and addresses the specifications to the letter. Nothing more, nothing less. Compliance is especially important in evaluated proposals because the evaluators frequently base their scores on the degree to which you have addressed their specifications, responded to their requirements, and provided the information they requested. If you fail to comply fully, you have failed the customer's first test:

Did you listen?
Can you read?
Do you understand what we need?
Will you give us what we need?
Can we trust that your solution will meet our needs?

Compliance is so basic that we should be able to assume it's done all the time. Who could fail to be compliant and still expect to win? Why would they even bother to submit a proposal if it weren't fully compliant?

However, in our years of experience we have seen thousands of proposals that failed this basic requirement. They were declared losers quickly and without reservation. And should a loser go to the effort to ask why they lost, the customer's terse answer is often "Price. Gee, need to get back to work." That is the quickest way ever devised to get a loser out the door or off the phone, and the fact that noncompliance was the real issue may never surface. Discussing the loss in those terms would take time and effort the customer rarely wishes to provide a loser.

The finest proposals not only answer the mail; they do it transparently. They are meticulous in following the customer's lead. They are scrupulous in addressing every requirement and in the order the customer listed them. They play back the customer's language, and they provide aids to help the evaluators see their compliance more easily. The best proposals make it easy for the evaluators to give them a perfect score, at least in terms of answering the mail.

However, if proposals are merely compliant, they may still be mediocre when the standard of compliance is easily met (by competent proposal writers) and therefore does not differentiate one proposal from others that are equally compliant. As we will discuss more fully later in this chapter, we've come to believe that if the customer were to grade proposals on a scale of A to F, a fully compliant one—again, providing nothing more, nothing less than what's required—would receive a C. You can't win deals and build your business getting Cs. You need As, and you need them consistently rather than once in a great while. Ultimately, that's your goal for investing in powerful proposals.

Be Responsive: Powerful Proposals Address Customers' Needs, Key Issues, Values, and Goals

To be truly successful, proposals must also be *responsive* to the customer's needs. Responsiveness goes well beyond mere compliance. Bear in mind that no RFP can ever fully capture the customer's intent. The RFP writers are human. They often work in a procurement function and may be restricted from describing everything that would be helpful for bidders to know. Even when no restrictions exist, few RFP writers are skillful enough to convey fully not only the customer's requirements but their goals, underlying concerns, key issues or hot buttons, and values.

In short, what most RFPs lack is insight. They present the superficial (although usually detailed) picture of *what* the customer wants, but not *why* the customer wants it. As a result, they generally fail to enlighten bidders about the more subtle and intangible factors that led to the customer's decision to purchase this product or service and the hopes, fears, and political concerns that will drive the customer's decision. Compliant proposals focus on the bidder's capability to deliver what the customer has specified in the RFP. Consequently, they focus on the supplier and the *features* of the supplier's solution rather than the customer and the *benefits* those features provide.

Responsive proposals do more. They demonstrate how the provider will help customers achieve their business goals, not just their project or procurement goals. The latter goals are not the end. They are the means to the business end, and a responsive proposal shows astute awareness of this distinction. What most proposals fail to recognize is that the customer is not in the problem-solving business. The millions they are about to invest are just that—an investment—and their ultimate goals define the ROI they must get as a business. The proposal that maps a clear path to that business goal is a proposal that truly understands what's driving the investment and what's at stake.

What Proposals Reveal About You

We spoke earlier about proposals as the endgame in a longer business development process. Briefly, the opening game in business development includes the marketing and positioning that companies do to condition the market and build bias toward themselves and their products or services. *Middle game* begins when you make contact with a prospect or current customer followed by the development of a specific opportunity. The call for proposals signals the end of middle game and the beginning of endgame.

Companies that have a solid opening game give themselves a decided advantage in their markets for the same reasons manufacturers spend billions of dollars on advertising: It pays to build your customer's awareness of and comfort with your product and your company. Middle game (which includes all intelligence-gathering, positioning, selling, and relationship-building activities prior to release of the RFP) is where the major battlefield lies. Middle-game prowess (or lack thereof) separates the winners from the losers. Middle-game intelligence on what's really driving the deal becomes the key informational differentiator for companies that have successfully deployed facilitative selling and relationship management up and down the customer organization. These middle-game insights are the difference between responsive proposals and those that are merely compliant.

In middle game, you undergo a chemistry test with customers. Once they have decided that you are competent—that you can do the job—the critical question in their decision making is not, "Who can do the work?" Rather it is, "With whom do we want to work?" In his book, *Managing the Professional Service Firm*, David Maister reinforces this point:

> *Unless their skills are truly unique, unmatched by any competitor, professionals are never hired because of their technical capabilities. Excellent capabilities are essential to get you into the final set to be considered, but it is other things that get you hired. Once I have decided which firms I will consider in the final set, my focus of enquiry shifts significantly. I am no longer asking "Can you do it?" but rather "Do I want to work with you?" I am no longer interested in the institutional characteristics of your firm, but am now trying to form a judgment about you. By the fact that you are sitting here talking to me, you can assume that you have successfully marketed your firm: Now the time has come to sell yourself.*[1]

Opening and middle games establish the impressions and perceptions you need to create: that you are competent, that you can be trusted, that you are people with whom the customer wants to work, that your solutions are right, and that your price is reasonable for the value you bring. Your proposal needs to reinforce and confirm these perceptions.

Because your proposal is often the first tangible evidence customers have of your ability to serve them, your proposal must make good on the "promises" made during your prior contacts and actions with the customer. If your proposals are compliant, creative, responsive, and insightful, then customers can reasonably assume that that's what you will be like to work with. Conversely, even if you talk a good game, if your proposals are noncompliant, dull, unresponsive, and devoid of insight, then customers may assume that the "real" you is what they saw in the proposal, not what they heard you promise. This means that the quality of your proposal is a critical element of your win probability because it formally sets forth what you will deliver and how you will deliver it.

(Our work in behavioral differentiation tells us that customers don't blithely believe what we say. They believe how we behave. They validate or invalidate our words with our observable behaviors because they know that we behave how we are, and we are how we behave. It follows, therefore, that we are judged in part by our proposal "behaviors"—for example, client-focused, responsive, clear, straightforward, honest—to calibrate how positive or negative the experience of working with us will be.)

Many proposal writers, especially engineers, assume that good proposals are ones that address the requirements, are logical and factual, and accurately describe the proposed technical solution. Although these are important features, they are insufficient because customers don't make decisions based purely on the facts. Of the many false assumptions a technical person can make, this is perhaps the greatest one. David Maister, writing as though he were the customer, explains:

> My impressions and perceptions are created by small actions that are meaningful for their symbolism, for what they reveal. How you behave during the interview (or proposal process) will be taken as a proxy for how you will deal with me after I retain you. Unlike the process of qualification, which is predominantly rational, logical, and based on facts, the selection stage is mostly intuitive, personal, and based on impressions.[2]

Thus, like all great marketing and sales documents, proposals are creators of impressions. Powerful proposals shape readers' perceptions and work as much on the intuitive and subliminal level as they do on the rational, descriptive level. Powerful proposals persuade on many levels and build the impressions they create from the complex interplay of language, design, emphasis, visualization, and packaging.

You can't be exemplary in middle game and perfunctory in endgame. Powerful proposals confirm and reinforce the A+ you earned on the chemistry test during middle game. By addressing not only the customer's bottom-line goals and requirements but also their underlying needs, concerns, values, and hot buttons, powerful proposals give the customer a formal basis for selecting you. They confirm the customer's belief that you can do the work and the customer's intuition that you are the one with whom they want to work.

Six Key Elements of High-Quality Proposals

While customer's impressions are shaped by compliance and responsiveness, there are other important elements of proposal quality: boilerplate, customer focus, page design, compelling story, executive summary, and ease of evaluation. Figure 1-1, The Powerful Proposal Matrix, shows how well these elements are handled in various types of proposals. However, before discussing the types of proposals, let's explore the quality criteria we use to assess how well crafted a proposal is.

Figure 1-1. **The Powerful Proposal Matrix.** The most powerful proposals establish standards of excellence by which other proposals are judged and found wanting.

Proposal Quality Criteria and Proposal Quality Types		Boilerplate (%)	Compliance (%)	Responsiveness (%)	Customer Focus	Creative Page Design	Compelling Story	Executive Summary	Ease of Evaluation
A +	Responsive, artful, and inspired	0	100	100	Best	Best	Best	Best	High
A −	Compliant, responsive, and helpful	10	100	90	Good	Good	Good	Fair	Medium
B	Compliant and generally responsive but uninspired	25	90	75	Fair	Fair	Fair	Fair	Low
C	Compliant but self-absorbed and self-focused	50	75	25	Poor	Fair	Poor	None	Low
D	Noncompliant descriptions of capability	90	25	10	None	Poor	Poor	None	Low
D −	Boilerplate proposals	100	0	0	None	None	None	None	Medium
F	Off-the-shelf brochures and price lists	100	0	0	None	None	None	None	High

1. Boilerplate

Boilerplate is the amount of recycled material included in a proposal. It consists of standardized text (résumés, experience lists, descriptions of previous projects, policies and procedures, standard methods and approaches, equipment descriptions or specifications) and visuals. Some companies create whole sections of proposals that can be recycled from one proposal to the next. Although boilerplate makes proposal writing faster and less expensive (just plug and play, so to speak, and "*voilà!*" you are done), it generally does not make the proposal better.

On numerous occasions, proposal writers have dropped a boilerplate section into a proposal and forgotten to change the previous customer's name. When that happens, there aren't enough *O*s in *doom* to describe the effect on the customer's evaluators. As a rule, the higher the quality of the proposal, the less boilerplate is used, and vice versa. Boilerplate is a convenience—but only for the proposal writer. The signal it sends is that you did not take the time to customize the proposal for your customer.

2. Customer Focus

A poorly written proposal focuses on the seller and what is being sold, not the buyer. The worst proposals are narcissistic and self-involved— they prattle on about the seller's experiences and capabilities as though customers will be as impressed with them as they are with themselves. The best proposals, on the other hand, link everything to the customer's goals, needs, and requirements. They provide a problem-solving roadmap for the customer rather than an advertisement for the seller's equipment and capabilities. In a seller-focused proposal, the seller's capabilities are the end; in a customer-focused proposal, the seller's capabilities are the means to the customer's end.

3. Creative Page Design

Presentation isn't everything, but it counts for a lot. Twenty-five years ago, when computers and proposal writers were less sophisticated, the standards for page design and format were lower. Today, anyone with a laptop and reasonable competence in Microsoft Word, Power-Point, and Excel (or equivalent programs) can create outstanding page layouts and visuals. The state of the art has advanced not only in computer equipment and software but also in the average proposal writer's knowledge of page design principles. It's inexcusable today not to bring design knowledge to bear in creating elegant proposals, with page designs that draw the reader's eye to the right places, emphasize what's important, and make comprehension of the offer and solution considerably easier. (For a fuller discussion of designing proposals, see Chapters 3 and 9.)

4. Compelling Story

A well-made proposal tells a compelling story of the offer and the offerer in the context of what the customer needs to succeed. It engages readers in the tale first by focusing on them and their problems and needs. Then it weaves in the seller's solution, showing how the choices being made are the best ones, how the solution addresses the problem in a convincing and elegant way, how the seller has thought through all the potential barriers and alternatives, and why the seller's solution is better than competing solutions. What makes it compelling is that the proposal answers the questions, "Why us?" and "Why not them?" (Chapter 2 provides discussion and examples of addressing the Big Four, including "Why us?" and "Why not them?")

5. Executive Summary

In the past twenty-five years, you can trace the development of the proposal by observing the development of the executive summary. In the past, executive summaries were optional and were often blocky narratives that simply summarized the key points in the proposal. Today, an outstanding proposal includes a separate, full-color, brochure-style executive summary that is well designed, highly customer focused, and succinct in telling the story of the offer. If you haven't mastered the brochure executive summary, then you aren't competing at the high end, and you are losing business to companies that *have* mastered this art (see Chapter 6).

6. Ease of Evaluation

Finally, a powerful proposal is easy to evaluate. It is reader friendly. The customer's evaluators have no difficulty finding what they need or understanding how your proposed solution addresses their goals, needs, and requirements. The irony, as Figure 1-1 shows, is that the worst proposals are relatively easy to evaluate; it is clear from a glance that they aren't compliant, aren't responsive, aren't customer focused, and don't tell a compelling story. In short, it's easy to discard them.

On the opposite end, the best proposals are easy to evaluate because their authors have used many techniques to make the relevant information easy to find and score. Middle-of-the-road proposals are actually the most difficult to evaluate because the information is often hard to find, and evaluators have to spend a lot of time searching before they realize that some of what they need simply isn't there.

Evaluating Proposals: The Best and the Worst

Looking again at Figure 1-1, you will see that we have classified proposals according to letter grades to make it easy to see the differences between the losers and the winners.

F

The worst proposals submitted are off-the-shelf brochures and price lists. They show no insight into the customer's problems and convey little desire for the work. They are a convenience to the seller. A potential customer calls for information, and the seller drops some standard brochures and a price list into an envelope and puts it in the mail. This type of response requires the least effort from the seller and provides the least information to the customer. It signals that the seller is not terribly interested in the work, has taken no time to learn more about customer's needs, and has made little effort to customize a response. These are easy proposals to evaluate because customers can determine quickly whether the equipment meets the specs, and brochures are easy to file away—or throw away.

D–

Boilerplate proposals are typically built by a salesperson from boilerplate components. We've seen fairly sophisticated operations where boilerplate proposal sections are kept on a server, and the salesperson downloads the relevant sections and assembles a completed proposal. There may or may not be a customized cover letter, but the contents are usually standard. If the boilerplate sections are well constructed, it may be easy for customer evaluators to sign off on whether the proposed equipment meets the specs. Otherwise, these kinds of proposals are little better than off-the-shelf brochures and price lists.

D

Next are noncompliant descriptions of capability. A surprising number of these types of proposals are submitted every year. In these proposals, the authors have looked at the RFP and tried to provide the information requested, but they haven't been meticulous in responding to every request or requirement, and they have focused almost exclusively on their own capabilities and products. These proposals are generally very difficult to evaluate because it isn't immediately clear whether the information that evaluators need is in the proposal. The biggest problem with these proposals is compliance. They generally lose because evaluators can't find the information they need, usually because the proposal writers have not answered the mail. These proposals often contain a disproportionately high amount of boilerplate and are not well designed. The primary signal they send to customers is, "We don't care enough to do a better job."

C

Considerably better in quality, but still not good, are proposals that are compliant but self-absorbed and self-focused. In these proposals, the writers have tried to answer the mail and often do a good job of it—enough to get high marks from the evaluators on the literal offer. However, they focus on themselves; don't link the features of their offer to the customer's goals, issues, and requirements via compelling benefits; and don't tell an engaging story. Many engineers and scientists who write proposals fall into this trap. They assume that well-written technical descriptions are compelling in and of themselves—and this is almost never true. Their attitude seems to be, "The customer asked how we approach XYZ, and here's how we approach it.

Period." These proposals fail to explore why XYZ is important, why the seller's approach to XYZ is preferable to other approaches, or how the seller's solution solves the problem created by XYZ. In short, C proposals don't sell; they describe.

B

Proposals that almost make the grade are those that are compliant and generally responsive but that are uninspired. These proposals answer the mail and show some insight into the customer's needs, but they do only a fair job of making a compelling case. Often, they don't link the customer's goals, issues, and requirements to the features of the offer, don't explain the benefits of those features, and don't provide enough proof of the benefits. Although okay, these proposals seem flat and disengaged. They are competent but not compelling. If you are well positioned going into the proposal evaluations, a B proposal won't cost you the win, but it also won't light anyone's fire or give you an additional edge in a tight race.

A−

Excellent proposals are compliant, responsive, and helpful. They are fully customized for the customer (i.e., they have no recognizable boilerplate), they are creative, and they show considerable insight. What makes them less than stellar is the degree of artfulness and creativity in their page design, executive summary, and visuals. These are good proposals—better than many companies are capable of creating—but are not quite the state of the art.

A+

These are the most outstanding proposals and warrant the highest rating. They are as well designed as the A− proposals but have even more creative page designs and customer focus. Generally, when writers have learned to create these kinds of proposals, they have also mastered executive summary design and are accomplished at telling a compelling story.

In our years of consulting on business development, we have seen A+ proposals that were so good they became collector's items. You know your proposal has achieved the highest grade when the customer calls and asks for more copies of it, or asks for your executive summary because they want more people to see it. You have mastered the proposal art when your work is so well done that your customers use it—with very little revision—to sell the project to their board. Or, after winning the award, when you debrief with the customer for lessons learned, and they tell you, "That is the finest proposal we've ever seen. If only all proposals could be like yours."

It just doesn't get any better than that, and you have learned the value of competing not by going head-to-head with competitors, but by raising your customer's expectations. Every time this happens, you have raised the bar for the competition. The powerful proposal is the highest achievement in proposal writing, and it occurs only when proposal writers meet all the criteria. In today's tough markets, you can't win with Cs in any aspect of business development, and getting an A+ on every proposal is what this book is all about.

There are many, many drivers of the buying decision outside the proposal and the evaluation process, such as the trust, credibility, and compatibility a company establishes pre-RFP; past performance on similar contracts; financial stability; or established positive relationships with local subcontractors and suppliers, to name but a few. The power of the A+ proposal is that it gives the customer a benchmark of excellence by which to judge other proposals and find them wanting. Furthermore, the A+ proposal basically tells the customer, "If you're going to look for a reason to eliminate us, you'll have to look elsewhere." When all those other factors combine to drive the buying decision, the proposal simply cannot overcome them. Still, to raise your probability (but never to absolute certainty) of winning to the highest possible level, an A+ proposal is a powerful investment for you and your customer. It tilts the playing field in your direction.

Although proposals are the products of the endgame in a long business development process, they are critically important because they reinforce the impressions you have created in your pre-RFP efforts and give your customers the justification for selecting you. There is an art to doing them well, and if you want to win more than your share of the business, you must master the proposal art.

Challenges for Readers

➤ How powerful are your company's proposals? Pull a couple of representative proposals off the shelf and assess them using our Powerful Proposal Matrix (see Figure 1-1). Grade them accordingly, and then begin mapping where your proposal philosophy, process, and tools can be adjusted to produce more powerful proposals.

➤ If you can legally and ethically gain copies of competitors' proposals, assess them with the Powerful Proposal Matrix. If any of them get a higher grade than your proposals, you've just discovered a positive differentiator for them, a negative differentiator for your company. It's time to develop next steps to reverse that situation.

➤ Debrief with your customers after each award is announced, win or lose. Among the many questions you may ask, be sure to include some that will help you to understand how much your customers value what we have called "powerful proposals." Offer your customers the criteria from Figure 1-1 and ask if they have value when evaluating proposals. The voice of your customers can and should drive your continuous process improvements for proposals.

Notes

1. David Maister, *Managing the Professional Service Firm* (New York: The Free Press, 1993), p. 112.
2. Ibid., p. 114.

Chapter 2

A SIMPLE NOTION

A Proposal Must Sell, Not Just Tell

GOLDEN RULE:

First and foremost, a proposal is a sales document.

A proposal is many things, depending on who is preparing it and who is reading it. Although the content will vary widely by industry and market, a typical proposal contains an abundance of technical, programmatic, personnel, scientific, product, background, legal, pricing, and/or contractual information in various combinations. Despite that, at the most fundamental level, a proposal is *not* a technical treatise, a scientific monograph, a textbook on project management, or a legally binding contract (at least not when submitted and evaluated, though it may eventually form the basis for a contract or be incorporated into the contract by reference). Rather, the "DNA" of a proposal is that it's a sales document. You have to sell your technical approach, your project management expertise, your scientific wizardry, your state-of-the-art solution. If all you do is clinically and bloodlessly describe these things, you are failing to give the customer compelling and substantive reasons to choose your offer rather than someone else's.

None of this is terribly new or innovative, as most proposal professionals and others who contribute to proposals would agree. Yet the very fact that this fundamental understanding of proposals as sales documents has been around for years and still the vast majority of proposals we critique—either in the draft stage or after they have gone to the customers—are *not even close* to being sales documents is nothing short of amazing. They describe. They define. They discuss. They illustrate. But they don't sell. Perhaps even more stunning is that the bedrock principles of selling (e.g., benefits, value added, the value proposition, solution selling, consultative selling, and so on) are hardly new to the selling scene.

(In our earlier book *The Behavioral Advantage*,[1] we trace these concepts as far back as the late nineteenth century. You would think that by now we would have at last gotten and implemented the message, yet that gap between knowing and doing is still there, memorialized in proposal after proposal. It's probably true that by now everyone *knows* about the role of benefits in selling, but it's equally true that they still aren't *acting* on what they know by consistently deploying those benefits in their proposals.)

The DNA of Proposals: How Organizations Buy Products and Services

Proposals are sales tools, but the product or service being proposed is often technical. That places proposals in the uncomfortable middle ground between marketing and engineering. They are technical documents, yet they differ from most other technical documents in at least four fundamental ways: purpose, audience, organization, and reader intent.

Purpose

The purpose of a proposal is to persuade readers to accept your offer to sell them a product or service. Most proposals are written in a competitive environment, so a further purpose of the proposal is to convince readers that your offer is superior to (or more beneficial than) your competitors' offers. A proposal is an offer that can be legally accepted, so the ideal proposal is one that closes the deal and results in a contract. Perhaps one definition of a perfect proposal, if one should ever be written, is that it would be incorporated into the contract by reference with no changes whatsoever.

Audience

The audience or readership of a proposal usually consists of a number of technical and nontechnical readers. Most other technical documents have a narrower and more technical audience, but a proposal must be written for a wide array of readers, including many who might not understand highly technical discussions. (Chapter 3 offers an extended discussion of designing technical proposals for mixed audiences.)

Organization

Most other technical documents are organized according to the logic of technical and scientific reports:

> ➤ Introduction
> ➤ Materials and Methods
> ➤ Results
> ➤ Conclusions
> ➤ Recommendations

In contrast, proposals are usually organized according to the customer's need for information. Most often the RFP dictates what topics will be covered and in what order. This order often reflects the way in which the customer's reviewers will look at the proposals and evaluate them. In fact, most proposals are broken apart into smaller sections, and evaluators receive only the portion of each competing proposal they will actually evaluate.

Reader Intent

A final fundamental difference between proposals and other types of technical documents is the reader's intent. Readers of proposals do not read for professional enlightenment. They do not read simply for information, nor do they read out of curiosity. They read proposals to make a buying decision or at least to recommend one to a decision maker. If it's a competitive situation, as it usually is, they read to differentiate among two or more providers of the product or service being procured.

As a result, proposal readers are evaluative. They differentiate among competitors based on evaluation or selection criteria, which may be formal or informal, stated or unstated, objective or subjective. Interestingly, even when the criteria are formal, stated, and objective, decisions are usually also based on informal, unstated, and subjective criteria. That's why it pays to know the customer well. You want to influence those hidden factors.

GOLDEN RULE:
To write an effective proposal, you must know and
address the customer's selection criteria—including the hidden,
subjective factors not revealed in the solicitation.

How Buying Decisions Are Made

One of the most important of the customer's selection criteria is price. In federal government procurements, the selection of any vendor other than the lowest-priced vendor must be justified. In business purchasing, lowest price is not mandated by law or regulation, but good business sense dictates that lowest price be a significant factor in supplier selection, and this indeed is the usual practice.

When price is not an issue (e.g., when several competitors' prices are close and within the customer's budget parameters), then other factors play an increasingly significant role in the selection. Knowing this, most bidders try to promote the added value they bring to the product, service, or business relationship. This concept—*value added*—is extremely important in today's highly competitive business environment.

The importance of value-added sales stems from the fact that so many competing firms are technically on a par. It's rare nowadays to find one firm technically head and shoulders above its competition. The leveling of technology has occurred for a variety of reasons:

> ➤ Scientific breakthroughs and technical innovations are rapidly communicated via the media, professional publications, trade shows, and so on.
> ➤ Talented engineers and scientists transfer among competing firms.
> ➤ Internal R&D and widespread reverse engineering are used to assimilate the state of the art as it develops.
> ➤ Many companies use benchmarking or related tools to reach state of the art with their competitors, which has the effect of eliminating or reducing differentiation among competing firms.
> ➤ The market's incessant effort to declare technical products and services as commodities drives prices even lower.

So we face a constant struggle in writing proposals: how to help the customer differentiate between us and our competitors. To do so, we must show that our firm adds value to every aspect of a project. We'll say more about this later, but the key point here is that value added is a customer-oriented concept. For us to even address the added value we bring, we must look at the project from the customer's perspective. That, in itself, is an achievement.

They Won't Buy, Unless You Sell

As we consider what we've learned from the field, we find a huge gap between what we know proposals need to be and what in reality they are. It's the gap between a cerebral grasp of something and the tactical development of it. It's the gap between what people in an organization *know* about proposals—theory, models, education, and philosophy— and what they actually *do* when they roll up their sleeves and set about creating proposals. That's the gap,[2] and it can be seen in a variety of ways in finished proposals:

> ➤ Unaltered product descriptions complete with technical specifications. Originally written for the precise and valid reason of describing the product, they don't sell because their original function had nothing to do with proposals and everything to do with satisfying product and packaging law.
> ➤ Generic descriptions, standard definitions, and graphics used in proposal after proposal without being tailored to the specific customer or recast to sell to that customer.
> ➤ Proposal text that, although generated for a specific proposal, does little more than passively describe, define, and discuss without addressing why the customer needs what is being offered and how it will benefit them. This conveys the attitude, "It is what it is. Enough said. And this is what it costs."
> ➤ A proposal design that does not recognize the diverse audience it needs to communicate with and doesn't include the appropriate steps to get its message through. (For a full discussion of this particular challenge, communicating with mixed audiences, see Chapter 3.)
> ➤ An obvious lack of strategy-driving proposal design and communication, which would highlight your strengths, ameliorate your weaknesses, neutralize the competitors' strengths, and ghost their weaknesses.

Powerful Proposals: Simple, Clear, and Precise

Another amazing gap we find in proposals as much today as ten or more years ago (especially in technology proposals) is the difference between what any competent proposal professional knows about quality written communication (e.g., clarity, concision, precision) and what actually ends up on the pages of a typical proposal. There we find nothing less than an engineering obsession with technical nuance, detail, elegance, and validity—a sort of bloodless inflation of the technical ego that has blinded the proposal contributors to what the customer really needs to buy and why. The assumption behind these pages is clearly, "Great technology sells itself, and anyone who understands the technology will readily agree. If we build it, they will come."

In the mid-1980s, a high-technology aerospace company was competing for a contract with the U.S. Air Force to design and manufacture a state-of-the-art camera to be mounted aboard military satellites orbiting Earth. Their proposal—a monument to engineering elegance, robustness, and complexity—got them to a shortlist of finalists and the opportunity to deliver a formal, oral presentation to the customer, including a three-star general. After two hours of technical jargon, algorithms, calculations, intricate schematics, high-density discussions of camera optics, and so on, they concluded by asking if anyone in the audience had any questions. Everyone fidgeted for several silent seconds until the general cleared his throat and asked, "Will it take a picture?"

Another gap amazes us whenever we posit the simple notion that a proposal is fundamentally a sales document. This is the gap that exists in people's minds between what they know and assume is valid (if only because no one has ever challenged it) and what they don't know that they don't know. Only slightly tongue in cheek, we call this the "knowing–not knowing gap." We see it expressed year after year in looks of incredulity on people's faces when we begin to discuss a proposal's DNA. After making the point that a proposal is a sales document, we often ask, "What does it mean to 'sell'?" The answers are slow in coming and unsure, as we see people for the first time confronting that gap between what they have done based on what they know, and what they need to do based on what they need to learn. The beauty of all this doesn't end with that discovery, but instead leads us back to the beginning, and the simple notion about selling now makes so much difference in creating superior proposals.

Look at it this way: Engineering is complicated, project management is complicated, contracting is complicated, and procurement law or policy is complicated. Add to these truths the fact that most customers today do what they do in a complex world where they invariably face complex problems requiring complex solutions. With all these layers of complexity, what do you suppose customers might value from providers? More complexity? A proposal so dense that only a handful of people on the planet Earth could possibly understand it, let alone appreciate and value how it directly and successfully addresses their problems and needs? No, they value simplicity (keeping in mind the critical distinction between something simple and something simplistic, the latter being unacceptable), clarity, and a clear path to success.

Four Compelling Questions
Every Proposal Must Answer

Understanding this much about a customer leads us to the real point: *Selling isn't complicated*. It's just very important in the tough markets you face every day to build your business. Why? Because what customers really crave from proposals is a clear and thoughtful response, set forth in ways both experts and nonexperts can comprehend, that convincingly demonstrates how they can close the gap between where they are now and where they need to be to achieve their business goals.

Understanding that provides the opportunity to create powerful differentiation not just in what you offer, but in how your offer is communicated, how it is sold. In fact, when you set out to sell in a proposal, you are really attempting to answer just four questions better than your competitors (who, based on our experience, won't even attempt to answer them, thereby giving you a tremendous advantage). We call these questions the Big Four:

1. Why us?
2. Why not them?
3. So what?
4. How so?

There they are. Four simple questions. If you provide powerful answers to them throughout your proposals, you will also provide your customers with compelling and substantive reasons to choose you, which is what selling is all about.

Question 1: Why Us?

Your best answers to "Why us?" are found in your positive differentiators (i.e., what you offer that's different and better, relative to the customer's needs, than what the competition offers). *These differentiators are your aces*, and you turn them into deal makers in your proposal.

What develops between you and your customer—trust, credibility, compatibility, information, insight, and so on—during the crucial middle game leading to the RFP will go a long way toward determining how well positioned you'll be when the customer's evaluators are faced with the often daunting task of assessing your proposal and those of your competitors. Which one will they use as a baseline of excellence? Which one provides powerful, customer-focused answers to the Big Four, answers that will move them to the right choice? (The Introduction provides a brief discussion of the chess game of business development. For an expanded discussion of business development and the game of chess, see also "Checkmate! How Business Development Is Like Chess" in our earlier book *The Behavioral Advantage*.[3])

To be sure, the customer shouldn't suddenly discover your answers for the first time when they appear in your proposal. Rather, they begin to take on shape and substance throughout your middle-game contacts with the customer, becoming more focused and compelling as more information is exchanged and insight gained. Then as the RFP approaches, your answers to "Why us?" are matured and validated, ready to be driven into the proposal as major, compelling messages during the evaluation process.

One definition of proposal excellence is that it formally confirms what the customer has already informally determined during middle game, namely, that they should choose your company and its offer over all the others. As Figure 2-1 shows, the best answers to "Why us?" are the positive differentiators that make up the *Sweet Spot*. Conversely, any negative differentiators—the *Sour Spot*—will make a competitor appear more attractive in the customer's eyes, something you can ill afford to have happen. After all, winning is tough enough in today's markets without giving your competition an undeserved assist.

The key to developing quality answers to "Why us?" lies in the willingness and ability to grow the Sweet Spot and shrink the Sour Spot, ideally into nonexistence. When you work to accomplish these two objectives, you are shaping and managing the customer's perceptions of your company and your competitors.

One of the best definitions of "business development" we've ever come across is that it is "the management of perception." Yet one of the most common problems we've encountered working with our clients on their proposals is that they wait too long to get serious about

The Sour Spot

Our Weaknesses   **Their Strengths**

Customer Needs

Our Strengths   **Their Weaknesses**

The Sweet Spot

Figure 2-1. **Sweet Spot and Sour Spot.** The Sweet and Sour Spots contain your positive and negative differentiators, respectively. The former are deal makers; the latter are deal breakers.

what it takes to grow that Sweet Spot with differentiating answers to "Why us?" and, likewise, to attack the Sour Spot's negative answers to the same question. Doing that successfully takes strategies (see Figure 2-2) that cannot suddenly be pulled out of a hat like so many rabbits after the RFP arrives but must be developed and deployed as early in middle game as you can determine that the opportunity is real.

When Price Is an Issue. Consider this simple and often unnerving fact: One differentiator the customer can *always* use to make the buying decision exists at the southeast corner of the spreadsheet: price. Therefore, if you are not the low-price provider, you are not just selling your approach, offer, solution, and company. *You need to sell your price*, and that means you need strategies to move your higher price from its natural location in the Sour Spot to a prominent place in the Sweet Spot, where it coexists with and relies on your other compelling answers to "Why us?" Those answers sell your price and allow the customer to conclude that although your price isn't low or lowest, all things considered your offer is truly worth it.

Our research into modern purchasing practices reveals some startling concepts that fly in the face of popular thought about low price as the only or principal selection criterion today. (For a full discussion

Figure 2-2. **Sweet Spot and Sour Spot with strategy elements.** You need middle-game strategies to move the circles, thereby expanding the Sweet Spot and shrinking the Sour Spot. Ideally, the latter disappears from the customer's mind when they issue the RFP.

and analysis of our research into today's procurement practices, see "The Changing World of Buying and Selling" in our earlier book *The Behavioral Advantage.*[4]) For example, almost all the senior executives who participated in our study agreed that lowest price simply cannot be the primary selection criterion when choosing providers. Instead, they are looking very closely at lowest total cost or lowest cost of ownership, the initial price being but one data point in a much larger calculation. Taking this tack as a major strategy for answering "Why us?" requires superb thoughtfulness not only about what to say but about where and when to begin delivering the message that will help to sell your price.

The process of winning begins long before the first word of an RFP is written. Certainly, you may need to develop some win strategies based on the solicitation, but key win strategies for pre-RFP positioning should have been developed in middle game as part of your opportunity pursuit and your efforts to manage customer perceptions. If, for example, you know that the customer places high value on the quality of your proposed project team, you would identify your

A-team in middle game so that they can connect with the customer to build trust, credibility, and compatibility.

Similarly, your proposal would focus on the team members' qualifications and accomplishments placed in the context of this customer's upcoming project. Likewise, if your company has innovated a technology solution, you would not want to keep it under wraps until you submitted the proposal. You would share at least enough of this technical breakthrough to ensure that the customer knows you've got it (but not so much that it could be copied or shared with other companies), and then develop it as the centerpiece solution in the proposal. By driving your middle-game strategies (or adjusted versions of them) into your endgame proposal, you clinch what they have come to know over time: whom to choose and why.

Question 2: Why Not Them?

The best way to answer "Why not them?" involves a technique called *ghosting*. Essentially, you know enough about the competition's offers/approaches/products/track record to discuss the disadvantages to the customer of using the competition (*them*) versus the advantages of using what *you* provide. To put it another way, you are using what's in your Sweet Spot not just to cast favorable light on your company and offer but to cast shadows of doubt on your competitors. The following example, which draws from a real federal government procurement for a state-of-the art airplane, illustrates this technique. The competitive field consisted of aerospace teams specializing in either single-engine or dual-engine aircraft. One of the latter teams used ghosting in both the executive summary and the proposal itself:

> Unlike a single-engine aircraft with **no power backup** in case of *engine failure*—thereby placing both the pilot and the plane at **ultimate risk**—our dual-engine design provides 100 percent redundancy for maximum safety and risk reduction with **only** a 12 percent increase in fuel consumption at required cruising speed and altitude [bold added for emphasis].

This ghost, well crafted and straightforward as it is, incorporated the additional strategy of *counterghosting* what this proposal team believed the competition would most likely ghost on them: additional cost of operation due to a second engine. By considering that ghost, they were simultaneously answering "Why us?" and "Why not them?" Furthermore, the knockout punch, so to speak, was the implication of the counterghost: a 12 percent increase in fuel consumption? What a small price to pay to protect a pilot's life and a multimillion-dollar airplane as well.

The critical factor here, of course, is the need to create your ghosts without ever mentioning a competitor by name. Doing so could back-fire, because not only have you made them the sympathetic underdog, but in the process you have willingly flirted with unethical behavior. One of the best ways to avoid the problem of a ghost even implying a specific competitor is to aim the ghost at your industry whenever your offer includes a Sweet Spot item that is unique, a best practice, or superior in some significant way to whatever the competition can pro-vide. If, for instance, your company's safety record is ranked number one by an independent agency such as OSHA (Occupational, Safety, and Health Administration), then by stressing the human, economic, and legal risk of safety infractions during the project, you compel the customer to consider safety as a heavily weighted selection criterion and to scrutinize all candidate companies accordingly.

Powerful answers to "Why not them?" demand a delicate touch, and ham-handed efforts at ghosting—exaggerations, distortions, par-tial truths, and the like—will invariably fail. What is more, effective ghosting allows you not just to sell yourself but to *unsell* the competi-tion. To put it another way, if you really want to compete on a level playing field, don't bother answering "Why not them?" before the RFP and in the endgame proposal. Just focus on your own strengths and hope that will be enough, but be warned, in most cases it won't be because the customer actually does need answers to this question to make an intelligent informed buying decision. Helping them to make that decision with honest, accurate answers is a major value you can and should add to your proposals.

Question 3: So What?

In more than twenty years of working with clients around the world, one of our favorite challenges has been providing great answers to "So what?" It may be the single most common question asked by custom-ers everywhere, culture, nationality, and procurement processes not-withstanding. What is most interesting, however, is how seldom that question is vocalized versus how often it is simply thought, accompa-nied by a slight furrowing of the brow. We've concluded that if it were possible to see a cartoon-like thought balloon next to a customer's head while he or she evaluated proposals, we would read the words

"So what?" in English-speaking countries—and "*Na und?*" in Germany, "*Et alors?*" in France, "*Nou en?*" in The Netherlands, "*En dan*" in Belgium, and "*Daka ra nani*" in Japan. In other words, this is true the world over, not just in the United States, so bear it in mind should you ever have to create a proposal for a customer in another country. Customer behavior in this regard appears to be universal, and so is the element in proposals prompting the question.

GOLDEN RULE:
Customers don't buy what it is; they buy what it *does* for them. They buy *benefits*, not features.

We began this chapter talking about the gap between what proposal teams know they *should* do and what they *actually* do in the heat of battle (read "response time from RFP receipt to submittal").

One of the most glaring gaps is the one created by *knowing* that a proposal that sells is benefits rich and then *producing* a proposal lacking benefits but stuffed with technical and other features. Indeed, clients often begin the discussion of selling with statements such as "Everybody knows about features and benefits," or "Hammering on selling benefits is just too basic for our organization. We traveled that road years ago." When we have looked at recent proposals, regardless of whether the client ultimately won or lost the deals, to determine whether they are indeed benefits rich, we have found, in practically every instance, that the proposals were laden with features of the offer, but that little was said about what those features would do for the customer.

Since proposals focus primarily on the details of the offer, which are often technical and/or programmatic in nature, they end up stuffed with the solution features, including endless technical and other details defining what the proposal team thinks and hopes the customer will buy. Yet those features actually cause the customer to ask, "So what?" For example, a company might state:

"Our team brings 233 years of collective experience to your project."

This is an impressive feature, but a feature nonetheless, and therefore rather meaningless to the customer unless you mention the compelling, bottom-line benefits associated with the feature, such as:

"Our team's 233 years of collective experience provides proactive problem solving, diminished learning curve, proven methodologies, and lowest possible risk of budget and schedule creep."

Features give rise to "So what?" Benefits answer the question. If a proposal's DNA defines it as a sales document, then by definition it must be benefits rich. In technical proposals, however, it's especially easy to be duped into believing that your answer to "So what?" is a benefit when, in fact, it's another feature masquerading as a benefit.

A technical person, for instance, might cite a state-of-the-art processing chip as a compelling reason to buy that company's computer, and if confronted with "So what?" would immediately answer, "It's faster." Well, it is, but speed is a feature, not a benefit, to a customer trying to decide where to spend a lot of money on computers as a business investment. We know its speed is a feature because, from the buyer's point of view, the question, "So what?" is still hanging in the air, waiting for an answer. If, however, the proposal cites greater productivity, lower long-distance charges, and less downtime for transmission of large files, then the answer has effectively responded to what the customer needs and is willing to pay for.

In a business context, this much seems certain: Customers spend large sums of money not to solve a problem—after all, they aren't in the problem-solving business—but to achieve certain business goals. The best benefits you can offer, therefore, are *bottom-line benefits that help the customer achieve their bottom-line goals*. In this context, we doggedly maintain that nobody needs a chain saw. Nobody. What they need is a method of cutting firewood that saves time and effort over alternate means (such as an axe) while increasing total output. In other words, for someone with this goal in mind, the chain saw, replete with technical features, provides the benefits that meet the goal. If, however, the person's goal is a soulful communion with nature in the forest primeval, punctuated with the occasional "thunk" of an axe in a tree trunk, then the chain saw's features and benefits are totally inappropriate. The key, then, is to understand what the customer needs to achieve in making the investment, and then align your offer and its benefits with their goal.

To develop the connection among features, benefits, and goals, we use an approach, shown in Figure 2-3, that links the customer's goals with their key issues, the features of the offer, and the benefits of those features. Finally, to build trust and credibility, we always provide proofs that those benefits are real for the customer.

The Decision-Making Process. Almost without exception the person or persons evaluating your proposal will not make the final buying decision. Their role is to make recommendations to the decision mak-

Figure 2-3. **GIFBP (goals, issues, features, benefits, proofs) Matrix.** The sum of the benefits you offer should get your customer to their goal.

Goals	Issues	Features	Benefits	Proofs
22 months to start-up to capture 23% share in emerging market	• Proven fast-track capability	• Complete in-house siting, licensing, engineering, procurement, and construction	• Minimizes duplication, administration, coordination • Accelerates problem solving • Single point of responsibility, accountability • Seamless transitions for all phases • Lowest possible risk of schedule creep	• Numerous projects fast-tracked with start-ups on or ahead of schedule (e.g., Norwood Refinery, Andreas Platform, ABC Ethylene Plant)

Bottom-Line Benefit

er(s) after carefully weighing the merits of each proposal as measured against their evaluation, or selection, criteria. Having reached a conclusion, they will communicate their recommendation to the appropriate executive for final approval to proceed to negotiations and contracting.

This is crucial because the minute these evaluators communicate their choice, they join your business development team. Your proposal needs to give them what they need to sell your company and its offer. If, drawing from the proposal's own language, they submit their recommendation in favor of ACME because their project team is horizontally organized, the decision maker's first question will be, "So what?" If, instead, the recommendation includes powerful benefits for that feature (e.g., responsiveness, less bureaucracy, one-to-one communication with customer counterparts), then your new business developers inside the customer's organization have what they need to sell effectively on your behalf. They also have what they need to appear fully capable of making a sound business decision in the executive's eyes, and that is the differentiating value added of a powerful proposal in this feature-intensive world in which we work.

Question 4: How So?

One of the quickest and surest ways to lose trust and credibility is to give the customer a "trust us" proposal—to ask for trust without having earned it. The proposal might claim the company's ability to compress the customer's project schedule by six months but never explain how that will be accomplished or provide any evidence of past successes in accelerating schedules. The proposal fairly oozes "trust us," and customers see the red flag of risk waving from every page.

One part of creating an excellent proposal is ensuring that, in addition to the features and the benefits getting the customer to their goals, it includes proofs and substantiations for all of its major claims. If you claim that you can reduce the customer's production costs by 16 percent with your process engineering efficiencies, anticipate that the customer will read that claim and immediately ask, "How so?" The question itself is not just a challenge; it's an opportunity to create significant differentiation. When you provide a convincing, detailed answer to that question, trust and credibility become key drivers of the buying decision; in tight competitions that alone can make the difference between winning and losing. Besides, selling is not pitching or dodging; it is communicating in ways that will cause the customer to want to work with your company rather than someone else's.

Keep in mind that your intent in using proofs should not be to prove that your offer has the features but rather that the benefits are real and will be realized by the customer. Developing such proofs can be frustrating, especially in the heat and rush of creating a proposal. Smart companies maintain a proofs database for all their services and product lines, then draw from it, quickly tailor the proofs to the current customer, and deploy them at the appropriate places throughout the proposal. While these proofs reside in the database as boilerplate, the careful customer-specific tailoring raises them above mere boilerplate (the difference between badly deployed and effectively managed boilerplate). Just as the finished document should be benefits rich, it should be proofs rich as well. Here are some possibilities for proofs in proposals:

- ➤ Facts, figures, and/or published information about your organization and its people, products, and services.
- ➤ Customer testimonials and references.
- ➤ Visuals of all kinds, especially those that incorporate photographs and other "hard" data.

➤ Other forms of "hard" data, such as technical specifications, cost figures, and quality/performance statistics.

➤ Created proofs, such as a graph showing that as productivity increases, cost of ownership declines; or a bar graph showing increasing production volume over a five-year period. (What these types of proofs reveal must be true; all you are doing is creating a new way of communicating it.)

➤ Facts, conclusions, or analyses from an independent industry oversight organization, particularly government agencies such as OSHA.

Never is the gap between knowing and doing more apparent in the world of proposals than when we revisit the simple notion that proposals must not just describe and define; they must sell. Smart companies today are working diligently to close those gaps and thereby create differentiated proposals. This effort is especially critical in markets where providers are commoditized and need every edge available to win clients and their business without entering into bidding wars for lowest price and without the low margins that typically result from those wars.

Challenges for Readers

➤ Pull a recent proposal off the shelf. Select ten or twelve pages as a sampling, and then develop a feature–benefit ratio. We recently did this exercise with a client and discovered that the ratio was 57:1. That is, there were 57 features for a single benefit. Regardless of whether the sampling is 100 percent representative of the entire proposal, that sort of ratio is a warning that must be heeded. On average, what do you think the ratio would be for, say, all *your* company's proposals during the past two years?

➤ If you consistently and effectively plant ghosts in your proposal to answer "Why not them?" then you are ahead of most companies responding to RFPs today. But what if you have a competitor who will ghost you in their proposal? Examine your Sour Spot, assume the role of your competitor to figure out how they would most likely ghost *you*, and then create a counterghost to neutralize their effort. The egg ends up on their faces instead of yours.

➤ As part of proposal review, consider using rubber stamps with the Big Four questions on them. Ink them and use them on the draft pages. It actually adds a bit of fun to a notoriously humorless process, and it generates relevant and productive discussion.

Engineers and other technical people intuitively understand the significance of the features they create and discuss in proposals. Automotive engineers can talk all day about gear ratios, cubic-inch displacement, and torque. They are happy to be communicating in their own special language, and often it doesn't naturally occur to them that nontechnical types might need a different message communicated differently. How could you help engineers contribute more effective answers to the Big Four? Training? Coaching? Models? Customer comments? Improving those answers can be a powerful way to compete.

Notes

1. Terry R. Bacon and David G. Pugh, *The Behavioral Advantage: What the Smartest, Most Successful Companies Do Differently to Win in the B2B Arena* (New York: AMACOM, 2004).
2. For an excellent examination of this gap, see Jeffrey Pfeffer and Robert I. Sutton, *The Knowing-Doing Gap: How Smart Companies Turn Knowledge into Action* (Boston: Harvard Business School, 2000).
3. Bacon and Pugh, *The Behavioral Advantage*.
4. Ibid.

Chapter 3

GETTING YOUR
MESSAGE ACROSS

Technical Proposals for Every Reader

GOLDEN RULE:

The audience, not the author, drives the design.

No matter how advanced or cutting edge a technology may be, it doesn't communicate itself, and, if poorly communicated, it may be rejected for that reason alone. In fact, our assessments of proposals ranging from mediocre to superior tell us that well-communicated, good technology will usually be chosen over poorly communicated, great technology, as long as the price is acceptable. There are two reasons for this: First, the message simply gets through more effectively, giving the customer understandable and substantive reasons to want that technology. Second, all the customer truly understands about the so-called superior technology is that it's profoundly more expensive, but exactly why remains unclear because the key messages are mired in elaborately complex technospeak.

The Competitive Advantage: Reader-Friendly
Proposals That Sell

In the tough markets technology providers face today, the issue of selling becomes largely an issue of communicating. That is, although excellent engineering design is mandatory in both a technical and business sense, it is also a commodity in most cases because all the first-tier companies in any technical industry will have the engineering prowess the market requires. If, therefore, several competing firms have impressive technology messages for their customers, the real issue is not which one has the best message because they all do in one form or another. The real issue is who gets their message through most effectively. (For an extended look at entropy in the marketplace—that is, the natural market force attempting to commoditize providers and drive down prices—see "We Will Assimilate You" in our earlier book *Winning Behavior*.[1])

GOLDEN RULE:
When capability becomes commodity,
competition becomes communication.

Most technology professionals, however, would rank sales communication, especially writing, as one of the least savory parts of their work. This view is largely understandable if only because most engineers, scientists, and other technical people are visual conceptualizers and their default preference in communicating will be visual media (e.g., drawings, schematics, flow diagrams, charts of all kinds, data displays). If you ask an engineer how something works, he or she will typically say, "Let me *show* you," and begin sketching a process flow diagram or other visual and spatial rendering of the answer. This form of communication is fine for technical professionals communicating with their technical colleagues and customer counterparts.

More than any other form of communication, printed documents that integrate visual communication will stimulate and sustain maximum interest throughout the business development process. Oral communication also has its place in that process and is often required by customers, but it makes both legal and common sense to understand that messages between providers and buyers must at some point be recorded, set down in various ways for a diverse customer audience to examine, weigh, and consider.

This need to document means that a critical factor in gaining acceptance and funding for a technology solution via a proposal is the ease and completeness with which your customer's evaluators and decision makers gain clear, compelling reasons to want your solution. They understand your offer, and they find it a powerful match with their needs and business goals. In other words, even though many of them lack technical expertise, they grasp what you provide and why they should buy it. Your printed messages got through better than anyone else's, and that's a hard-copy fact.

For this reason, designing the most persuasive, reader-friendly proposal becomes a critical step in moving technology from those who created it to those who need it. Yet technical contributors to proposals typically want to propose their technology by attempting to establish technical superiority in technical terms. Problem? Relatively few people in the customer's procurement chain care about technical superiority per se and even fewer understand the technical nuances that establish that superiority. Would a decision maker in a global oil and gas company really be swayed by the technical superiority of a particular data-logging system? Or would that decision maker focus on how such a system could increase the probability of finding and extracting profitable petroleum reserves? In other words, what they care about is getting the job done the right way with the right technology for the right price to achieve the right business goals as the right return on their investment. Right? That's the message that has to get through.

Compete by Communicating

Winning business today means competing with communication. For today's top-line/bottom-line–driven customers, it's not enough to know in some technically elegant sense *what* the solution is; they need to know *why* they should buy it, and that crucial message may be anything but technical. Knowing this, the technical contributors, proposal managers, and support staff who create your proposals can build the business by addressing (in addition to the myriad questions and requirements from the customer) this crucial communication question:

> *Knowing how many people get directly or indirectly involved in the customer's procurement process, how can we effectively get our message through to all, or at least most, of them?*

The buying process can involve multiple people, including decision makers and those who directly or indirectly influence them. We refer to this widely dissimilar group of people collectively as "the customer."

Our challenge is to provide this diverse audience with compelling answers to those four critical questions: Why us? Why not them? So what? and How so? These are the same Big Four questions we discussed in Chapter 2, but dealing with them in technology proposals adds layers of complexity if only because technology has a legitimate language of its own, one that many of the people in the customer's procurement process are not conversant in. Outside technical circles, for example, "nanosecond" may be used as a figure of speech meaning "extremely fast," but few people could accurately define such speed, neither would they need to. They are not communicating a technical concept, so pinpoint accuracy is not the issue.

Anyone buying technology needs answers to the Big Four, each one easily recast to represent the customer's perspective:

1. Why should we buy your company's third generation telecommunication technology?
2. Why shouldn't we buy theirs?
3. Regarding your claim of state of the art, so what? That doesn't mean your technology is either unique or better for our business, so what's it going to do for us in our markets?
4. And, finally, regarding your claim that your integrated technology can shorten my launch schedule by three months, how so? Why should we trust a message that's unclear and unsubstantiated?

Know Your Audience

Having great answers to these or any other version of the Big Four solves only half the communication problem. The other half involves getting the answers through to a mixed, remarkably diverse audience: a series of people constituting the buying "food chain" who may have nothing in common except that they all must contribute to a complicated, binary decision that ultimately gives a thumbs-up to one offer and a thumbs-down to the others. You can understand this mixed audience if you see it not simply as a series of different people but as a series of human communication "filters," as depicted in Figure 3-1.

Figure 3-1. **The eight communication filters in technology proposals.** Your proposal must successfully run a communications gauntlet on its way to the award.

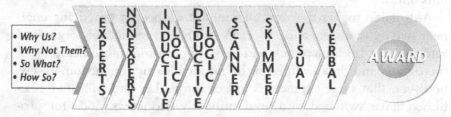

The main messages (i.e., your best answers to the Big Four) must successfully pass through these filters to win the communication competition.

Knowing that the customer's people are diverse is perfectly irrelevant unless you also understand that different people process information differently, and, therefore, knowing how to address those differences, those filters, can be a powerful competitive advantage for selling technology.

In light of what Figure 3-1 shows, a brief discussion of each of these communication filters seems in order.

Experts and Nonexperts. In complex selling, which large technology contracts almost always involve, the seller has to answer the Big Four for both *experts* and *nonexperts* in the technical subject matter. The danger here is an attitude all too prevalent in technology-driven organizations:

If the customer uses nonexperts to buy our technology, that's their problem. There's just no getting around the fact that it takes a sophisticated mind to appreciate a sophisticated technology such as ours. Period.

Fine . . . but prepare for a huge business development disappointment because this mind-set telegraphs massive arrogance, and it dismisses almost every decision maker who ever made a technology buying decision. In fact, we've learned that the higher the technology being sold, the more likely it is that your decision maker is a nonexpert who nonetheless must have powerful answers to the Big Four.

Inductive and Deductive Processors. Simply stated, logic is the way a person prefers to organize and transmit outgoing information and process incoming information. We don't carry a logic chromosome in our DNA. Logic is acquired behavior initially practiced consciously but over time and many repetitions, embedded as an unconscious, default behavior. Most technical and scientific people automatically deploy *inductive* logic (details/data leading to an idea), whereas most nontechnical people prefer *deductive* logic (an idea supported by details/data).

A decision maker, for example, may have been a practicing engineer twenty years ago and, therefore, preferred inductively organized information, both incoming and outgoing: a thorough rehearsing of the details and data leading to the major idea or conclusion. Today, however, that same engineer is a decision maker and will in all likelihood have switched to a predominately deductive mode for processing and communicating information: big-picture, bottom-line conclusions first supported by the details and data, much of which will be skimmed as a quick credibility check rather than scanned for absolute accuracy at the subatomic level.

Thus, in communicating and selling your technology in a proposal, you achieve maximum reader friendliness if you can convey your message both inductively (for technical people in the customer's organization) and deductively (for nontechnical people). *Caution: As illustrated above, most decision makers and executives are deductive processors, so don't discount the importance of the deductive mode, even in a highly technical proposal.*

Scanners and Skimmers. Depending on certain variables, such as level of expertise and vested interest, a person confronted with printed matter will be either a *scanner* or a *skimmer*. The scanner scrutinizes the page, examining each detail, challenging every claim, seeking the hidden flaw. Scanners will read every word or close to it. Thus, engineers in your customer's organization may well scan your proposal's technical offer because that's what experts do: Experts study other experts' work to determine whether it passes muster. Skimmers, typically nonexperts, haven't the time, the inclination, or the motivation to pore over pages and pages of technical discussions. The skimmers want to hit the high notes: main ideas, important proofs, and big-picture (sometimes quite literally) concepts.

Visual and Verbal Conceptualizers. We're convinced that most technical people are *visual thinkers* and nontechnical people tend to be *verbal thinkers*. Technical people prefer to share their thoughts with a process flow diagram rather than an essay, but nontechnical people would probably try to explain first with words, either oral or written. It has long been accepted that most technical people don't feel comfortable writing and nontechnical folks fail to see the charm of staring at a schematic. In either case, the message won't get through very effectively because, however great the medium may be, if it's not right for the recipient, that's a working definition of a non-reader-friendly proposal.

Overcome Differences

These filters become nothing less than a communications gauntlet through which your technology messages must successfully pass to secure the number-one ranking from the customer's evaluators. One solution, then, would be to hit these filters head-on by developing a separate message for each one, a commonsense but highly impractical approach. We have enough problems getting one proposal pulled together, let alone eight versions of it, to communicate with all members of that mixed audience.

Fortunately, the task at hand is not quite as daunting as it may first appear because these eight filters, as shown in Figure 3-2, quite naturally group into two major clusters. Once we understand that, we can begin to design effective communications that will get the messages through to all, or most, of the customer's people: decision makers, evaluators, and influencers alike.

Engineers, scientists, and other technical professionals can be generally profiled with the following four filters for processing incoming technology messages: *Experts* using *inductive logic* who are *scanners* conceptualizing *visually*. Conversely, nontechnical people processing that same technology message could be profiled with these four filters: *Nonexperts* using *deductive logic* who are *skimmers* conceptualizing *verbally*. A notable variation could be executive decision makers because they typically fit most of the latter profile—*nonexpert, deductive, skimmer*—but instead of conceptualizing verbally, they, like technical people, tend to think in *visual* ways. (We demonstrate this concept much more fully in Chapter 6.)

The issue now becomes one of communication design. How can we craft our proposal's technology messages so that they get through both processors with clarity and positive impact?

Designing the Proposal

One answer to the previous question may have been right in front of us all along in the form of a fundamental publishing principle: Inte-

Figure 3-2. **The eight communication filters merged into two groups.** By clustering the filters into two groups—experts and nonexperts—you can design your proposal to communicate most effectively with a mixed audience.

- Why Us?
- Why Not Them?
- So What?
- How So?

EXPERTS · NONEXPERTS · INDUCTIVE LOGIC · DEDUCTIVE LOGIC · SCANNER · SKIMMER · VISUAL · VERBAL · AWARD

grate graphics and text (as opposed to attaching the proposal's figures at the end, as we did in the precomputer heyday of typewriters). Consider for a moment the monumental reader unfriendliness of, let's say, *National Geographic* if it published its articles as straight text with those magnificent photographs inserted at the end. That will never happen (even though it might be more cost-effective) because professional publishers know how to get the message through to a mixed audience, some of whom will read the article while others will look at the pictures. Still others will look at the pictures first to sort their reading, to set priorities, which means that some of those articles never get read based on a graphics-driven decision.

Two Messages, One Proposal

The key point here is that two different processing modes—those filters described above—have been integrated into a single expression of the message and each reader can access the message according to a predisposition to either read or look, or some combination of the two. In any case, those who have designed the message have ensured the highest probability that it will get through. Taking that same principle and extending it to cover the audience for most technology proposals, you can design your messages so that your proposals accommodate both experts and nonexperts alike, the classic mixed audience.

We design proposal messages as a *double exposure on a single plane*, not unlike a double-exposed sheet of photographic paper with two overlapping images on it. One "exposure" is for the expert-inductive-scanner-visual audience and the other exposure is for the non-expert-deductive-skimmer-verbal audience. Figure 3-3 shows the model for double-exposure proposal design.

Double-Exposure Techniques

How does the concept of a double exposure on a single plane actually work in communication design? Consider these specific techniques for getting your technology messages through better than the competitors and thereby winning the communication competition:

Experts and Nonexperts

➤ For the *expert* members of the customer's evaluation team, be sure to provide as much substantiating data/detail/features as necessary

Figure 3-3. **Communicating with a double exposure on a single plane.** Having designed the proposal to communicate effectively with each group, you can overlay them to communicate effectively with both in a single proposal.

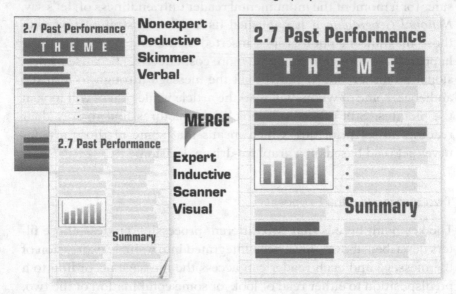

to convince them that your technology is not just the best but the best buy, too. This will be especially important when your price is not low or lowest, because in addition to selling your technology offer in the proposal, you will have to *sell your price*. Furthermore, one of an expert's highest callings (and most satisfying tasks) is to seek and find errors committed by other experts. This is what experts do. It is how they assert themselves as experts.

➤ For the *nonexperts*, state the main ideas and support them selectively with the best data/detail but no more than necessary to validate the main ideas. And because nonexperts won't understand or fully value the technical features of your offer, be sure to correlate those features to compelling, customer-focused benefits. Listen to the nonexpert whispering in your ear, "I'm not sure I grasp all or even most of the technology you're describing (nor do I particularly want to), but I definitely need to understand what it will do for my business." (Chapter 2 provides an extensive discussion of the features-benefits correlation in proposals.)

Inductive and Deductive Thinkers

➤ For those technical professionals in your proposal audience who typically employ *inductive logic*, rehearse your data/details/features first, then state the main idea, or conclusion, derived from them. Faced with the main idea first, inductive thinkers will most likely ignore or discount it until they have examined the data or other proofs that the idea is valid. The data lead them to the idea.

➤ Conversely, for the nonexperts who use *deductive logic*, state the main idea, or conclusion, first, then support it with the data/details/features. These readers resent having to wade through what seems like an endless recitation of data and detail to get what's really important to them: the main idea. They prefer to know what it is immediately and then see if the ensuing information supports it. And once satisfied that the main idea is valid, they often stop reading altogether.

Scanners and Skimmers

➤ Because technology experts tend to be *scanners*, be certain your discussion (textual and graphic) of the subject matter is bulletproof, airtight, or whatever metaphor you need to make you examine your message with an electron microscope. Why? Because your customer's scanner probably owns an electron microscope and will use it on your proposal before deciding to give you that contract and money.

➤ On the other hand, for those customer personnel who tend to be *skimmers*, be sure your messages are emphasized by design (e.g., italics; boldface; one-sentence paragraphs; prominently displayed main ideas or themes; plenty of white space; and a format that is skimmer friendly, such as double or message column). At least some of the visuals need to be nontechnical, more conceptual, and designed to be understood and valued in eight to ten seconds.

Visual and Verbal Conceptualizers

➤ For the *visual* conceptualizers in your mixed audience, ensure that at least one-third of your message is captured and expressed via powerful graphics, figures, visuals, or whatever term you choose to define nontextual communication (even though a good visual contains some words and should always have a powerful, full-sentence caption for explanation and interpretation).

➤ Then, for the *verbal* conceptualizers, ensure that your text is well written (e.g., in the active voice rather than the passive), well edited, and "punched up" with effective but not overdone emphatic devices.

Once you've determined the key messages you need to get through to the customer, you're ready to design the proposal so that it will deliver the messages unscathed through the filters that people use to process information and determine the right technical direction for their company. You help them make that decision by soundly defeating the competition with the quality of your message and how it's communicated.

GOLDEN RULE:
Excellent technical capability or technology poorly communicated
is a surefire way to lose on price.
When that happens, you don't *really* lose on price.
You lose on communication.

If your technology's key feature is blazing speed, unless that message and its potential business impact (e.g., greater efficiencies, increased productivity, lower production costs) are made clear, the proposal will falter. If the customer doesn't understand how valuable your technology is for meeting their needs, they certainly won't understand your pricing. When this happens, you lose revenue, your customer loses an optimum business solution, and the only winner is the competition. For a far better end, therefore, Figure 3-4 provides an example of a finished, reader-friendly proposal using the double-exposure model and the techniques we've addressed here.

By consciously addressing the communication challenges posed by a mixed audience, your communication design results in much more reader-friendly proposals. That's a win for you, a win for your customers, and a loss for the competition. When all is said and done, that provides a much happier ending to the story your proposals need to deliver.

Bulleted list with abundant white space for nonexpert skimmers

Ample text with detail for the expert, inductive scanners

Ample text with detail for the expert, inductive scanners

Graphic with an interpretive caption for the nonexpert skimmers and visual conceptualizers

A summary paragraph at the end of the section would paraphrase the theme at the top of the section for the inductive readers who, having processed all the discussion and detail, will now accept the main idea as an acceptable conclusion.

United Nations Environmental Oversight Council
Worldwide Environmental Remediation Project (WERP)

TECHNICAL APPROACH

2.2 Turnkey Environmental Remediation Operation

Worldwide will provide timely, cost-conscious responses to remedial action assignments at UNEOC sites, using experienced environmental engineers and support personnel employing the latest, most cost-effective, and environmentally friendly remediation technologies

Worldwide Environmental Services has been working with the U.S. Government on environmental remediation projects for over 20 years. Several large-scale remediation programs are in progress or have been completed successfully. Treatments range from simple: removal or incineration to sophisticated packages such as ultraviolet, bioremediation, and jet grouting. All work will be overseen by Professional Engineers registered in the country and state or province where the work is to be done, supported by other properly licensed environmental remediation specialists as necessary.

This section presents our capabilities in the following areas:

- Treatment Facilities at Priority Sites
- Soil Excavation, Treatment, and Disposal

2.2.1 Treatment Facilities at Priority WERP Sites

Worldwide Environmental Services uses the experience gained in the construction, deployment, and operation of our treatment facilities to evaluate and to utilize proven and commercially available treatment technologies.

At the five UNEOC priority sites already identified, we propose to employ the technologies shown in Figure 2.2.1.1 (right). All five technologies are either WES developed or licensed.

Contaminated soil can be treated by our Obbivnisator system or our licensed Biocorrosive Organic Blasting Incinerator Technology System (BOBITS). The Obbivnisator is for black stabilization and slurry wall construction projects up to 60 feet deep. BOBITS is a transportable counter-rotating air-based system.

Contaminated soil and groundwater can be treated simultaneously by our licensed Microbial Soil or Groundwater Remediation (MSOGR) system. Our Ultrahydrivonne process can be used to treat groundwater. Our Jetwall barrier system can be used to create slurry walls in support of treatment and containment projects. State of the art continuous air monitoring systems and air pollution control systems are used to monitor and control our excavation, ventilation, and treatment operations.

MSOGR uses air injection and extraction wells to strip organics and accelerate bioremediation. Ultrahydrivonne uses UVB rays, hydrogenated vegetable oil, and ozone

WES Remediation Technologies and Applications

Remediation Technologies	Highbid 7	Crivelcoosaht 20	Prestbillation Renmarine	Cuspidabvisomphis	Polistan Wilderness
Obbivnisator	•				
Biconnerv Organic Blasting Incinerator Technology System (MSOGR)		•	•		
Ultrahydrivonne			•	•	
Jetwall	•			•	•

Figure 2.2.1.1. Worldwide Environmental Services will use its own or licensed technologies to address the specific environmental challenges of the five priority sites identified in UNEOC's Site Characterization document.

Worldwide
Environmental Services

112

---

*Figure 3-4. **Sample proposal: double exposure on a single plane.** Proposals designed for a mixed audience could look like this sample page.*

Challenges for Readers

➤ Take one of your company's recent technical proposals off the shelf. Give it to someone who isn't a technical professional: a spouse, perhaps, or a friend, or even a colleague. Ask them to read a couple of sections. Then ask for their opinions. Did the messages get through? If not, why? Since that person could very well be one of the customer people who will evaluate your proposal, do you have a potential problem here? What can you do to begin addressing this problem?

➤ Pick up a recent technical proposal your company submitted to a customer. Try skimming it. Does it allow you to do that and get a fair amount of information? Do you have to "get into the grass" to find meaning and messages? If skimming is a fruitless approach to your proposals, what could you do to make future proposals more reader friendly for skimmers?

➤ Pick up a recent technical proposal your company submitted to a customer. Study it as a scanner would. Does it provide proofs, substantiations, and supporting detail/data for all of its claims, or is it to some degree a trust-me-please proposal? Would experts representing the customer find this a reader-friendly (and credible) proposal if they scanned it? If not, what could you do to make future ones more reader friendly for skimmers?

Note

1. Terry R. Bacon and David G. Pugh, *Winning Behavior: What the Smartest, Most Successful Companies Do Differently* (New York: AMACOM, 2003).

Chapter 4

SELLING THE BENEFITS
Customer-Oriented Proposals

GOLDEN RULE:

You have to sell the sizzle to sell the steak.

It's hard to find heroes in the world of sales and marketing. The feats of the most prolific sellers are generally unknown except to those who pay their bonuses, and if they gain too much notoriety, the rest of us usually resent them.

Now and then, however, a folk hero emerges among that group of humans purported to be able to sell gasoline to a bicyclist. Recent sales heroes include Zig Zigler and Buck Rodgers of IBM. Back in the late 1940s and 1950s, the hero of selling was Elmer Wheeler, who advised his fellow salespeople to sell the sizzle, not the steak.

In a way, this is our story. Educated, in one case, in the liberal arts and, in the other, in engineering, we were dragged kicking and screaming into selling. Before writing our first proposals, we held the typical, even stereotypical, view of salespeople: loudmouthed, overbearing, full of hype, lacking subtlety and substance. When we first heard Elmer Wheeler's advice, it confirmed our prejudice that selling is an impure world of gab and guile and glitz.

Why Steak Without Sizzle Is Not Enough

Our world, in contrast, was one in which substance mattered—almost all our early work was with engineering and other technical organizations. We shared our clients' concern with functionality, with reliability, with robustness, with *elegance*. That last element is crucial. Elegance in engineering does not necessarily mean complexity. It means that the design or solution solves an engineering problem in a particularly effective and satisfying way. The most elegant solutions are often the simplest, but you may have to work through great complexity to reach simple elegance. Anyone who has accomplished that knows that, in engineering, we all are heroes. Every time we tackle some new problem, we slay another beast. As professional problem solvers, that's what engineers do.

What sets us apart from other dragon slayers is our pragmatism. As complicated as a problem might become, we strive for practical, workable solutions—and we appreciate it when others are equally practical. That's why, when we are forced to write proposals, we describe our "steak," so to speak, in fine detail and ignore the "sizzle" altogether. The steak, after all, *is* the thing. It's what's being sold. It's what will be cooked and eaten. Buyers who are educated enough to appreciate the qualities of our lean sirloin will not need to be sold by a salesperson making *sizzling* sounds in their ears.

At least that was our attitude. Then we began writing proposals—*losing* proposals. And we wondered why we were losing. We spoke to the people who were reading those proposals. Often, these people were engineers. We learned—albeit slowly and painfully—that proposals are *not* engineering documents. They're *not* technical reports, specifications, dissertations, or treatises. They are sales tools. Their purpose is to *sell* something to somebody. Understanding that distinction has made all the difference in our proposals. Now we think Elmer was at least half right: *In proposals, you have to sell the sizzle to sell the steak*. (For a full discussion of proposals as sales tools, see Chapter 2.)

Customer-Oriented Proposals

Although we believe Elmer Wheeler was right about what you sell to buyers, we still find that his advice goes down hard with engineers and other technical or scientific professionals, especially those purists who believe that potential buyers ought to be able to base their buying decisions on a circuit diagram, a list of parts, and a price. So we frame our advice a little differently. We focus on what we call *customer-oriented proposals*—proposals written from the customer's point of view, proposals that take a "you" attitude rather than a "me" attitude. Before we describe these types of proposals more fully and offer some tips on how to write them, let's discuss the nature of proposals and their function in the acquisition or procurement process typical to government, business, and industry.

Who Are the Buyers?

To appreciate the importance of writing proposals oriented toward customers, we need to ask ourselves who makes the selection decision and what they look for in an offer. In our experience, the buyers and evaluators include:

➤ *Technical Specialists and Mid-Level Managers:* An important part of the evaluation team, to be sure, but generally not the real powers.
➤ *Purchasing or Procurement Managers*: Generators and reviewers of the terms and conditions. Although dealing with a narrow range of issues, they wield considerable influence.
➤ *Pricing Specialists:* Their areas of concern are pricing, discounts, life-cycle costing, compliance, cost-estimating methodology, warranties, payment schedules, and other critical business issues. They're generally more influential than the contracts people within the procurement/purchasing function.
➤ *Senior Executives:* These individuals include the general manager, vice presidents, functional directors, and other organizational barons who often either have nontechnical backgrounds or have become far removed from technical issues. Here is the real power. We have been involved in a number of sales efforts in which a single individual in this group soured a deal that everyone else up the customer's buying food chain had already approved and supported.

What Buyers Look For

As this list of people demonstrates, a purely technical presentation of an offer is doomed to failure. A review of the questions an evaluation team usually asks indicates why:

➤ Will this supplier *deliver on time* (so that we, in turn, can meet our deliveries)?
➤ Will this supplier have any labor, safety, or other *problems* that could threaten us? Similarly, could this supplier have (or have they already had) environmental or legal problems that could embarrass us?
➤ Will this supplier's products or services meet our *quality* standards?

> Will there be any *hidden costs* in doing business with this supplier? Could any unforeseen problems raise the life cycle or support costs of our products?
> Will this supplier provide adequate and timely *project management?*
> In summary, how will it be to work with this supplier? Will it be a good *business relationship?* Even if they can deliver, *can we work with them?* Do they have *both the capability and the chemistry* we're seeking?

These last questions are the proverbial bottom line. Remember that in today's marketplace, most customers can find several competent suppliers who can meet their technical requirements. So if you are the buyer, the key question becomes, "Which supplier would you prefer to do business with?"

As you no doubt noticed, our list of selection criteria excluded technical issues. Of course, technical issues do play an important role in buying decisions, but you may be surprised by the kinds of technical questions buyers are asking these days:

> Is the product *comfortably state of the art?* Products on the far reaches of technology are usually unproven and potentially full of bugs. They smell of risk and skyrocketing cost of ownership. Most customers are wary of the performance risks of too much innovation.
> What is the *growth* capability of the product? How much flexibility does the product have? Can it be grown without significant retooling or additional cost?
> How can we *protect our investment?* An increasing concern among buyers is protecting their existing investment in hardware, software, and systems.
> How easy will the product be to *maintain* and *support?* Logistical support has been one of the fastest-growing fields in the last two decades; today it falls under the rubric of supply chain management. Why? Because, like all of us, today's budget-conscious firms are trying to get more for their money.
> Can the product or service be *customized* to meet our needs? Here's another wave of the future. More customers are demanding customized products or services, and more suppliers are building customizing into their offers. Today, customization is added value; tomorrow, you won't get a contract without it.

Customization, ease of maintenance and support, protection of investment, growth capability, proven and reliable hardware—all these are technical and design issues. But notice that *not one of them favors you, the seller*.

Today, even the technical criteria reflect customers' concerns with the long-term usefulness of products and services; with the reliability, supportability, life-cycle cost, total cost of ownership of every product; and with the kinds of business relationships that result in long-term equity *for both parties*.

In an article for the *Harvard Business Review*, Theodore Levitt argues that all products are to some degree *intangible*.[1] From the buyer's point of view, says Levitt, "the product is a promise, a cluster of value expectations." Further, "The way the product is packaged (how the promise is presented in brochure, letter, design appearance), how it is personally presented, and by whom—all these become central to the product itself because they are elements of what the customer finally decides to buy or reject."[2]

The "Me" Proposal

A remarkable number of proposals not only don't sell the sizzle; they try to turn meat eaters into vegetarians. The customer says, "I'd like a sirloin steak," and the proposal offers spinach quiche. Let's look at an example from an actual RFP and proposal response in the telecommunications industry. The customer wanted a statewide telecommunications system. In the RFP, the customer specified a number of features this system should include. Here is one such requirement:

The system shall provide the ability to program a minimum of 20 different stations to each automatically dial an individually programmed telephone number upon going off hook on the station. At a minimum, the number dialed may be programmed to be "0" for an attendant, an unrestricted PBX extension, or an outside number that may be either local or long distance. The responder shall state the maximum number of stations that can be programmed as Hot Line/Ring Down stations and any limits on the numbers that can be automatically dialed.

Here is how one bidder responded:

The Model 1066 PBX allows up to 64,528 Hot Line numbers, with up to 24 digits stored per Hot Line number. This number is reduced by the number of individual and group Quick Dialing numbers assigned for purposes other than Hot Line. Included in the numbers that can be called using Hot Line service are all required numbers.

Even this short example demonstrates a couple of the worst abuses of "me" proposals:

➤ They ignore at least some of the customer's requirements or requests for information.
➤ They often redefine the problem in the seller's terms.

Note that the proposal response fails to address the customer's primary concern: How many *stations* can be programmed as Hot Line/ Ring Down stations? (The number of Hot Line *numbers* allowable is a different issue.) "Me" proposals often have the following additional problems:

➤ They often confuse complexity with sophistication and are consequently unclear.
➤ They are often organized according to the writer's perspective, not the customer's.
➤ They often include options the customer hasn't asked for.
➤ They are often arrogant and unresponsive, solving the seller's problem (the need to push products), not the customer's.

The following example shows some of these problems. The left column contains an outline of the customer's RFP; the right column shows the table of contents of one bidder's response, which, incidentally, was a loser. Can you see *any* correspondence between the RFP and the proposal?

REQUEST FOR PROPOSAL

Customer Order Fulfillment System

1. Introduction
   1.1 Project Objective and Scope
   1.2 System Overview
   1.3 Evaluation Process and Criteria
   1.4 Timeframe Guidelines
   1.5 Technical Edit Approach

PROPOSAL

Technical Design & Implementation

1. Technical Design
   1.1 Technical Architecture Definition
   1.2 Hardware/System Software/Network Overview
   1.3 Database Design and Distribution

1.6 Personality System

2. Purchasing Terms and
   Conditions

3. System Processing
   Requirements

   3.1 Distributed Processing

   3.2 Response Time Go

1.4 Application Program
    Architecture

1.5 Performance, Security,
    and Controls

1.6 Development Approach

1.7 Product Descriptions

2. Conversion

Admittedly, organizing proposals so that they are consistent with the RFP and also allow you to present a clear picture of your offer is sometimes difficult. Nevertheless, the proposal outlined above appears to have little correspondence to the RFP. For all we know, they could have been dealing with two different projects.

Reading the Customer's Mind: The "You" Proposal

We once received what we think must be the ultimate compliment for a proposal writer. Our company, at the time, submitted a bid to McDonnell-Douglas Astronautics Company (MDAC) for the contract to train the proposal team MDAC was assembling to write its proposal to NASA for the Space Station program. After we won the award, we had the opportunity to meet with the MDAC representative who wrote the RFP, then read and evaluated the proposals. Not knowing that we had written the proposal, he remarked on its quality and comprehensiveness. Then he said something intriguing: "When I read it, I had the uncanny feeling that I was reading our own thoughts."

It occurred to us then that *that* is the real secret to writing good proposals—reading the customer's mind, making the customer feel comfortable with your grasp of the issues, presenting a conception of the problem and solution that *precisely* matches the customer's conception of the problem and solution. Now the questions were, "What had we done?" and "Could we do it again?" In retrospect, the steps seem simple:

➤ We had followed MDAC's RFP to the letter. We proposed providing precisely what MDAC asked for.

➤ We organized our proposal precisely as the RFP was organized. We made a checklist of the points they wanted covered and covered them in that order.

➤ We used MDAC's terminology. When our terms differed from theirs, we used their terms.

> We explained, throughout the proposal, how what we were offering would benefit them. We were careful to state how our design was the right design *for MDAC*.

> When we didn't understand a requirement, we called and asked them what it meant. In short, we never allowed our ignorance to turn against us.

> We used every legitimate trick up our sleeve to make our message clear and easy to read and evaluate.

> We incorporated what we had learned into the training we subsequently developed and conducted for MDAC. We'd like to think that what we taught them about customer-oriented proposals helped them win that NASA contract worth hundreds of millions of dollars.

Five Essential Components of a Customer-Focused Proposal

Since that time, we have refined our concept of the customer-oriented proposal. To craft a truly powerful proposal, you must:

1. Respond to the customer's *real* issues and problems.
2. Address *all* of the customer's requirements and requests.
3. Reflect the customer's conception of the project by mirroring the RFP in organization and coverage of topics.
4. Use the customer's terminology.
5. Emphasize the benefits to the customer of your offer, particularly the intangible benefits of doing business with you.

Uncover and Respond to the Customer's *Underlying* Need

This is a subtle but significant factor. The requirements stated in the RFP rarely reflect the whole truth about the customer's needs. Underlying the requirements are the issues that caused the customer to specify those requirements. Even deeper are the problems that gave rise to the issues, yet in an RFP you generally see only the requirements.

In one procurement process in which we were involved, the customer specified a rapid electronic mail system to be installed between its regional offices and its headquarters. Of particular concern to the customer was the speed of transmission and turnaround the system would allow. Specifically, they wanted direct routing of messages to addressees so that "same-day response" to messages was not only possible but routine.

Upon analyzing this opportunity, we discovered several issues underlying the requirement. First, the customer's existing electronic mail system was configured such that incoming messages entered a queue. When traffic was heavy, these messages could remain in the queue for days. Second, their existing system had no means of sorting messages by priority; routine messages were treated the same as important queries from customers. Those issues gave us insight into their real problem—loss of business to competitors because they were not resolving their customers' problems or complaints in a timely manner. *That* was the real problem, and it was fundamentally a *business* problem, not just a technical one.

All of the issues and problems underlying the requirements rarely appear in an RFP. The RFP may state some of them, but you won't know *all* of them unless you work with the customer and ask probing questions to uncover the "hidden" issues and problems.

Address All of the Requirements and Requests

For every requirement in an RFP, ask these key questions:

"Where did this requirement come from?"
"Why do they require this and not something else?"

These questions signify both a technique and an attitude. They help you identify the customer's hot buttons, discover the appropriate technical solutions, and then sell those solutions in the most effective manner. Simply identifying each requirement and responding with a general statement like "We will do it" or "We will provide it" or "We will comply" does not mean that you have truly *addressed* that requirement by demonstrating your understanding of it, your approach to delivering on it, and how your approach will benefit the customer.

Mirror the RFP

One of our golden rules says that ease of evaluation is a very real factor of success in a proposal, and we've heard that message countless times from customers whom we've asked to reflect on their procurement process. One of the techniques they value highly is found in proposals that are organized to follow the RFP's structure. Therefore, if the solicitation sets forth requirements for past performance, project team, and safety in that order, the proposal responding to that RFP should address those three sets of requirements in sections presented in the same order as they were in the RFP. In one major proposal we reviewed, over half of the 260 sections in the proposal failed to address topics required by the RFP. That sort of noncompliance is nothing short of reckless, and it is no wonder they lost the bid.

GOLDEN RULE:
When the customer asks you to address topics A, B, C, D, and E,
you address topics A, B, C, D, and E—in that order.

How much mirroring your proposals can accomplish depends in large part on the customer to whom you are responding. For instance, in U.S. government RFPs, Section L specifies the key features of the proposal and includes everything from organization, font, point, margins, characters per line and page, to the number of pages. Following the Section L instructions is a fundamental compliance issue, and it must be followed precisely.

Private sector and some lower echelon (state, county, municipal) government RFPs are not typically prescriptive about proposal design, which gives you a lot more room for creating positive differentiation through ease of evaluation and a more reader-friendly proposal. If your proposal "tracks" the RFP and is not randomly organized or organized according to your company's standardized outline for proposals, it will be easier and quicker to assess. If, however, the RFP is so chaotic that mirroring it would only make the problem worse, turn to the evaluation/selection criteria and use that for your outline. These criteria become first-level heads, and the requirements are given a "home" beneath them. You are still mirroring the RFP but in this case you are using the customer's criteria as the structural framework of your proposal.

Another aspect of mirroring involves recognizing that the terms the customer uses to signify events, activities, products, or operations may differ from those you would use and responding in ways that will differentiate your proposal from those of the competitors.

For example, "Hot Line/Ring Down" originated as one company's terminology for describing a particular feature available on a PBX system. If your company sold PBXs, you might call your "Hot Line/Ring Down" feature something else, for example, "Direct Access Dialing" or "Off Hook Dialing." However, if the customer asks for "Hot Line/Ring Down" service, use that terminology in your proposal. If you switch terms, you risk alienating the customer and confusing the discussion. We've read proposals that complied with the requirements but didn't *seem* to because the writers had switched terms. Even if the customer ultimately concludes that your offer does meet the requirement, you've made them work a lot harder to get to that conclusion than was necessary.

GOLDEN RULE:

Use key words in the RFP to cue readers to the fact that your proposal is addressing the required key topics.

To write a mirroring, customer-oriented proposal, treat the RFP as a list of key words and phrases. Repeat those key words and phrases in your proposal as a way to cue the reader. If, for example, the RFP asks providers to state "any limits on the numbers that can be automatically dialed," *limits* is the key word. Your proposal response should not only repeat that key word but emphasize it (with italics). If you are uncertain and have an electronic copy of the RFP (or can get one), do a global search for the word in question. If it comes up multiple times throughout the solicitation, that's hard evidence that that term is important to the customer, especially when you consider that most RFPs are written by committees. Thus, it's a word on the minds of several people, not just one person who has a verbal hobbyhorse.

Emphasize Benefits, Especially Intangible Ones

Benefits come in all shapes and sizes and are often either tangible or at least measurable. A faster computer (feature) will increase productivity (benefit) as measured by reduced time to complete repeatable tasks. Any customer would welcome this and similar benefits, of course, but we may often ignore the more intangible, but nonetheless compelling, benefits associated with working with Company A rather than Company B. In most cases, both companies could provide these intangible benefits, the differentiator being that Company A actually included them in their proposal and Company B didn't.

Thus, a client of ours in the construction business, knowing that their prospective customer held a dim view of all construction companies, recently put a running footer in their proposal and on their presentation slides that stated, "In executing your project, we will positively change your perception of our industry." After awarding this company their contract, the key customer contact said his jaw dropped when he saw that statement. He also accepted their claim and told them that if they succeeded, it would be a huge win for everyone. Similarly, a theme running through another proposal and executive summary on which we worked centered on the ease of doing business with this bidder as opposed to most other companies in that industry (a broad-spectrum ghost on all competitors). In so many words, this told the customer they would be able to sleep at night because they wouldn't be bringing headaches home from work.

Develop an Effective Proposal Strategy

Understanding the customer's real problem allows you to devise a more effective strategy, which is the ultimate purpose of analyzing the issues and problems underlying the customer's requirements. We might have given our client the same electronic mail system regardless, but knowing they needed faster resolution of queries and customer complaints told us *how* to sell it.

Understanding what problem the customer is trying to solve helps you develop an effective proposal strategy. We can't overemphasize this point. The issues and problems underlying the requirements are the customer's *hot buttons*, and it is the hot buttons that keep the customer awake at night. They are the reasons the customer is procuring a solution, and they form the basis for the selection criteria. By pushing the customer's hot buttons, you show that you understand their problems in depth and that your offer is going to meet their real needs.

In proposals, marketing and writing are synonymous. All the issues we've been discussing are related to sound customer-oriented sales writing:

➤ Knowing and understanding your readers
➤ Writing so that the document meets the reader's needs
➤ Thoughtfully organizing the document for clarity and impact

The most effective way to sell that cluster of values is to write a customer-oriented proposal—one that's oriented toward *them*, that meets *their* needs, addresses *their* problems, reflects *their* conception of the project, uses *their* terminology, and presents the offer in terms of how it benefits *them*. That, in any kind of proposal, is how you sell the sizzle to sell the steak.

Challenges for Readers

➤ Open the electronic files for a recent proposal. Do a global search through the entire document to count the number of times the proposal uses words such as "you," "your," and the customer's organizational name. Then do the same type of search for "we," "our," and your company's name. What do the numbers suggest? Is the proposal a "me" proposal or a customer-oriented proposal?

➤ Get an electronic copy of a recent RFP. Determine from a quick visual scan some key words and terms. Conduct a global scan of the document to verify multiple uses of those words and terms. Now open the electronic version of the proposal submitted in response to that RFP. Conduct a global scan for the RFP's key words and terms. Has the proposal played back the customer's language? Did the proposal require evaluators to learn your terminology as substitutes for theirs?

➤ Examine a couple of recent proposals you submitted on must-win opportunities. Can you plainly see that these submissions to the customer not only addressed stated requirements but also "drilled down" to the issues and problems beneath, or behind, the requirements? If not, would future proposals on major opportunities be better received if they addressed all three procurement drivers: requirements, issues, and problems?

Notes

1. Theodore Levitt, "Marketing Intangible Products and Product Intangibles," reprinted in *The Marketing Imagination* (New York: The Free Press, 1983), pp. 94–110.
2. Ibid., p. 99.

Chapter 5

WHAT IT TAKES TO WIN

Credibility, Acceptability, and Preference

GOLDEN RULE:

If customers want to work with you, they will. If they don't want to work with you, they won't. In either case, they will fully document the decision during proposal evaluation.

It's the largest contract from the National Science Foundation (NSF) in nearly ten years, and Bob Cullen is determined to win it for his company. This win will not only achieve Bob's sales goal for the year; it will represent nearly one-quarter of the company's annual goal. Clearly, this is a "must-win opportunity," and the company spares no expense pursuing it.

As soon as the RFP is released, Bob marshals his resources and the team hunkers down to analyze the RFP and plot their response. They don't know who in the NSF will make the selection decision, but the scope of the work is clear, and they have an excellent solution to propose to the customer. They have built sophisticated facilities in extreme environments before, and that's what is called for here, so they have the right experience. Further, they can offer one of the finest project managers in the world. As his team scans the competition, Bob becomes convinced that no one will be able to offer a finer solution than his company. No one.

The challenge, Bob knows, will be finding a price that satisfies the customer while giving his company a satisfactory margin. They decide to be very competitive on price, to find cost savings wherever possible, and to pass those savings on to the NSF. Moreover, the bid review committee agrees to accept a slightly lower margin than they typically seek on their contracts. In this must-win situation, they pull out all the stops.

The proposal itself is a work of beauty—well written, well designed, compliant, and colorful. They tell their story clearly and are confident that their document answers all the customer's questions, requirements, and specifications. After they deliver their bid, the president of their division hosts a champagne party to celebrate the team's accomplishment. Then, almost before the cheers have faded, they learn that they have lost.

Convinced that no one could have had a better solution or a more competitive price, Bob is devastated. He begins to doubt himself, wondering if he has what it takes. Then he becomes angry and entertains the thought that the win must have been fixed. Had it been a full, open, and fair competition, they surely would have won. He considers talking to legal to see if they should lodge a protest. As these thoughts are roiling in his head, he receives a call from the procurement officer in the NSF, who explains that, although their proposal received high technical marks, the winner was rated slightly higher. "What about price?" Bob asks. "Your price was lower," the procurement officer replies, "but the winner's price was within acceptable budget parameters."

Months later, Bob is able to talk to a contact at the NSF, who confirms that the evaluation scores Bob's company received were very close to the scores the winner received, but the winning company was preferred by the NSF authorities who made the selection decision.

What Bob learned the hard way is that having a good solution and a competitive price is not enough to win today, especially when the evaluation scores of the top competitors are nearly equal. To win a competitive bid, you must build *preference* on top of two solid foundations: *credibility* and *acceptability*. You must have a credible solution to the customer's problems and needs, and you must be acceptable to them as a provider. However, as Bob learned, credibility and acceptability alone will not seal the deal. You must also establish a *preferred position* with the people in the customer's organization who will make or influence the selection decision.

How do you establish credibility, acceptability, and—most important—create preference?

Establishing Credibility

Credibility is the price of admission. Without it, you won't be in the game. So the first foundation to lay with customers is your credibility as a provider. You lay this foundation not only in your proposal but, even more important, in your market positioning, advertising, trade shows, product demonstrations, third-party product evaluations, strategic account management, and all preproposal activities that occur while you are pursuing an opportunity. In short, you build credibility through every aspect of your marketing, sales, and ongoing product or service delivery activities during what we've described as the opening and middle game preceding your endgame proposal. (For an expanded discussion of business development and the game of chess, see "Checkmate! How Business Development Is Like Chess" in our earlier book *The Behavioral Advantage.*[1])

Everything you do as a company either adds to or detracts from your credibility with customers. How you establish credibility for a particular opportunity depends on whether you can offer the right experience, the right solution, the right technology, and the right team. Moreover, our research and experience combine to tell us that up to 90 percent of what it takes to win today occurs before the proposal, and that means that you can ill afford to wait until the RFP arrives to begin communicating your experience, solution, technology, and team.

The Right Experience

You must prove to customers that you have the right experience for the solution they need. If all else is equal, buyers will prefer the company with more experience because it implies a shorter learning curve. More experienced providers should be better at diagnosing and solving problems because they've seen it all before. They should know where the trouble spots typically occur. They should be able to anticipate the roadblocks and know where they can tighten the schedule, eliminate costs, and find the right subcontractors. More experience also suggests that they will be most efficient at addressing the customer's needs (which adds up to lower risk for the customer) and conducting value engineering (which reduces the customer's costs).

At some point, of course, enough experience is enough. There may be little difference in the customer's mind between a company with thirty-five years' experience and another with twenty years' experience. What is more important to most customers is that your experience aligns with what they need—the closer the better. If you have built the same kind of plant they need, using the same processes, in a similar location, with the same regulatory and environmental conditions, and you can use the same team you used before, you are more credible than another provider who can offer everything you can except "the same team that did it last time." By and large, the more exact your experience is, the more credible you will be to customers.

Consequently, it is important in proposals to highlight the similarities between your experiences and the customer's wants, needs, requirements, and goals. A general overview of your vast experience, whether or not it applies to the customer's needs, is less effective and can appear as whitewash, and this is a mistake many bidders make. They stuff the experience section of their proposals with boilerplate descriptions of past projects, and they fail to make the relevance of that experience clear to the customer's evaluators.

The Right Solution

The right solution is one that meets the customer's needs, solves the problems in the most efficient and effective way, satisfies their expectations, and gets them to their goals. It isn't necessarily the most elegant, state-of-the-art, or creative solution. Here, it is important to know what the customer values and how the customer thinks, neither of which will be revealed fully, if at all, in an RFP. Some buyers are open to creative alternatives and are willing to take some risks; others are leery of value-added solutions that could introduce unnecessary costs, risks, or delays because the bugs haven't been worked out. For this reason, it's crucial to understand how the customer views the solution, what latitude they will allow in proposing solutions, and how closely they are required to follow any standard specifications or requirements.

Furthermore, you must understand how much ownership they have of the solution specified in their RFP. If they've spent a fair amount of time researching solutions and developing what they think they need—and if their key people have a lot of ego invested in seeing that solution through—then you run a high risk in challenging their view of the solution, even though you could provide something better, more sophisticated, more elegant, or more robust. We've seen many bids fail because the bidders proposed what they felt was a superior solution to what the customer specified—and they hadn't done the advance work with the customer to presell their alternative approach. This tack leaves the customer with two possible conclusions: This provider is "gold plating" the offer to justify a higher price, and/or they can't actually deliver what's been scoped and requested so they're attempting to dodge that bullet by proposing what they *can* offer and selling it as a superior response to what we've requested. Either conclusion takes a cynical view of the provider and is not a positive step toward winning the award.

It's important for you to distinguish between the *good*, *better*, and *best* solutions. A good solution may be what the customer has specified and what would work for them. A better solution might include some value-added enhancements whose value you can establish and prove to the customer's satisfaction—and that they are willing to pay for. The best solution may be an elegant and creative alternative that is simply too far beyond what they can reasonably consider doing for budgetary or other reasons.

It is often difficult for us to propose solutions that are less elegant, interesting, creative, and state of the art than we would like. What drives professionals is the desire to be the best, to advance the state of the art, and to be clever and creative in finding solutions to problems. For this reason, we prefer solutions that are interesting and exciting to us, which typically means that they incorporate the latest thinking, the best ideas we've seen, and perhaps the most creative applications we can envision. Customers usually lag behind us, which is why they come to us for solutions to their problems and fulfillment of their needs. One of their biggest concerns, for instance, is managing risk, so they will naturally prefer solutions they know about and are comfortable with, ones they know will work. Your challenge in proposing a solution is to find the one that solves the problem efficiently and creatively without substantially increasing the risk to the customer—as the customer sees it.

Bidders accused of being arrogant are generally guilty of assuming they are smarter than the customer and proposing what they think the customer *really* needs in spite of what the customer has asked for. If you do this, you are not providing the right solution.

The Right Technology

The right technology is usually compatible with the customer's existing technology base and has one foot in the present and the other in the future. Technology today is especially tricky because the state of the art is advancing so rapidly in many fields. Today's technological "aha!" may be tomorrow's "ho hum." So you have to balance wizardry with practicality.

It is good to remember that for most customers technology is the means to an end, not the end in itself, and they generally view technology as a necessary investment, if not a necessary evil. They have made a wise investment if the technology enables them to produce their goods and services better, faster, or cheaper; if the technology integrates with their existing technology and does not require a wholesale replacement of other items; if their people can easily learn, use, and maintain the technology; and if the technology investment can be justified to their stakeholders.

So the key questions to ask about technology are:

➤ Is the technology you are proposing the best fit for the customer at this time?
➤ Is it compatible with their existing technology base?
➤ Does it minimize the time and expense they may incur in retooling, modifying existing facilities or equipment, revising their processes and systems, and reeducating their people?
➤ At the same time, does it enable them to streamline production, achieve greater efficiencies, reduce cost, or improve quality or speed?
➤ Further, will it give them a competitive advantage in their industry? Will it enable them to compete more effectively against their competitors?

When introducing new technologies, we sometimes talk about people as being "early adopters," "late adopters," or "laggards." The early adopters are quick to experiment with new technology and are greater risk takers. The late adopters wait until the technology is widely used and proven. They are risk avoiders who wait until the thing is failsafe. Most people are in the middle of the pack—they wait until the technology has been established and the early bugs have been found and fixed, but they don't wait as long as the laggards. Companies are like this, too. Some are early adopters of new technology and have a big appetite for risk. Others are laggards. It is helpful to know whether your customer is an early adopter and how much technological risk they are willing to accept. If they want the latest technology without the risk, then the right solution may include installation assistance, 24/7 technical support, and provisions for upgrades.

The Right Team

Finally, your credibility depends on your having the right team to serve the customer. More bidders lose because they fail to provide the right team than lose because they don't have the right solution, technology, or experience. The right team has the following character-istics:

- It has an effective leader—someone who can build the team, give it direction, and provide leadership both internally and to the customer.
- It has the right composition—all the requisite skills are repre-sented.
- Its individual members have the right experience. Your company as a whole may have the right experience, but that's not enough. The people you propose must also be experienced in the right ways.
- It acts like a team. The members know each other, have worked with each other, and have a common sense of purpose, values, and goals.
- There are no interpersonal or other issues that could prevent its members from working together effectively.
- Its members have good chemistry with their counterparts in the customer's organization.
- It knows and understands the customer's specific needs, wants, requirements, and goals.

The last item is extremely important. It's not uncommon for bid-ders to assemble their teams at the last moment and for their team members not to have participated in responding to the RFP or devel-oping the proposal. If your team members are recent imports, they will probably look that way, which does not enhance your credibility with the customer. Smart bidders assemble their teams early and en-sure that they participate in developing the solution and the proposal. They think and act like a team, so that's what the customer sees.

In the case of Bob Cullen's company, credibility was not an issue. They had established their credibility as a provider to the NSF, but that wasn't enough. It's not uncommon in major bids for there to be a dozen providers who meet the credibility test. Being credible means you have passed through the first gate. It almost never guarantees you the win.

Establishing Acceptability

If customers find you credible, they will next want to determine if you are *acceptable*. Acceptability hinges on two factors you can control (negotiable terms and a competitive price) and on one you cannot (the political environment).

Negotiable Terms

First, customers want to know if they can work with you. Are your terms and conditions acceptable to them, which usually means, are you willing to negotiate the terms of the contract? You should have the same questions about them. Are they willing to negotiate the terms so the two of you can work together?

The terms and conditions of an agreement vary considerably depending on the nature of your products and services and on the types of conditions customers feel are necessary to protect their rights (and enable you to protect yours, though they usually are not as concerned about that). The terms may include conditions of manufacture, quality standards, inspection requirements, permits, bonding, contingency, insurance, and warranties. Generally, customers will ask for terms that are highly favorable to them, and they may ask that providers assume all or most of the risk. In the construction world, for example, customers (often referred to as "owners") and the construction management company commonly elect a contractual relationship called "CM at Risk," or construction management at risk. By legal definition, most if not all the risk (e.g., budget overruns, schedule slippage, subcontractor performance, safety) falls on the CM provider. Thus, willingness to accept risk and a proven ability to manage it favorably become major acceptability criteria in the customer's decision-making and negotiating processes.

In determining whether you are acceptable as a provider, customers want to know whether your terms are negotiable, whether you are willing to meet them somewhere in the middle, or whether your legal position is so intransigent that it makes them assume too much risk or liability. They will also want to know if you can meet the nonnegotiable requirements of the contract, which usually are imposed by the government. These are such things as EEO compliance, EPA emission standards, and other applicable federal, state, or local laws and regulations.

Nonnegotiable requirements are rarely an issue, but it's not uncommon for a company's legal and sales departments to disagree strongly about how flexible to be in areas where the terms are negotiable. There are no easy answers, but you should recognize that you create a powerful differentiator for a competitor if both companies are credible but your competitor is more flexible on terms than you are. If your prices are roughly equivalent, then your competitor's greater willingness to meet the customer on terms may be enough to swing the decision in their favor.

Competitive Price

Within reason, you can control how negotiable your terms are. Within reason, you can also control another important part of acceptability: your price.

The notion that price is the most important factor in most competitive bids is so common it's virtually legendary. From space shuttles to bridges, from accounting services to coffee cups, there are legions of bidders who will swear that they lost a bid based on price and price alone.

If lowest price is truly the only driver of the buying decision in your markets, then reduce overhead and increase margins by simply closing down your marketing/sales/business development functions. Why would you need them? Just find out what the customer wants, quickly and as cheaply as possible show them that you've got it, and give them a price. No advanced conditioning of the customer and the deal, no relationship building, no credibility or acceptability issues, just a number. How would your business fare? If your answer is, "We would be ruined," then there has to be a lot more to winning than just low price, which we've seen used too often as the explanation for losing.

The surprising truth is that price is rarely the decisive factor in provider selection except where all else is equal—in short, where what you are selling is a commodity. In the highly competitive world we live in today, it is convenient to think that many goods and services have been reduced to commodities, but Harvard's Theodore Levitt argues differently. In his book, *The Marketing Imagination*, he says, "There is no such thing as a commodity. All goods and services can be differentiated and usually are."[2]

We once asked the worldwide purchasing director for a Top 5 engineering and construction firm whether he ever told providers and subcontractors that they lost bids based on price when in fact it was something else. He laughed and said, "All the time." "How often do you do that?" we asked. He estimated that at least 60 percent of the time higher price was not the determining factor, but he said it was easier to tell them that because he wasn't prepared to argue about the other factors—the real reasons they lost. Also, price is a convenient way to avoid a lengthy discussion with a loser simply because he's not about to disclose pricing data for the other competitors, including the winner.

So what were his real reasons? He said it could be anything: less comfort with their team, a bad experience someone had had with them previously, less apparent commitment on their part to the contract. "Sometimes," he said, "a company just doesn't seem to want the work as badly as the winner does."

Nothing that two different competitors offer will ever be the same, precisely because the product—even something as straightforward as raw materials (often called "commodities")—is offered by providers with different strategies, messages, people, systems, policies, locations, channels, distribution networks, communication skills, terms and conditions, and so on. Bidders imagine that there is a level playing field and that price is the primary differentiator, but that is simply not true. The playing field is never level, nor should you want it to be. Price will always be a key factor in competitive bids. It must be. But your price doesn't always have to be lowest for you to win. However, it must be in the *competitive range*, and this is a crucial concept.

The competitive range may be defined as the highest and lowest prices the customer is willing to pay for the goods and services received. Competitive range is a set of expectations based on what they've paid before for this product or service, what they understand to be the range of prices currently being paid by others in the marketplace, and the relative value of what they are getting for their money. Note that we said the highest *and* lowest prices they would be willing to pay. No sensible customer will pay more for the product or service than it is worth to them, but they also don't want to pay less. Bidders whose prices are too far below the customer's price expectations raise suspicion. Did they not understand the requirements? Are they omitting something important? Will quality suffer? Are there hidden costs that will only become apparent later? Are these bidders lowballing the bid to get the contract and then planning to recover more money later by means of change orders, legal hairsplitting, squeezing subcontractors and suppliers, and the like?

Having the right price means having a price that is neither too much higher than the average bidder is asking nor too much lower. Further, if your price is higher or highest (but still in the competitive range), can selecting you be justified by the higher value you offer? Does your proposal offer justifiably higher quality, speed, reliability, maintainability, usability, or other performance measures important to the customer? Does it make a compelling and proven argument that although the front-end price is higher, the cost of ownership is significantly lower through lower maintenance cost, longer production runs, and so on?

The key question to ask yourself is, "Could my customer justify to their board or senior management selecting me over other providers if my price is higher than the prices my competitors quoted?" Having the right price means your customer can justify it to anyone who asks. It also means that when your customer argues for your higher price as the right price to decision makers, your customer has joined your business development team. When that happens, your proposal must provide all that's needed to make the case on your price airtight.

Conducive Political Environment

Now we come to the aspect of acceptability you cannot control, at least not completely: the political environment. In many bidding situations, political considerations play a role in determining which provider is acceptable, either internally in the customer's organization or externally in the political, economic, and social domains in which the customer operates. Some examples of political situations that could affect the outcome of a bid are:

➤ The customer has a high profile or is extremely important in the country in which it operates. The country's politicians become concerned about and try to influence who works with the customer or supplies its raw materials or services. This is obviously true with nationalized companies in many parts of the world, but political influence is likely to be felt whenever the bid has some degree of national importance.

➤ The customer is located in a country that is hostile toward or out of favor with the country in which your company is located.

➤ The customer is under pressure to use local providers or labor, and in your offer you must find some way to show substantial "local presence" or to make maximum use of "local content" (e.g., sources of labor, supplies, and/or raw materials).

➤ Your customer is a government entity that has to "share the wealth" among providers. Your company won a recent contract, and it's now another provider's turn to win (though it would rarely be expressed this straightforwardly). Or one of your competitors must win this contract to stay in business—and the customer knows that. In the heyday of the Cold War, it was common practice for the U.S. Department of Defense to award contracts that seemed designed to keep certain defense industry providers healthy not only for the purpose of maximum choice for the buyer but also to bolster depressed geographic areas with federal dollars.

> Your company recently had a high-profile problem—an oil spill or other environmental disaster, a product safety lawsuit, a serious violation of a law or regulation, a sexual harassment complaint, or some other social or legal issue. Consequently, awarding you the contract could cause the customer more public scrutiny than they want.

> Your company failed to deliver on a previous contract to the customer or had some other notable product quality or delivery problem, so giving you this contract would cause the decision maker more internal scrutiny than they wish.

Many of these situations are beyond your control, but you should assess the political environment as you consider bidding on a contract. If any political factors could prevent you from winning the contract, then you need to strategize about how to overcome those factors, or perhaps decline to bid for this work.

Returning to Bob Cullen for a moment, we see that his company's bid was acceptable to the NSF. Their terms were negotiable, and their price was lower than the winning company's price. It would be difficult to assess any political factors that may have influenced the decision because we don't know what they might have been. However, everything we know suggests that Bob's company also passed the acceptability test. So why did they lose?

Creating Preference

It should be obvious that merely establishing credibility and being acceptable to the customer do not win bids. They just open the gates so the customer feels confident in awarding you the contract. The reality of competition in the new millennium is that many bidders can pass through those gates, and that's what happened in Bob's case. If no company bidding on a contract did anything more than establish credibility and acceptability, then the playing field truly would be level and low price would be the decisive factor in all bids. But that's not how the game is played.

Everyone tries to create preference. Getting others to prefer you is so ingrained in human behavior that it would be difficult to imagine life without it. We learn it as children, experience it in every aspect of our lives, and understand it as one of the most operational aspects of competition. It's the entire purpose of dating and courtship. We want to create a bias in our favor. We want to tip that level playing field for our benefit. In competitive bidding, as in courtship, creating preference comes down to three things: building the right relationships, telling a compelling story, and behaving in ways that differentiate us from our competitors.

The Right Relationships

Since people decide who should receive a contract, you must have relationships with the right people in the customer's organization to build preference. The right people include the decision maker and everyone else who can influence the decision. Clearly, if these people prefer you, then your odds of winning the contract increase enormously. This is nothing new, but the implications are important for three reasons:

1. You have to know who the right people are, and this is not a trivial requirement. Sometimes, you don't know who will make the final decision. Other times, you know the decision maker, but you are unlikely to know everyone who will influence the buying decision. The influencers include advisers to the decision maker (usually other high-level executives); the people in the organization who will manage or use the product or service being purchased; the gatekeepers who conduct the purchasing process; the people who evaluate your proposal as part of that process; and perhaps some external advisers, such as consultants, lawyers, government officials, and bankers.

   The network of power and influence in any organization is dynamic and complex. It's often difficult even for insiders to fully comprehend all the influences on a decision, so it is certain that outsiders will have only a proximate view of the situation. Moreover, the group of people advising and influencing the decision maker is likely to change from one contract to the next. So, although you may know who influenced a previous contract, you are unlikely to know everyone who will influence the next decision.

2. Relationships don't spring to maturity overnight. It takes time to build a good relationship with anyone. So the implication of having

the right relationships is that you have to build those relationships over time. This is why getting work from new customers is harder than getting more work from existing customers. Many providers have developed strategic account management programs whose aim is to ensure that they have the right relationships established long before key opportunities arise.

3. Resting on your laurels with people is likely to lead to permanent rest. You can't depend on existing relationships to carry the day. You have to work those relationships actively while the opportunity develops. Any personal or professional relationship will decline in quality and intensity if left unattended. This means meeting with the people you know, asking about the opportunity and listening to what they say, discussing their needs, and exploring alternatives. Your goal should be to presell your solution, *to prepare the way for the proposal*, and you do that by testing the solution ahead of time, discovering what works and what doesn't, and seeing what excites them and what leaves them cold.

GOLDEN RULE:
A proposal is not an isolated event but a critical part of a larger process. As such, the proposal doesn't introduce the solution but confirms what has already been offered to the customer, unofficially validated, and now must be formally defined to be accepted.

Having the right relationships also depends on preselling your team. Since you build credibility, in part, by having the right team to serve the customer's needs, it is imperative to introduce that team not only before you submit your proposal but also before the customer releases an RFP. The earlier you can make the customer comfortable with the people who will work with them if you get the contract, the better off you are. When they read about your proposed team in your proposal, customers should think of the team members as old friends.

If you read Bob's story carefully, it should be apparent that he and his company did not have the right relationships in the customer's organization. They weren't sure who would be making the selection decision. They didn't get started on their bid until the RFP was released; they weren't able to work the hallways, develop the relationships, and begin building bias in their favor. In fact, much of their bid process was focused internally, not on the customer.

A Compelling Story

Now we get to the art in preference building: telling a compelling story. A great story told poorly will lose every time to a good story told well. Assuming all else is equal—that you and your key competitors are credible and acceptable and that each company has good relationships in the customer's organization—the winning team will be the one that has been most compelling in the presentation of its offer. Artistry matters.

It is a fundamental fact of human behavior that what is most compelling to most people is themselves. When something new comes along, what they most want to know is how it affects them. Likewise, when customers want to buy something, they want most to know what it will do for them. How does it meet their needs and solve their problem? How does the solution benefit them? The remarkable irony of most proposals and customer presentations is that they are focused on the provider instead of on the customer. Most proposals are about as compelling as last year's phone book because they center on the provider's qualifications and products or services instead of on what the customer needs and how the provider's solution benefits the customer.

For example, as a key element in their pursuit of a major opportunity, a technology company never failed to tell the customer, "When it comes to customer focus, we have 20-20 vision 24/7/365." They provided generic information about their capabilities in pretty-picture brochures totally focused on themselves rather than placed in the context of this customer's needs. Their proposal was heavily boilerplated with their own logo prominently displayed on every page. Their final presentation focused on them for the first twenty-three slides, finally shifting to the customer for the last eight slides. They lost. The customer didn't believe the words. They believed how the people who said those words actually behaved.

Most proposals are "we" focused instead of "you" focused. So the first lesson in making your offer compelling is to focus your proposal and presentation on the customer. If you can do that, everything else you do will be icing on the cake. In Bob's case, they told a good story, but they were focused on their own approach, their team, and their solution—not on the problem the NSF was trying to solve, the need they were trying to fulfill. Here are five points that, in addition to customer focus, make your story compelling:

1. Your story should have clear messages about why the customer should choose you. Like billboards, headlines, and sound bytes, your messages should be bold, crisp, and memorable.

2. Your story should address each of the customer's needs and requirements—in the order the customer stated them in the bid request. Being compliant is critical because when customers start to evaluate proposals they are looking for losers, not winners. They need to clear the clutter so they can focus on the serious contenders, and the best way for them to narrow the field is to eliminate the bidders who were noncompliant to their request for information.

3. Your story should explain why you made the choices you did in crafting your solution. You chose one distribution channel instead of others. Why? And how does that choice benefit the customer? You chose one technology over another. Why? And what positive business impact will that have on the customer? You proposed John Doe as your project manager instead of all the other people you might have proposed. Why? What does John Doe bring to this customer that no one else (in your organization and among your competitors) does?

   Your choices are the features of your offer, and those choices say a lot about how you have approached the customer's problem. If you have made smart choices, and the customer can see that, then your story will be more compelling. Incidentally, in explaining your choices you have a great opportunity to ghost your competitors, who presumably have made different choices.

4. Your story should be told visually as well as verbally. Even before the age of video games and short attention spans, many readers were more affected by visuals than by words. Visuals draw the eye and engage the imagination. One well-designed visual, presented well, has more power than pages and pages of text. Annotated visuals are especially compelling. These have short interpretive captions that draw readers to and explain important parts of the illustration. A well-annotated visual is like a walking tour of the illustration; it draws the reader's eyes to what the bidder wants to emphasize and makes the journey more enlightening.

5. Finally, your story should meet each of its audiences' needs. For the customer's technical evaluators, who are primarily interested in whether the offer meets the specifications, the proposal shows—often point by point—how the proposed solution complies with the requirements. For the customer's financial evaluators, the proposal presents the bidder's costs in ways that facilitate financial analysis

(one best practice today is to include an electronic spreadsheet for the customer's accountants).

For the customer's executive readers, including the primary decision maker and key advisers, the best practice is to tell the story in a well-designed, separately bound executive summary. This summary gives the top-management perspective. It usually links the customer's key issues and needs to the bidder's primary features and benefits, and if it's done well it highlights how the bidder's solution is differentiated from competing solutions. The best executive summaries are designed for maximum visual impact. They make good use of color and follow the "one-third" rule: 1/3 text, 1/3 visuals, and 1/3 white space. They end with an "elevator speech"—a concise statement of the most compelling reasons for choosing your solution and bid over others. Chapter 6 provides an extensive examination of what executive summaries must accomplish, what they look like, and how best to create them.

Winning Behaviors

The third thing it takes to build preference is behaving as though you really want the work. This is easier said than done, but it is a real and powerful differentiator in the marketplace. Companies have won and lost hundreds of millions of dollars based on whether they distinguished themselves behaviorally.[3] *Behavioral differentiation* occurs when you do something your competitors fail to do—when you show more interest, pay special attention, take more care, or in some other way go the extra mile. Here are some examples of behavioral differentiation:

- ➤ Your CEO meets with the customer's CEO and conveys your company's commitment to the relationship and desire to get the job.
- ➤ Senior executives in your company are dedicated to your customer and show an ongoing commitment to meeting their counterparts in the customer's organization and building relationships from top to top.
- ➤ You move some people to a location at or near the customer's location to ensure that you understand their local needs and environment and show your commitment to them.
- ➤ You engage in joint planning with the customer to ensure that you understand their needs and have the wherewithal to serve them with excellence.

➤ You make frequent, value-added contact with customer representatives at all levels in their organization. These contacts help demonstrate that you want their business.

➤ You are proactive with your customer. You tactfully point out opportunities and pitfalls to them.

➤ You take the time to get to know your customer's customers. You talk to them, survey them, and develop insight into their buying habits and preferences. You can therefore talk intelligently to your customer about their customers' needs and wants.

➤ When opportunities arise, you are quick to discuss them with your customer. You take advantage of every opportunity to question them about their needs and to understand their business goals, the barriers to achieving those goals, and the alternatives the customer has.

➤ You make valuable connections for the customer. You introduce them to other people who can help them or otherwise add value to their business.

➤ You show a deep interest in their business and industry. You become knowledgeable enough for them to value you as consultants.

➤ If you will be proposing a team of people to serve them, you assign and introduce the key members of your team well before the customer releases an RFP.

➤ At preliminary meetings, you prepare an executive summary that hits the high points, and you leave copies of these summaries with them.

➤ If possible, you demonstrate your products or services for them. You give them the hands-on experience to help them feel more comfortable.

➤ You send thank-you notes after meetings.

➤ You send them business articles, news clippings, or other information that would be helpful to them. You do this periodically enough to maintain the sense of your continuing commitment to them as individuals and to their company.

➤ You care about their share price and show it by being concerned about their market performance.

➤ You read and comment on their annual report, their quarterly reports, and any other news that becomes available about them.

➤ When they have an open house or a similar event, you attend.

➤ When they have company anniversaries or other notable events, you send a card or make a call.

➤ If you have a personal relationship, you note the important events in their lives and celebrate or commiserate appropriately.
➤ You return their calls promptly.
➤ If you make a commitment to them, you keep it—no matter what.
➤ If you are giving them a presentation, you do it professionally and leave copies of a presentation summary prepared especially for that occasion.
➤ You hand-deliver proposals if at all possible.
➤ When problems occur, you personally get on the phone and stay there until you resolve them.

Behavioral differentiation is not easy. It takes attention and effort. It can't be faked. You either care about the customer and the business or you don't, and you demonstrate it.

No one in business is indifferent to customers, but many people lack the commitment, the intensity, the drive, or the time to do what they should to make themselves stand out. Consequently, the people who do take time to do it right create an enormous advantage for themselves. You should be thinking *winning behavior* from the moment you decide to pursue a customer and a particular opportunity with them. How can you show them, through your behavior, that you are deeply committed to them and really want their business?

Ultimately, this is why Bob's company lost. They were not as proactive as the winning provider in differentiating themselves through their behavior, so the customer wound up preferring someone else. In the homestretch of a highly competitive bid, the company that is better at positively setting themselves apart from the pack will score many points over their competitors, and there are countless examples of that being enough to capture the win. Smart companies try to differentiate themselves behaviorally in every bid, but they can't do so unless they bid selectively. The cost of behavioral differentiation is too high.

In virtually every competition we have been involved with, the competing bidders devote a remarkable amount of time and energy to proving that they are credible and acceptable. It would be fair to say that companies spend hundreds of millions of dollars annually trying to convince customers that their company can pass these two tests. Are those dollars misspent? We think the right answer is "not entirely." Clearly, you must show customers that you are credible and acceptable. However, if you could save 20 percent of that time and money, you could invest in what really makes the difference: *creating preference*.

That's what it takes to win customers and competitive bids.

Challenges for Readers

➤ We always consider behavior as something that people do either singly or together. But think about how behavior occurs in proposals. How does your company behave in their proposals? For instance, if you claim powerful customer focus as one good reason customers should choose you, how can that be observed in your proposals? Are they customer focused? How would the reader know? Do you display the customer's logo prominently on every page and at the upper left? Or is your logo where theirs should be? Examine the subject-verb clusters in your proposal text. How many of them express your company as the subject, including pronoun references to your own organization, versus how often your sentences use your customer as the subject? If you cite benefits of your offer, are they linked to the customer's bottom-line goals or do they exist in a customerless vacuum? Do you include an executive summary with each proposal that isn't just a textual summary of the offer but is organized according to the customer's key issue or selection criteria? Does your proposal address the customer's key issues, those things that keep them awake at night, rather than addressing only requirements and specifications? The challenge, then, is to examine some of your recent, representative proposals and calibrate how well they are "behaving" in ways the customer can observe.

➤ On average, what percentage of your business developers' workweek is spent in direct face time with prospects and customers? And what percentage of the information gleaned during the face time is being captured, analyzed, and incorporated in your proposals to those customers? Is there a powerful communication link between what is captured in middle game and what drives the endgame proposal? How can that link be formed? Strengthened? Made to be a powerful differentiator for your organization and in the eyes of your customers?

➤ What strategies can your organization develop and deploy to build credibility, acceptability, and preference? What knowl-

> edge and skills would be required to implement those strate-
> gies? What would the investment be and what kind of return
> could you achieve in today's tough markets?
>
> ➤ Consider how often people in your company claim that they
> submitted a fine proposal and then lost to the low bidder.
> Then consider this question: "Did we lose to a lower price or
> did we fail to win because we beat ourselves (i.e., we didn't
> adequately sell our own price, both before the proposal and
> in it)?"

Notes

1. Terry R. Bacon and David G. Pugh, *The Behavioral Advantage: What the Smartest, Most Successful Companies Do Differently to Win in the B2B Arena* (New York: AMACOM, 2004).
2. Theodore Levitt, *The Marketing Imagination* (New York: The Free Press, 1986), p. 72.
3. The whole topic of behavioral differentiation has become so important and has taken on such a life of its own that we have devoted two books to the subject. See Terry R. Bacon and David G. Pugh, *Winning Behavior: What the Smartest, Most Successful Companies Do Differently* (New York: AMACOM, 2003) and *The Behavioral Advantage*. The former focuses primarily but not exclusively on business-to-consumer behavioral differentiation, whereas the latter focuses on business-to-business, including business-to-govern-ment, behavioral differentiation.

Chapter 6

WINNING EXECUTIVE SUMMARIES

Your Most Powerful Selling Tool

GOLDEN RULE:

A compelling executive summary gives the customer's evaluators what they need to sell your company to their decision makers. When they do that, they become de facto members of your sales force.

One of the finest red wines in the world is Penfold's Grange Hermitage from South Australia. The label on each bottle advises purchasers to age the wine for twenty years or more to allow it to reach perfection. That's a long time to get it right, and it has taken even longer than that for the concept of the executive summary to mature.

In their earliest incarnation, prior to and after World War II, many proposals did not have executive summaries. They were mainly workmanlike responses to a list of technical specifications and, in many cases, were offered and accepted by handshake. If an executive summary was prepared, it simply summarized the key elements or features of the offer. It was not intended to be a selling tool. The selling was done on the golf course, in the restaurant or bar, or in the president's office. Even into the 1970s some companies prided themselves on cutting deals through the oral agreements of their directors or owners.

As the complexity of the projects increased, proposals exploded in size. It was not uncommon (and still isn't) for complex, multiyear U.S. government procurements to require multivolume proposals. When documents become that long and complex, an executive summary is virtually mandatory. Somewhere the story had to be told in a more readable, comprehensive fashion, especially for nonexperts, which decision makers typically are. Initially, these executive summaries were mirrors of the entire proposal. If a topic was addressed in the proposal, then it had to be covered in the summary.

Clearly, if you take this approach, you write the proposal first and extract its key points later as you create the summary. Form follows function, and the summary will be a kind of miniproposal. The problem with this approach is that not all of the content of a proposal is worth summarizing. Some of it merely responds to project, product, or standard contractual requirements and is not *crucial* in the customer's mind, nor does it differentiate you from your competitors. Consequently, these executive summaries are full of fat, use color ineffectively, and aren't effective selling tools.

Other executive summaries are treated like introductions or cover letters. They say how pleased your company is to respond to the customer's request for proposal, promise to comply with their requirements, introduce the proposal content, and identify the sections in the proposal. These are the legitimate functions of an introduction and cover letter and belong in those documents, but they do not constitute an executive summary.

During the past two decades, global competition has increased dramatically, with many more bidders vying for pieces of the pie. It is probable that, for any particular project, dozens of companies are capable of bidding the work and executing it well if they are awarded the contract. Under these conditions, you have to work harder than ever to make your bid stand out. Every part of the proposal becomes an important selling tool, and none is more important than the executive summary. It *is* what the key executives are likely to read, and as bidders realized this, they took a new look at the executive summary, and proposal writers began to:

➤ Reject the mirror image concept and focus on the aspects of their offer that differentiated them. *In short, the summary became the primary instrument of their win strategy.*

➤ Move away from completely narrative summaries. Newer summaries contain visuals, color, graphic design elements, and lessons from the advertising and marketing worlds.

> View summaries as key selling tools, so they focused on the information key executives would need to make favorable buying decisions.

Today, the executive summary is typically seen as *the single most important part of a proposal.* As a result they are demonstrably more powerful and impressive.

The State of the Art: High-Tech Summaries

These days, companies submitting proposals without powerful executive summaries risk appearing unsophisticated, almost like novices, because those companies that set best practices for business development across their industries are those that constantly seek innovations in how they communicate with customers. A state-of-the-art executive summary is such an innovation; indeed, it continues to evolve along with improvements in print media and information management technologies. More and more proposers create state-of-the-art executive summaries that are:

> Separately bound (i.e., saddle-stitched) brochures
> Prepared by professional designers, following excellent design principles
> Primarily visual and visually exciting
> Spatially designed to avoid overcrowding the pages
> Sophisticated in their use of representational graphics, where the graphics actually represent what is being promoted (as opposed to purely ornamental graphics and clip art) and use color effectively
> Professionally printed on high-quality paper
> Written specifically for the decision makers, with compelling high-level sales messages rather than technical detail
> Interactive, using electronic programs and media such as PowerPoint, CD-ROMs, or the World Wide Web

One particularly exciting development is the executive summary on the Web. The proposer creates a confidential Web site and the customer's decision makers and influencers go there to *experience*, not just read, the executive summary. The Web environment enables levels of richness and user definition not possible on paper or even CD-ROM. Flash technology and other forms of animation deliver the sales messages with interest and impact, and each user is free to navigate the site to learn more about what interests him or her. For example, a page about the proposed team might include links to the individuals' résumés. The pages might even include video and audio clips of the team members describing their roles and what they commit to provide the customer as added value and compelling benefits. Instead of reading a letter of commitment, the customer actually hears it from the executive sponsor. Today, what you can do with an executive summary is limited only by the pace of technology—and that's faster than most of us can keep up with.

The bad news is, many of your competitors are sparing no expense to prepare and submit state-of-the-art executive summaries—or if they're not, they'll soon start. The good news is, by and large, they will fail to comprehend the full potential impact and will submit executive summaries that look pretty or are even technologically dazzling, but totally miss the mark.

If you view your proposal and executive summary as embodying a set of value-enhancing behaviors and weave as many as you can throughout the pages, you'll vastly improve your chances of winning. Many of your competitors, in contrast, are likely to engage in *value-diminishing* behaviors in their preproposal business development efforts, their proposals, and their executive summaries, inadvertently handing you a major opportunity for creating positive differentiation.

Keep in mind that a very real question the customer is seeking to answer is not only "Who can do the work?" but "With whom do we *want* to work?" Basically, business development at any customer contact point is a chemistry test, and a powerful executive summary helps you pass it.

A Powerful Executive Summary: Focus on the Benefits

The main purpose of an executive summary is *not* to summarize the offer or preview the content of a larger proposal, or even to describe and demonstrate knowledge of the requirements. An executive summary:

➤ Tells the story of your offer in terms of the customer's issues and priorities, thereby demonstrating your attention to these issues and, most important, your ability to help them achieve their goals

➤ Answers the "Big Four" questions every customer asks: "Why us?" "Why not them?" "So what?" and "How so?"—by

- Stating the key reason(s) for choosing you ("Why us?")
- Stating, without mentioning your competitors by name, the reasons for *not* choosing them ("Why not them?")
- Communicating the value in your offer by linking features to specific benefits ("So what?") and by providing proof of your ability to deliver the benefits ("How so?")

➤ Behaviorally differentiate your company in the mind of the customer—help them decide not just if they can work with you, but if they *want* to work with you (in other words, pass the chemistry test)

➤ Deepen your relationship with the customer and position yourself for the long term, win or lose (recognizing that sometimes it really does come down to price, and it has to be the other guy's turn at least occasionally)

An executive summary is your best opportunity to reach your customer's key decision makers and convince them that your offer or solution is the one they want. It "tells the story" of your offer, solution, and proposal in a way that they can relate to and will make them want it: by showing how their goals are achieved. Too often we forget that whenever a customer calls for proposals, that call is part of a larger procurement process seeking an optimum and affordable solution to a problem. Since your customers are not in the problem-solving business, they have decided to solve this particular problem and are willing to make the investment to achieve business or organizational goals.

Thus, a compelling executive summary doesn't focus on the details of the solution. It focuses on the customer goals, and how they will be achieved as the necessary return on investment. In other words, *the executive summary becomes the primary vehicle for demonstrating to your customer at the highest levels that the bottom-line benefit of working with you is that you will get them to their goal(s)*. And as long as your competitors continue the standard practice of focusing their proposals and executive summaries almost exclusively on themselves and the features of their offer, your executive summary provides you with significant positive differentiation in the selection process.

Preparing to Create an Executive Summary

To create the kind of executive summary we've been talking about—the kind that makes it nearly impossible for the customer *not* to want to choose you—you must have four things:

1. Intimate knowledge of the customer, the opportunity, and your competition
2. A good solution at an acceptable price
3. A thoughtful win strategy that mitigates your weaknesses and highlights your strengths, as it addresses your competitors' strengths and weaknesses
4. A compelling story line, or set of sales messages

Develop Your Win Strategy

Developing and applying a thoughtful win strategy for your executive summary requires an in-depth understanding of the customer's key issues in selecting a provider. A successful business development effort prior to the RFP will surface these key issues and help the customer define, refine, and/or expand them. Furthermore, whenever helping the customer to identify a key issue will genuinely provide them value as well as cast your approach in a favorable light, you should do so.

If, for example, your project team will include a full-time, certified safety engineer and you know that at least one of your competitors will attempt to win with a lower price by not offering that position on their team, you serve your customer (and, by extension, your own company) by influencing them to make a tangible commitment to safety. Your objective in doing this is to ensure that key issues prior to the RFP become that solicitation's formal selection criteria. Typical customer key issues might include:

➤ Cost—initial and/or life cycle (always a high priority)
➤ Schedule/delivery
➤ Related experience
➤ Key personnel
➤ Compatibility with existing systems
➤ Local presence
➤ Technology
➤ Legal/regulatory compliance
➤ Safety
➤ Past performance/track record
➤ Reliability
➤ Proven technology
➤ Turnkey solution

Seeing that you have influenced those criteria to the customer's and your advantage is hard evidence that as you enter the proposal phase you are perceived by the customer as their preferred provider. Understanding those key issues/selection criteria helps you develop a comprehensive set of strategies for the final push to winning the award. The trick is to understand not only the key issues but how the customer sees you and your competitors relative to each one—because those perceptions ultimately define each company's strengths and weaknesses. For example, if your company has a strong track record in technology development, but your customer doesn't know about it, their perception will be that you are weak in that area, which is a key issue for them. You need a strategy to change that perception, and until you have one, you'll suffer the consequences of a simple and sometimes painful truth: *Customer perception is reality*.

One key element in creating a winning executive summary is developing a strategy that differentiates you from your competitors and shows customers why they should choose you. Developing such a win strategy requires a thorough understanding of the customer's key issues, the competition, and your own strengths and weaknesses. An effective win strategy does four things:

1. Highlights your strengths
2. Ghosts (i.e., subtly points out) your competitors' weaknesses
3. Mitigates your weaknesses
4. Neutralizes your competitors' strengths

These are the basic elements of proposal strategy, and you should always invoke all four in developing your executive summary. Strategies provide your executive summary with your best answers to the Big Four: "Why us?" "Why not them?" "So what?" "How so?" (Chapter 2 provides an extensive discussion of the Big Four.) Effective strategies are linked to the customer's issues and consist of an objective plus one or more actions to achieve it (see Table 6-1).

Build a Compelling Story Line

For years we have used a specific tool for helping our customers develop their most compelling sales messages in executive summaries, proposals, and presentations. We call this tool the *GIFBP Matrix* because it links the customer's goals and issues to the most significant features, benefits, and proofs of your offer. It helps you develop the theme statements that will provide compelling answers to the Big Four. Doing this requires an understanding of the linkage of goals, issues, features, benefits, and proofs, illustrated next.

Table 6-1. **Sample strategies.**

Key Issue	Objective	Action
Safety	Highlight our strength	We will highlight our safety record, which is far better than the industry average, and stress the benefits of lower insurance and workers compensation rates, along with those of a safe workplace.
Credibility-based relationships	Mitigate our weakness	To mitigate our lack of close relationships in the customer's project management group, we will subcontract to Boron Labs, which has been working with the customer for eight years and has excellent top-to-top relationships.
Personnel qualifications/ experience	Neutralize a competitor strength	We will establish our team's credibility with tailored résumés beginning with "Projects Successfully Completed." In addition, a "Recent Performance Matrix" will cross-reference the team members with names of projects, brief project descriptions, and customer references.
Cost risk	Ghost a competitor weakness	We will illustrate potential problems with Competitor A's discount service center approach to maintenance by showing data on the incidence of critical component failure in the field, ghosting it as an unacceptably high-risk approach to lower cost.

Goals   What the customer needs to achieve

Issues   Concerns with selecting a provider to get them to the goals

Features   The definition of how you will address the issues

Benefits   What value the features provide the customer in achieving the goals

Proofs   Validation and substantiation that the benefits are real

By effectively linking goals, issues, features, benefits, and proofs, you are presenting your offer in a way that responds directly to the needs and interests of the customer's decision makers and influencers, which gives you a critical edge on the competition. You can revisit Figure 2-3 to see the thought line in the GIFBP Matrix, one that links the collective impact of the benefits to the achievement of the customer's goal.

The GIFBP Matrix

You can develop a more general GIFBP Matrix for a specific market or market segment, customer group, product line, or key account before an opportunity with them begins to surface. From this GIFBP Matrix, you can extract and adjust relevant information for the opportunity-specific GIFBPs that will drive the executive summary messages. To build a GIFBP Matrix:

1. List the business goal(s) driving the customer's need for your product or service.
2. List the key issues by linking them to the goal(s).
3. List the features of your offer that address each issue. You'll probably have several features for each issue.
4. For each feature, ask "So what?" to brainstorm the benefits. Again, you may have several. State them in terms of what the features will do for the customer. *Caution:* Especially in technical offers, people will determine what they think are benefits but in fact are features masquerading as benefits. A new computer may have the fastest processor available, but the benefit is not speed because "So what?" still applies. Rather, the benefit is greater efficiency and productivity multiplied by the number of people using the new computers. *Whenever possible, think of benefits in terms of business impact.*
5. List the proofs for each benefit that will substantiate its value and show that it is real. The customer can expect to receive not just the features of the offer but the benefits they create. Proofs can include:

- Facts, figures, or published information on your company or its products and services
- Customer testimonials or references
- Visuals (especially those incorporating photographs or other "hard" data)
- Hard data (e.g., technical/cost data, production, and other performance statistics)

Figure 6-1 shows a completed GIFBP linkage and the sales message, or theme statement, that "falls" out of the raw GIFBP information. We transferred that theme statement—one of several we created while working with a client on a major must-win opportunity—to the top of the page in their executive summary, where we addressed the issue of "proven fast-track capability."

Figure 6-1. **GIFBP Matrix and theme statement.** Once a rich GIFBP linkage has been developed, a proposal theme statement "drops" out of it, giving the customer compelling and substantive reasons for choosing you.

Goals	Issues	Features	Benefits	Proofs
• 22 months to start-up to capture 23% share in emerging market	• Proven fast-track capability	• Complete in-house siting, licensing, engineering, procurement, and construction	• Minimizes duplication, administration, coordination • Accelerates problem solving • Single point of responsibility, accountability • Seamless transitions for all phases • Lowest possible risk of schedule creep	• Numerous projects fast-tracked with start-ups on or ahead of schedule (e.g., Norwood Refinery, Andreas Platform, ABC Ethylene Plant)

Bottom-Line Benefit

To meet your 22-month startup goal for capturing an initial 23% share in an emerging market, B&B offers complete in-house siting, licensing, engineering, procurement, and construction. Our single-supplier approach ensures quick problem solving, seamless transitions, and the lowest possible risk of schedule creep.

A compelling theme statement forged from the GIFBP Matrix has these characteristics:

➤ It identifies a primary feature of the offer addressing the issue (which, in turn, links to the customer's goal) and ties that feature to one, perhaps two, significant benefits it provides the customer. Those benefits—individually for a given key issue and collectively for the whole executive summary—create your best answers to "Why us?" and "So what?" *Features create the latter question; benefits answer it.*

➤ Whenever possible (it won't be 100 percent of the time), communicate legitimate benefits that impact the customer's bottom-line goals (e.g., price, increased market share, public image, regulatory compliance). When you do this, in effect you're telling your customer that the bottom-line benefit of working with your company is that you will get them to their bottom-line goals. And when your win strategy is not lowest price, *that message is a powerful way to sell your price.*

➤ If you have developed a win strategy to ghost your competition on a specific weakness, there is no better place to plant that ghost than the theme statement. The ghost will answer the question, "Why not them?" without, of course, ever mentioning "them" by name. The executive summary in Figure B-1 (Appendix B) includes a theme statement containing the ghost "the widest array of benefits available through a single vendor." Our client was the only proposing company that didn't need to team with one or more other companies for a total solution. The ghost in this case represents a significant feature so we were sure to follow it in the first paragraph of text with a compelling, bottom-line benefit to the customer: "a single provider who assumes the administrative costs for you."

Having answered at least two, possibly three, of the Big Four questions at the top of the executive summary—thereby communicating the main message to the customer about one of their key issues—the space below the theme can now be used to prove the message. In other words, we use a top-down, deductive design for executive summary pages: key issue and theme at the top, proofs from the GIFBP Matrix supporting, substantiating, and reinforcing it. While answering most of the Big Four questions, the theme statement also creates one in the reader's mind: "How so?" The proofs on the page answer that question.

It is usually challenging, if not impossible, to achieve perfect horizontal alignment across all the columns of a GIFBP Matrix. That's because features often link to multiple issues, benefits link to multiple features, proofs link to multiple benefits, and vice versa. The idea is to achieve good approximate horizontal alignment, with minimal repetition in each column.

As you review your features and benefits, think about the features and benefits your competitors are likely to offer. Highlight the features and benefits that make your offer *uniquely advantageous* to the customer in contrast to competing offers. These are your differentiators, your deal makers, your best effort at selling your price.

How to Design an Executive Summary with Impact

Once conceived, a message is not automatically compelling. It must be made compelling or it will fail to get through as intended. A major cause of communication breakdown can be found in the simple fact that the person creating and communicating the message failed to account for the different types of people who will receive it. That is, the target audience for an executive summary typically consists of executive decision makers and those who influence their decisions, such as junior executives, line managers, and/or the people who will actually use your product or service. Within these audience groups, we find a not altogether unpredictable mix of preferences for processing printed information (which are discussed in more detail in Chapter 3):

➤ *Skimmers:* Typically nonexperts who spot-check text by reading sentences at the tops of paragraphs and glance at visuals, reading the captions before moving on

➤ *Scanners:* Typically experts who examine the information, both textual and visual, slowly and in great detail to verify or question the expertise of others

➤ *Visual Conceptualizers:* Typically technical and scientific professionals who think spatially rather than verbally

➤ *Verbal Conceptualizers:* Typically nontechnical professionals who prefer to think and communicate with language, either oral or written

Whereas decision makers tend to be skimmers and visual thinkers, the other audience groups for executive summaries may include both skimmers and scanners, and the visual and verbal thinkers will populate both groups as well.

Dealing with the visual versus the verbal thinkers is fairly simple:

Create a visual for one, write a full-sentence caption for the other; write a paragraph for one, follow it with a visual for the other. This approach means that the executive summary should contain a mix of text and visuals. However, because executives are your primary audience and they tend to be skimmers, we don't recommend trying too hard to satisfy the scanners with lengthy narrative. Instead, make your executive summary highly visual and provide explanatory wording where appropriate but sparely. Address the needs of the skimmers and capture their attention through the liberal use of emphatic devices such as headings, lists, boxes, rules, different fonts, boldface, italics, and shading. Last but not least, use white space as a communication ally to draw attention to the ideas you want to telegraph to the skimmers.

Brochure Format: Your Best Sales Tool

The brochure-style executive summary is your best sales tool for communicating with customer personnel who, in all likelihood, will never read your proposal and may never even see it. Its key advantage is being separately bound, so it can be reproduced in greater numbers and handed out to all the key influencers as well as the decision makers. You can print extra copies to accompany the proposal or leave on a customer's desk, and they'll probably be passed around.

Picture this scene: At a proposal presentation for a $500 million project in Indonesia, the bidder places six copies of the proposal on the customer's conference table along with two dozen copies of the executive summary, which is bound separately as a brochure. After the presentation, only a few copies of the proposal are taken by customer team members, but all of the executive summaries disappear, and the client later calls and requests fifty more.

We've seen this scenario repeated hundreds of times with all types of projects and customers in many different industries. We've heard scores of customer comments on the quality of the executive summaries and how they made the selection decision easier. Why is the executive summary such a powerful tool? The answer is simple:

It's the only part of a proposal the key decision makers are likely to read in its entirety.

After we worked with one of our global engineering and construction clients to improve the quality of their proposals and executive summaries, their win rate improved dramatically. In fact, they won seven out of the next eight projects they chased. Knowing full well that there are many drivers of winning outside the proposal, they wanted to know just how much impact their newfound techniques were producing. So they hired an independent research firm to study if and how their proposals were making a positive difference on their business development efforts. The resulting data showed that when this company invested (time, information, people, effort) in a brochure executive summary as part of their proposal, *their probability of winning increased by 249 percent.*

This company set a new standard for proposals and executive summaries in their industry, a standard some of their competitors have imitated with varying degrees of success but others still can't figure out.

Brochure-style executive summaries should be primarily visual—one to three key visuals on a page, surrounded by captions and theme statements and white space and precious little text. In general, a brochure executive summary should:

➤ Follow the customer's instructions or expressed preferences, if any.

➤ Visually convey your key differentiator—preferably on the cover.

➤ Develop a consistent "look" within the executive summary by using running headers and footers, consistent placement of theme statements, a uniform graphics style, and so on. You want to create the impression that your executive summary was developed by a single mind, not a committee.

➤ Maintain consistent fonts and type styles (bold, italics, etc.) for headings, body text, and so on. Printing conventions suggest sans serif type for headers, serif for text.

➤ Maintain consistent styles for lists (embedded versus displayed, numbers versus bullets, indentation, etc.), captions, themes, and visuals.

➤ Address the customer's key issues and priorities.

➤ Embody your four-point win strategy by systematically highlighting your strengths, mitigating your weaknesses, neutralizing competitor strengths, and ghosting their weaknesses.

➤ Offer compelling reasons for choosing you.

➤ Answer the Big Four.

➤ Demonstrate to the customer that your bottom-line benefits equal their bottom-line goals.

➤ Use color effectively.
➤ Be designed to satisfy the needs of executive readers, with 1/3 visuals, 1/3 text, and 1/3 white space.
➤ Be bound separately from a proposal.
➤ Be laid out in multiples of four pages (four, eight, twelve, sixteen) on 11″ × 17″ sheets to be printed, folded, and saddle stitched (two staples).

The four-page brochure is the most difficult to work with. Invariably, there's so much essential information that fitting it all in while still following the 1/3-1/3-1/3 rule is a real challenge. We find that an eight-page brochure summary is ideal for most readers and is about the right size for many proposals. Larger proposals with more key issues can go to twelve pages or, if necessary, to sixteen pages. It's generally best to go with eight or twelve pages. Even skimmers disengage at some point with longer versions.

A brochure executive summary *tells a story*—the customer's story. It tells how you translated their problems and needs to a solution, how you are partnering with them to solve their problems and achieve their goals.

To tell a good story, you must do three things:

1. Synthesize the primary reasons for choosing you.
2. Be clear yourself about why they should choose you.
3. View the opportunity from the customer's perspective.

The customer shouldn't have to think about the "Why us?" You write the rationale for them.

Above all, a brochure-style executive summary that accompanies a proposal should drive the proposal. That means it should be prepared first, not last, and the proposal sections should echo and expand on the themes. The brochure executive summary tells your story to the people who make the decisions. Therefore, it must be compelling. Furthermore, we consider it a best practice (based on our experience in the field with our clients) that for large, must-win opportunities, the identification of key issues, the preparation of the GIFBP Matrix, and the creation of a full executive summary draft should all happen *prior to* receipt of the RFP. Doing so gives you a major jump start on writing your proposal and on your competitors, and it will pay huge dividends at crunch time toward the end of the proposal preparation period.

Later in the chapter we offer specific techniques for creating the different types of brochure executive summaries, but first consider these general recommendations, applicable to all of them:

> Create the executive summary first and let it "drive" your proposal.
> Make it stand-alone. Don't refer to other sections of the proposal or map out its content.
> Put a simple, strong visual on the cover, preferably conveying your strongest positive differentiator. It's even better if you can somehow incorporate the customer's goal along with your key differentiator in this image.
> Address all of the customer's key issues, linking them to your features, benefits, and proofs on every page.
> Design each page around one or more strong themes, preferably your key positive differentiators addressing each key issue.
> Use every opportunity to demonstrate that your bottom-line benefit equals the customer's bottom-line goal. If possible, do it on every page—if not in a theme, then in a visual or a caption.
> Save your strongest visual and verbal content for the executive summary. It's preferable to design it specially. Don't just look around for something to fill a particular space.
> Use as many quality visuals as you can find or time allows you to create.
> Keep it brief: Use as few pages as you can, while addressing all the issues and following the 1/3-1/3-1/3 rule.
> Write an *elevator speech* and place it at the end (usually on the back cover). This is a short list of the key reasons for choosing you. As a rule, you shouldn't exceed five or six points, and the text should be concise and tightly focused on issues, features, and benefits.

Brochure-style summaries offer a great deal of opportunity for creativity as long as you don't go overboard. The pages should be colorful and interesting, yet clean, and never busy or overwhelming. Figures B-1 and B-2 in Appendix B show two finished brochure executive summaries, one a straightforward, issues-driven style and the other an issues-driven, advertisement style.

Issues-Driven Executive Summary

In an issues-driven, brochure-style executive summary, each page typically has a theme or major content focus. The pages convey a sequence of themes that should match the customer's key issues and priorities or follow some other, customer-connected sequence. The easiest and most effective way to organize your brochure, especially when you're working with RFP evaluation criteria or another customer-supplied list of issues and priorities, is to follow one or the other.

Here is how we organize the four parts of an issues-driven executive summary:

1. *Front Cover:* A graphic depicting your key differentiator, preferably along with the customer's bottom-line business goal.
2. *Inside Front Cover:* A hot-button list. This is a list of the customer's issues in descending order of priority, with the key features and benefits of your offer linked to them. Those linkages can be taken directly from your GIFBP Matrix (see Figure 6-1).
3. *Interior Pages:* The key issues—one or two per page, depending on the number of issues. An eight-page brochure, for example, lends itself to five key issues, each on its own page.
4. *Back Cover:* An elevator speech.

Here's a sample outline for an eight-page brochure based on a typical set of issues (it has room for five key issues on the interior pages):

➤ *Front Cover (page 1):* Logos, title, and so on, plus a visual of our key differentiator. Why we're unique and what that will do for you, the customer. Graphically connecting that differentiator to the customer's goal is a powerful message to send to someone who has just picked up your executive summary and wonders if it will be worth the effort to read it.
➤ *Why Us? (page 2):* A "hot-button list": your key issues and the primary reasons for choosing us.
➤ *Our Approach (page 3):* How it meets your needs and solves your problem; plus the unique advantages we offer.
➤ *Our Team (page 4):* People you can trust to deliver on time, within budget, and with excellence.
➤ *Fast-Track Schedule (page 5):* How and why we can deliver faster than you thought possible.
➤ *Relevant Experience (page 6):* Our long history of success proves that we can deliver as promised.
➤ *Innovative Pricing (page 7):* Our rates may be higher, but your overall cost is lower because of fast-track scheduling and incentive subcontracting.

➤ *Elevator Speech (back cover, page 8):* In summary, why choose us?

A twelve-page brochure has room for nine key issues, or fewer if you need multiple pages to cover one or more issues. We don't recommend a sixteen-page brochure, except for the largest and most complex of offers. Also, a four-page brochure, unless it's a small proposal or there are only three or four key issues, is generally too short.

One nice thing about the issues-driven structure is that it enables you to address each issue in one location, as opposed to having them scattered throughout the document. Also, because it follows the customer's order of priority, it tends to put your most powerful messages up front—that is, if you've done a good job of strategizing. Even if you have a weakness on the customer's highest-priority issue, if you effectively mitigate that weakness, you will eliminate a perception problem.

Finally, addressing the issues in order of priority is a subtle way of demonstrating customer focus and understanding of their needs.

Ad-Style Executive Summary

This style differs from the basic issues-driven style because it is slicker, selling more overtly with softer benefits. It addresses the customer's key issues, but the issues don't follow in lockstep. Instead, it addresses the most critical issues in a minimal, emotionally evocative way—much like a series of magazine ads.

Here are some conditions under which you could consider this type of executive summary:

➤ You know the customer and the job very well and are comfortable enough to take risks.

➤ You're a long shot, and you have nothing to lose by being bold.

➤ Your customer's business invites this approach (e.g., an advertising agency or high-end graphics company), and they would find this sort of brochure "behavior" not only acceptable but empathetic.

➤ Your strategy for winning includes pointing out, or ghosting, the pitfalls of a particular approach, getting the customer to think about the problem in a new way.

➤ You want to break from a pack of ho-hum competitors.

➤ If you want the customer to take a risk, an ad-style brochure can lead the way by demonstrating your willingness to break with convention and extend your creativity.

➤ You need to display your commitment to an emotionally driven (as opposed to financially driven) business goal, such as social or environmental responsibility or image enhancement. The ad-style brochure plays well to any number of concerns that go in directions other than straight down to the financial bottom line.

As with all executive summaries, a full suite of win strategies and themes and the tools for preparing them form the foundation on which it is built. The objective, rather than telling the complete story, is to communicate a few believable points imaginatively so the reader supports them with conviction.

Here are twelve keys to creating an ad-style brochure executive summary:

1. Emphasize your key differentiator, either by visualizing it on the cover or by dedicating space to it in the interior.
2. Address the issues in order of priority, but narrow your focus to a handful of critical issues—say, three to five.
3. Create a colorful, flexible, offbeat layout for the interior pages. Choose your colors to reinforce what you're trying to do. Colors can shout, "Wait a minute—you're going about it all wrong!" or say, "Look, this thing here is more important than that other thing over there." They can convey a sense of professional coolness in a heated battle or a lean, mean approach to a weighty and expensive problem.
4. Spare no expense. Quality paper, printing, images, and the people who excel at creating them are expensive, but so is not winning the contract. To have an impact, an ad-style brochure has to look professional. Anything less than first-class production values will look like a cheap impersonation of the real thing.
5. Dedicate each two-page interior spread to a single issue or a combination of related issues that can be expressed in a few words. Think of it as a billboard for that issue. With three issues, you'll have an eight-page brochure with three billboards plus a front and back cover. Likewise, five issues form a twelve-page brochure.
6. Fill each billboard with one or two strong graphics, bold copy, and lots of white (or colored) space. The objective is to "nail" the issue on two pages, with a few compelling words and images.
7. To select the words and images, explore the customer's emotions. What drives and provokes them? What words and images play to them? What do they value above all else?

8. Work the words very carefully. Pare the message down to its core and deliver it with the fewest, most powerful words at your disposal.
9. Arrange the words and images on the page, linking them in ways that draw the eye from one key point to the next.
10. Resist the urge to keep adding elements. One billboard shouldn't take more than a few seconds to consume. Then the reader should want to explore and ponder the issue. Make them dwell on it by choice, not necessity. Don't clutter the reader's mind with nonessential thoughts or statements that lead to questions straying from the issue at hand. Make them *feel* as well as think.
11. Make it fun. So much of work, including evaluating proposals, is drudgery. Look for ways to lighten it up and make it an enjoyable experience. Use humor where appropriate. Consider a well-placed pun or double entendre. Feel free to poke fun at things you know the customer is also capable of laughing at—but make sure that you're laughing with them, not at them, or, worse still, that they're not laughing at you.
12. If you're working alone, seek feedback from others who know the customer and the opportunity. Ask them to step into the customer's shoes and react to your mock-up as a first-time reader. Where do they ask unwanted questions? Where do they share your conviction? Where do they feel stretched, and where do they feel you've left the comfort zone?

The ad-style executive summary is a bold, even courageous, approach to winning the customer and their work. Its success may well depend on knowing the customer almost as well as they know themselves.

Above all, you have to consider the customer's culture. Identify their boundaries and stretch them a little. Figure out what the rules are and break some of them. A bit of a shock can be good—for example, when you're trying to tell the customer they're going down the same old worn-out path. Demonstrate that you're capable of looking at the situation with fresh eyes, a beginner's mind, and a spark of creativity. When using the shock treatment, remember—the current must be very carefully directed and contained. You must address the right issue with the right feature, the right benefit, and the right proof. *The shock value must equal the level of goal satisfaction.*

And don't be afraid to experiment. Just because you didn't succeed by going outside the norm with one customer on one opportunity doesn't mean it won't work the next time. Try different approaches with different customers, and keep refining them until you succeed more often than not.

The keys to institutionalizing this type of brochure executive summary are creative people and quality images. Commit to building an image library. Buy good-quality photos from an image bank, along with the rights to reuse them. When a specific image plays well to a specific theme and wins you some work, you can build on it. Bring it back to the customer as a reminder of a past positive experience—a visual calling card, a clue that you were there. Thus, the ad-style executive summary can also be an effective branding tool—one that hits right in the center of the customer's emotional generator.

Four-Page Executive Summary

The four-page brochure executive summary is the easiest for customers to absorb—and the hardest for proposers to create. Space limitations create a formidable design challenge, even with fewer key issues. If you use the issues-driven structure, with a hot-button list on the inside front cover, you've only got one internal page on which to address the issues.

Few opportunities are small enough to lend themselves to a four-page brochure without a great deal of paring down and editing and editing and paring down some more. However, if it's done well, the four-pager makes a neat, compact presentation and is highly desirable to the customer. Following are some suggestions for using this type of executive summary effectively:

➤ Consider using a format other than the basic issues-driven format. If you have enough to fill the inside front cover with a hot-button list, you probably have too much to be able to fully address the issues on the opposite page.

➤ If you use the issues-driven format, use no more than half the inside front cover for the hot-button list.

➤ Pick three to six high-priority issues to address in the interior of your brochure; then allocate a set amount of space to each issue, giving the most space to the highest-priority issue. For example, if you have three issues, you could put a hot-button list at the top of page 2 and address the first issue below that, then address the third and fourth issues at the top and bottom of page 3, respectively.

With five issues, you could address the highest-priority issue at the bottom of page 2, then address the remaining four issues on page 3 with small, simple visuals and minimal text. Or you could forego the hot-button list and block out space on the two interior pages for four, five, or even six issues.

➤ Edit, edit, edit. Even if you think you can't possibly eliminate any more words, someone else probably can.

➤ As always, it's a good idea to use an image to convey your key differentiator on the front cover and put an elevator speech on the back.

Brevity and creativity are the keys to an effective four-page brochure executive summary.

Product-Emulation Executive Summary

One way to demonstrate your understanding of and commitment to your customer's business goals is to emulate the customer's product. There are about as many ways to do it as there are products to emulate, and most of them involve more than just a brochure.

For example, when making a proposal to an automotive manufacturer or supplier, you could package your proposal in a faux-leather folder or wallet envelope, like the manual that comes with a new car. Or when submitting to the Postal Service, you could put all the sections in separate envelopes and deliver them in a mailbag.

Several years ago, we worked on a proposal to a major ballet company in the western United States. Their long-term goal was to become first a nationally, then internationally, recognized troupe without losing their unique identity based on location. Thus, our cover graphic showed a pair of ballerina slippers—their product, so to speak—with spurs on them.

A broadcast entertainment company might appreciate a proposal on videotape, with the brochure executive summary as a companion piece: "The Discriminating Viewer's Guide to [Title of Your Proposal]." For a software developer, an executive summary on CD would have impact. And a Web-based executive summary is certainly apropos for a dot-com customer.

Time-consuming? Risky? Expensive? Yes. But emulating the customer's product doesn't have to involve extraordinary media or elaborate packaging. It can be as simple as choosing a background and images that represent what the customer does. For example, the pages of an executive summary for a furniture maker could have a subtle wood-grain background. For a home builder, the cover could be made to look like the front door of a new home, and the interior laid out like a floor plan. The theme statements could appear in boxes that look like windows.

Page headings and themes, too, could incorporate the customer's terminology and play off of the images. For an electric utility, you could put photos of transmission towers on the outside edges of the pages, with lines extending from the tops of the towers to goal-oriented headlines like "Recharge your billing capability" and "Plug into customer satisfaction." For a biotech firm, you'd use words like "replicate" and "splice," with a double helix in the background. As in an ad-style brochure, the words and images should work together for emotional impact.

When emulating the customer's product, make sure you understand how your proposal will be evaluated and take care to select media and packaging methods that don't interfere with the task. Beyond that, the only real rules are:

1. Don't get carried away.
2. Don't take too many liberties.

You don't want to be perceived as being too cute or disrespectful, or trying too hard.

Customer-Empathy Executive Summary

One way to win with your executive summary is to demonstrate customer empathy. This comes from having an in-depth understanding of the customer's needs and a close fit between the two organizations (your alignment with their values, structure, goals, and people).

With customer empathy comes inside knowledge of the customer's requirements, concerns, and culture—things your competitors aren't in a position or didn't take the time to find out. Obviously, if you're not already working for the customer, this requires some intensive preselling and relationship building. The customer must agree that you're an insider, and even then you don't want to say so.

The key to demonstrating customer empathy is subtlety. You don't want to appear presumptuous or overstep your bounds. Here are some suggestions for demonstrating customer empathy:

➤ *Look for ways to show your depth of understanding and present yourself as an insider*. Arrange meetings with the customer's people and yours. Don't just meet for the sake of meeting. Meet with a purpose—preferably discovering and understanding their needs, problems, and goals.

➤ *Join or participate in the customer's trade associations*. Invite them to your trade association meetings and functions, always with the purpose of helping them solve a problem or achieve a goal—even if it's only to gain a better understanding of your solution or approach.

➤ *Don't attempt to portray your competitors as outsiders*. They may be doing as much preselling and relationship building as you are, and you'll look bad if you suggest you're more knowledgeable or harder working. That said, you should still have a full suite of win strategies that deal with your competitors' strengths and weaknesses as well as your own. Inside knowledge can help you highlight your strengths, mitigate your weaknesses, neutralize your competitors' strengths, and ghost their weaknesses, but it should call more attention to you than to your competitors.

➤ *Use the customer's language*. Recall things they told you in conversation, aside from an RFP. And always, even when referencing written requirements, use the customer's terminology rather than your own. If you change their words, they may not realize where you got your information.

➤ *Don't remind them that they told you*. They'll remember when they see their words and the information they gave you being used to solve their problems and achieve their goals.

➤ *Link your features and benefits to their issues and goals*. Inside information isn't worth much if you don't do anything with it. Take care to show them that you used the information to improve your offer and to tell them how it helps them. The way to do that is through the linkage of goals, issues, features, and benefits from your GIFBP Matrix.

➤ *Don't merely repeat their requirements back to them*. Repeating the requirements is a good technique, as long as you use their words and link your features and benefits to their issues and goals. However, many proposers repeat the requirements without the GIFBP linkage, in a way that seems presumptuous. For example: "You require a system that will do this, that, and the other thing." They already know that. Telling them sounds very condescending, as if they're simpletons.

➤ *Don't favor what you've been told privately over RFP requirements.*

➤ *Take care to address all the requirements, written and unwritten.* If what you've been told privately is in conflict with what's in writing, go with what's in writing.

➤ *Don't explicitly state that you're an insider or an incumbent.* If you're an incumbent, constant explicit reminders of your position and past performance (however stellar you may think it is) could easily backfire. They are, after all, going out for bids. A better way to capitalize on your incumbency would be to weave examples of what you've learned and how you plan to use it to their future benefit throughout the body of your executive summary.

When attempting to demonstrate customer empathy, it's easy to appear presumptuous and arrogant. The key to avoiding that perception is to remember that they know what they told you, and they still know more than you do.

Living Executive Summary: An Evolving Sales Tool

Executive summaries are most commonly submitted along with larger, formal proposals. However, an executive summary can also replace or serve as a proposal where no formal written presentation is required. It can also be used throughout the sales process as an evolutionary sales tool—a "living" executive summary.

GOLDEN RULE:
Differentiation does not simply occur. It must be created.

The Five Steps

Returning to our chess analogy, Figure 6-2 shows how as many as five versions of the living executive summary could be deployed to create significant positive differentiation both in your markets and with your customers.

Much of opening game is devoted to either planning middle game success or conditioning the market, not a particular customer, to think about your company in positive and different ways than it thinks about your industry. For example, we are always struck by how companies exhibiting at trade shows and conferences—a classic opening game investment—try to use attractive and clever ways of demonstrating their products and services, yet their behaviors are nothing less than commodity. That is, we can stop at any booth in the hall

Figure 6-2. **The living executive summary.** As many as five versions of an executive summary can create powerful differentiation for you to condition the market, condition the customer, and condition the deal.

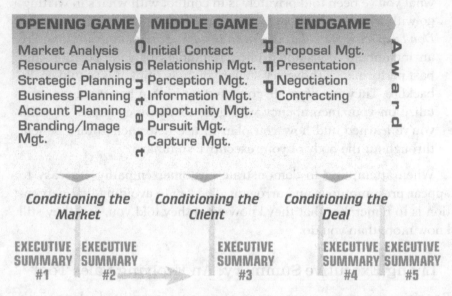

and receive a generic, pretty-picture brochure totally focused on the provider's organization, products, and/or services. It's all about them. Yet the large sign on a tripod next to the brochure table says, "When you count on us, you can count on customer focus first, last, and always." Alas, their behavior betrays their words, and it's the behavior we believe first, last, and always. (This disconnect between what we claim and how we behave forms the basis for two of our previous works, *The Behavioral Advantage*[1] and *Winning Behavior.*[2])

Living Executive Summary 1. Instead of shelves stacked high with generic, self-focused brochures, look at a market or market segment your company has chosen to serve and ask, "In this market/segment what are the key issues driving procurement of what we sell?" In other words, if we keep in mind that a market can be defined as two or more companies with common needs, problems, challenges, and issues, then we can understand that although each company in that market has its own fingerprints, all of them share certain things in common, including issues related to buying goods and services. They could include price, experience, location, distribution, and full service. The point is to figure them out and do something significant with that knowledge long before the competition has even taken notice.

As part of your opening game effort to condition the market for your company and to create positive differentiation as early and often as possible, use your market's key issues to develop an issues-driven, brochure executive summary for the trade show, the conference, and even the coffee table in your lobby. When a potential prospect picks up your executive summary focused on his world—health care, for example, or oil exploration and extraction, or financial services, and so on—watch for a far different and much more positive reaction. At that moment, you are different from and better than the competitor in the booth next door who behaves like everyone else in the industry. They and their brochures are commodities; you and your brochure are no longer seen as part of that pack.

When a stranger approaches your trade show booth, that person is really a suspect, not in any sinister way, of course, but in a business sense. It's your job to determine, as quickly as possible, if this suspect might be a prospect, and that's what most of your conversation is designed to determine. Next, as part of the booth ritual, you exchange business cards and other relevant information, because those cards help you identify qualified prospects according to your company's established criteria. Still in opening game, you then convert Living Executive Summary 1 into a new executive summary for the qualified prospect before calling on that organization, which initiates the middle game of business development. In all likelihood, at least some of your competitors have also decided to call on this qualified prospect; the difference is that on the way out the door to make the call, they stop by the marketing department to pick up a few more copies of those generic, pretty-picture brochures focused totally on themselves.

Living Executive Summary 2. We have seen bold evidence over the years that smart companies work to win customers before they work to win their business. That's a fundamental tenet of relationship-based selling and customer relationship management. Thus, making that first face-to-face contact in early middle game armed with a brochure executive summary focused on this prospective customer's key issues in buying what you sell can, all by itself, convert a cold call into a warm call. Before a specific opportunity emerges, Living Executive Summary 2 provides a new kind of capabilities presentation, one not communicated in the typical, self-focused "we're wonderful and here's why" sort of way your competitors deliver but in a truly customer-focused one. What you're providing that customer is a pre-opportunity discussion of their goals, needs, and key issues in getting what they need to achieve those goals.

A critical part of customers' reactions to this approach, we've found, is that they are typically much more willing to open up and reveal additional information and insight into what's driving their businesses. That is a differentiating way to launch a relationship based on trust, credibility, and compatibility—none of which is made possible by a generic sales call that includes a generic brochure.

Living Executive Summary 3. Once an opportunity emerges and begins to develop in mid-middle game, you might refine your executive summary to address opportunity-specific issues, helping the customer further define the requirements and determine the optimum solution, one that brings mutual advantage to both you and them. Living Executive Summary 3 also becomes one of your most effective techniques for your final positioning efforts to win the deal.

Keep in mind that a winning middle game has been designed to achieve one of two objectives:

1. The highest objective would be to keep the RFP from ever being issued. Doing so provides value to your customer (through shorter procurement schedule, earlier launch, lower procurement cost, and earlier business impact) and to your company as well (through shorter sales cycle, lower cost of sales, and, therefore, increased margin on the sale).
2. If, for legal or other reasons, you can't avoid a call for proposals, then you want to enter endgame being perceived by the customer as the preferred provider (i.e., all else being equal, they would prefer to work with you). Our experience tells us that if you enter endgame in this position, you have between a 60 and 70 percent probability of winning. It's essentially yours to lose. In today's marketplace, we can live with those numbers and sleep better, too.

Living Executive Summary 4. Upon receiving an invitation to submit a proposal, you would revise the opportunity-specific executive summary from middle game and submit it with your proposal. This version of the living document demonstrates a tight focus on the customer's final and formal definition of their key issues in selecting a solution provider. With few exceptions, we've found that the RFP's selection or evaluation criteria define the issues that should be used as the outline for this executive summary, which will present your best, benefits-based answers to why the customer should choose you rather than your competitor. These are the answers you want the decision makers and influencer to have even though they will never read your proposal. In short, Living Executive Summary 4 helps to confirm, as part of the customer's endgame selection process, their late middle game inclination to choose your company.

Living Executive Summary 5. This final step in the evolution of the living executive summary is optional, depending on your customer's endgame rules of engagement. That is, you may or may not be permitted to communicate with them outside the proposal and any specific instructions they issue for a shortlist presentation. If that's the case, by all means obey the rules. If, however, you have the opportunity to visit with the customer after the proposal and before the presentation, then you also have the opportunity to create additional value and differentiation to knock the remaining competitors out of the race.

In talking with your customer prior to the presentation, try to get answers to as many of these questions as possible:

➤ Did we identify and fully address the right key issues? If not, where could we improve? Are there any key issues we missed?
➤ Did you find the features and benefits we linked to your key issues compelling and convincing?
➤ Have we offered sufficient proofs that the benefits we've defined will, in fact, be delivered to you? If not, what proofs would convince you that we can and will deliver as promised?
➤ Are there specific areas of our offer that we've fully and correctly addressed? If so, what other areas should we concentrate on to bring them to this level as well?

Given the details of a specific opportunity, many other questions might potentially be raised. These questions are broad enough, however, to get you started toward your objective of bringing with you to the endgame presentation a fifth and amended executive summary as your one-of-a-kind, leave-behind handout.

Based on endgame customer feedback, you may have deleted your treatment of one or more key issues because the customer is fully impressed with your approach. In that case use the additional space to expand on those issues that were less well received. You might also include one or more key issues that you missed in Living Executive Summary 4. And if you missed something, it's highly likely your competitors did, too, so Living Executive Summary 5 will be an impressive and differentiating recovery for your presenter(s) and your company.

The incarnations of your living executive summary should be

Figure 6-3. **Executive summary review tool.** A consistent set of standards for draft executive summaries will result in better drafts over time. When people know what the standards are, they can design to them.

Executive Summary Review
Page 1 of 2

Company:	**Instructions:** Put an x or a check mark in the box that represents your answer—yes (Y), partially (P), or no (N)—to each question. Then explain your answer in specific, constructive terms and assign a score of 0–5 for each question. Total the scores for each group of questions. Add the four totals at the bottom of the form. Recommended scoring: no = 0–1; partially = 2–3; yes = 4–5.
Proposal:	
Reviewer:	
Review Type: Pink Team ____ Red Team ____	

Criteria	Y	P	N	Comments	Score
A. Is it compliant?					
1. Does the executive summary adhere to all customer instructions regarding the content and design of the proposal?					
				Total: Is it compliant?	
B. Is it responsive?					
1. Does the cover—through the graphic or a heading—convey a key benefit or the achievement of a customer goal?					
2. Does the first interior page (if a brochure) or section include a hot-button list linking our key features and benefits to the customer's key issues or evaluation criteria in order of priority to the customer?					

3. Is the document organized in a similar fashion—i.e., key issues in order of priority?				
4. Does it demonstrate customer focus by frequently acknowledging the customer's goals, problems, and business drivers and by mentioning the customer or the customer's issue first more often than it mentions us first?				
5. Does it appear to have been wholly designed and written for this customer and this opportunity?				
Total: Is it responsive?				
C. Does it sell throughout?				
1. Does it articulate a compelling set of reasons for choosing us?				
2. Does it differentiate us from the competition by highlighting our strengths, mitigating our weaknesses, neutralizing our competitors' strengths, and ghosting their weaknesses? Does it answer "Why not them?" as well as "Why us?"?				
3. Does it clearly and prominently display our most powerful differentiator, preferably in the cover graphic?				

(continues)

Figure 6-3. (Continued).

Executive Summary Review

4. Is each section or page (if a brochure) designed around a single key issue, with a prominently displayed theme statement and one or more visuals supporting the theme?				
5. Does each theme statement state a customer issue, the features addressing that issue, and the benefits associated with those features? Are the features and benefits specific and appropriately quantified?				
6. Do all the visuals convey clear and compelling sales messages?				
7. Does each one include a full-sentence, interpretive caption linking features and benefits?				
8. Does it end with an elevator speech or other quick summary of the three to six most powerful reasons for choosing us, succinctly stated in terms of benefits to the customer?				

9. Does it associate substantive, bottom-line benefits with all key features?			
10. Is it free of summaries and references to other areas of the proposal?			
Total: Does it sell throughout?			
D. Does it communicate?			
1. Is it attractively designed with approximately one-third visual, one-third text, and one-third white (or colored) space?			
2. Do the visuals communicate their main messages in 8 seconds or less?			
3. When you look at each page or section as a whole, do the important sales messages "jump out at you"?			
4. Is the writing conversational and confident without sounding arrogant or demanding unwarranted trust?			
Total: Does it communicate?			
Grand Total			

Best Possible Score: 100

Additional Comments and Recommendations

significantly different and strategically timed. The point is not to keep assaulting them with your sales messages—powerful as they may be—but to continually demonstrate your evolving understanding of their world, their business, their goals, their needs, and their key issues, all dovetailed with your capability and commitment to helping them get what they need to solve their problems and achieve their goals.

The living executive summary is a cutting-edge method for achieving true partnerships with customers. Meanwhile, some (if not all) of your competitors are spinning their rhetorical tributes to partnership; touting their capabilities; focusing on themselves; and generally making it more problematic, rather than less, for the customer to choose them. You, in contrast, have found yet another way to make it not only easier, but a pleasure, to choose you.

Executive Summary Quality Check

Reviewing a draft proposal and revising it before production is not only a good idea; it's mandatory unless you enjoy living on the edge of business development disaster. When a formal process, such as pink and red team reviews, is used, we see it as a best practice (one that we explore in great detail in Chapter 10). Often either companies don't understand the power of superior executive summaries and, therefore, don't commit to creating them, or they do generate executive summaries of varying quality but have no means of calibrating the level of quality they're achieving. Those companies also typically know about reviewing and revising their draft proposals but have never extended that concept to executive summaries, at least not with a simple, systematic, and repeatable process.

To evaluate the executive summary, use a methodology that is compatible with (though not identical to) the red team review of the draft proposal. Figure 6-3 on the preceding pages illustrates a tool to consistently produce the highest-quality executive summaries possible.

By consistently applying standards for how your executive summaries will be developed and what they must accomplish, those who create them know what needs to be done to design and produce them. When we see this initiative embedded in a company's business development process, we've also seen increased probability of winning, positive customer reactions, and a ratcheting up of customer expectations. Once a customer is exposed to this differentiating, brochure-style executive summary, they will expect the same thing from your competitors. When that doesn't happen, you have raised the bar for your competitors while maintaining your focus on the customer, and that is a powerful way to compete.

Challenges for Readers

> Study some of your company's generic, full-color marketing brochures. Could the techniques used to create them also be used to create customer- and opportunity-specific executive summaries? Could you use them to focus on the customer with as much intensity as you focus on yourselves in the generic brochures? If so, what impact could that create?

> What is the current practice for creating executive summaries in your industry? Benchmark on that practice and then decide if that's the best that can be done. If not, can you break from the pack to set a new standard that will raise your customers' expectations? If so, have you raised the bar on your competitors?

> Revisit a proposal you submitted recently and see if an executive summary accompanied it to the customer. If not, you have an open field ahead of you for innovation. If so, would a brochure executive summary have been more effective in selling to decision makers and those who influence them? Use that completed proposal to practice developing a superior executive summary. Work with colleagues on another one or two completed proposals to refine your abilities. Present the before-and-after versions to the right people within your company who can drive this initiative on upcoming proposals.

> Hold a brown-bag or similarly informal meeting to present the concept of the Living Executive Summary. If your company has marketing professionals, be sure to include them along with colleagues from business development/sales, proposal production, and any other functional areas you think would value a differentiating approach that works at the market level, the customer level, and the opportunity level.

Notes

1. Terry R. Bacon and David G. Pugh, *The Behavioral Advantage: What the Smartest, Most Successful Companies Do Differently to Win in the B2B Arena* (New York: AMACOM, 2004).
2. Terry R. Bacon and David G. Pugh, *Winning Behavior: What the Smartest, Most Successful Companies Do Differently* (New York: AMACOM, 2003).

Chapter 7

TIMING IS EVERYTHING

Positioning to Win

*Procrastination: To intentionally and habitually put
off doing something that should be done.*
—MERRIAM WEBSTER'S COLLEGIATE DICTIONARY

GOLDEN RULE:

Winners are working while losers are waiting.

According to an old adage, "If it weren't for the last minute, a lot of things would never get done." Does that describe your business development efforts? Do you start late and not finish the proposal until the last moment? Does this describe the way you normally work?

Donald Marquis said that "procrastination is the art of keeping up with yesterday." That's how it is. There's always so much to do that you can never get ahead; you can only keep from falling farther behind. Still, would anyone argue with the idea that you should start early when pursuing new business development opportunities? It's self-evident that starting earlier is better.

How to Position Your Company to Be a Key Player

Companies also procrastinate. They have to run lean or they aren't efficient; they can't have people sitting on the bench waiting for new opportunities. Everyone has to be kept occupied. When everyone is too busy putting out today's fires, it's difficult to devote the time, people, and resources to preventing the potential fires of tomorrow.

Like people, companies pay more attention to the short term than the long term, devote more time to the tangible than the intangible, and worry more about tomorrow's deadlines than next month's early warnings, let alone next year's. It's easier, more concrete, and more urgent to spend time working on the opportunities that are coming due quickly—the ones that are so close you can practically reach out and touch them. Compounding the problem is the fact that many companies chase too many opportunities. They chase some that are ill suited for them, that other competitors have sewn up, or that they can't realistically capture because they can't devote the requisite pursuit time. Still, they pursue the opportunity, as if by some miracle it might come through.

As a result, they create the pressure and resource constraints that prevent them from starting earlier on the opportunities they should be chasing. This knee-jerk reaction to bidding makes it very difficult to chase anything effectively. Why don't companies get started earlier? Table 7-1 shows some of the classic reasons and the prescriptions for change.

Begin Early: Build Relationships, Develop Influence, and Win the Customer

It may help to consider once again the chess game of business development. Both unfold over a finite period. Both require effective strategy and tactics. Both have an opening game, a middle game, and an endgame, and the outcomes in both are largely determined by what happens early in the game, particularly middle game.

Middle game starts when you make initial contact with either a prospect or a current customer with a high potential for repeat business. This is the point where starting early has meaning, and from this point forward we like to divide middle game into three phases: early, mid-, and late middle game.

GOLDEN RULE:
Whenever possible, work to win customers
first; then work to win their business.

Early middle game involves breaking the ice; creating quality face time by ensuring that value is moving in both directions; and thereby building relationships based on trust, credibility, and compatibility. In these terms, early middle game is predominantly behavioral and

Table 7-1. **Causes and cures.**

Symptom	Prescription
Everyone is too busy to devote much time to new opportunities until they become pressing. In short, every opportunity becomes a priority only when it becomes urgent.	➤ Be more selective in the opportunities you pursue. By chasing fewer, you make more time for the ones you do pursue. ➤ Focus your salespeople and account managers on creating and identifying opportunities and building position with customers; have others focus on writing proposals.
The account manager has too many other customers and opportunities to pursue or other items of business that take too much of his or her time.	➤ Limit the number of accounts your salespeople handle. Their effectiveness is inversely proportional to the number of accounts they are expected to handle. ➤ Ensure that your salespeople are spending 90 percent of their time on customers; limit the amount of time they spend on administration, record keeping, and internal matters.
It's difficult to bring the right people together to make the bid decision.	➤ Enforce a policy of weekly bid review meetings with all key people present. ➤ Alternatively, use electronic tools such as eRooms, NetMeeting, WebEx, or internal Web sites to post opportunities for review and set time limits for approvals. If key people are too busy, they should lose the opportunity to vote. Don't allow anyone to become the bottleneck in your process.
The management group is misaligned on whether to bid, and they don't gain alignment until the opportunity is well along in development.	➤ Investigate the way you are presenting opportunities. Ensure that there is enough information for managers to make sound decisions. ➤ For major opportunities, consider including a draft executive summary to present to managers who need high-level insight into the opportunity and why they should commit to capturing it.

	➤ Restrict decision authority on bidding to a smaller group of managers. ➤ Set more tangible and specific go/no-go guidelines for bids.
Managers don't have a strong sense of urgency about pursuing work in middle game.	➤ That sense of urgency must come from the top. Make sure the message to senior and middle management is clear. ➤ Educate them on the folly of starting late.
No one is aware that the opportunity exists. No one is talking to the right people in the customer's organization.	➤ Examine your early warning systems; you have a serious flaw somewhere. ➤ Institute a strategic account management program. ➤ Improve your ability to manage your sales pipeline. ➤ Develop better relationships with your customers. If you aren't aware of opportunities, you don't have good relationships.
People are encouraged to maximize their time charged to billable projects. There is no allocation for time spent pursuing new business, so people are not motivated and incented to devote any time up front on opportunities until they become urgent near the end of middle game.	➤ You have a serious structural barrier to starting early; examine your policy on maximizing billable hours and consider relaxing this requirement. ➤ Devote some portion of the relevant people's hours to middle game activities.
There isn't a clear process for starting early.	➤ Create one. ➤ Examine your sales process. If it does not demand early starts on opportunities, then revise it and educate people on the revisions.
The only people who can start early are the account managers—and they're preoccupied with other matters, including finishing proposals for the most urgent "must-win" situations (which they started late).	➤ Create a separate group of proposal managers. Have your account managers hand off the opportunities to them during late middle game. ➤ Ensure that you have a clear division of responsibilities so your salespeople are not expected to track all opportunities from cradle to grave. It isn't efficient, and it compromises your ability to win by hampering your middle game.

(continues)

Table 7-1. (Continued).

Symptom	Prescription
You convince yourself—or you're "convinced" by higher-ups—that the buying decision will go to the lowest bidder, which your company is not.	➤ Either scrub your price to the bare margins you have to make, or ➤ Develop and follow better, more realistic criteria for qualifying customers for pursuit before qualifying specific opportunities with them. One criterion would be customers who understand the risks of using low bidders and, therefore, are willing to pay for added value in various forms: e.g., more educated, experienced people; proven technology; better safety record; full service; single source provider.

will establish the nature of the relationship (substantive versus superficial, formal versus casual, open versus guarded) for the rest of the business development cycle.

Mid-middle game includes the customer's initial work in identifying the problem to be solved, gaining alignment on the need for a solution, discussing alternatives, estimating the scope and budget of the solution, and identifying potential suppliers or thought partners. If you have the relationship developed and in place, mid-middle game is your golden opportunity to influence the opportunity by sharing knowledge and experience, lessons learned, latest innovations, risk mitigation strategies, current costing data, and value engineering. The value list is endless, and it opens the door for you to be perceived by this potential customer as an indispensable resource.

This approach to pre-RFP positioning goes by many labels, none of them particularly new to the business development scene: consultative selling, facilitative selling, value selling, solution selling, value added, and so on. (For an extended discussion of how these approaches to selling have been largely commoditized, see "The Death of Selling" in our earlier book *The Behavioral Advantage.*[1]) What this means for the organization that takes them seriously and deploys them consistently well is that they can create powerful middle game differentiation either to keep the RFP from being released at all (the ultimate victory but in most markets also the rare exception) or to send them into endgame perceived by the customer as the preferred provider. If that happens, they would have, on average across industries, between a 60 and 70 percent probability of ultimately winning the award. Those are good numbers in today's tough markets and worth the middle game investment to achieve them.

By late middle game, the customer is usually developing specifications, finalizing the procurement budget, writing their request for proposal, defining their bid process and procedures, and meeting with suppliers to learn more about their products and services. By working hand in glove with the customer in the days or weeks preceding the RFP, you are in the final push to build preference for you, your company, and your solution. You are also learning a great deal about what your endgame proposal and presentation must accomplish—and that's insight and information a company with nothing to work with except the RFP will never possess. In business development as in chess, the power and quality of your opening and middle game drive the power and quality of your endgame, leading to the ultimate prize: winning.

If all you do to win a deal is wait for the RFP and submit a proposal, you'll have about a 10 percent probability of winning. You can't build, or even sustain, your business with that win rate. The tough markets we face around the world put highly competitive companies into rigorous competitions. When that happens and there is no clear winner heading into endgame, the difference between first and second place will be as close as it is in the Olympic finals of the 100-meter dash, and that 10 percent will be the most important 10 percent you may have ever experienced. A single mistake could lose the whole thing.

Is it possible to win in endgame alone? Yes, miracles do happen, but we wouldn't advocate building your business model on them. For that specific, aberrant opportunity, however, where your instinct tells you that you might just have a chance of winning even though you didn't know about the opportunity until an RFP dropped on your desk, make sure that you don't have crippling liabilities coming into endgame, that the playing field is relatively level, and that none of your competitors has played a masterful middle game. If any of these conditions is, in fact, operative, you need to say the two most dreaded words in a business development vocabulary—"No bid" or "No go"—and then move on. Next time, find the customer first, then the potential opportunity, and, of course, execute a powerful middle game that will transform your proposal into a new standard by which your customer can judge your competitors—and find them lacking.

What you lose when you start too late is considerable, even potentially devastating, so it always surprises us that that there are still companies out there who do not even learn about opportunities until an RFP flies through the transom. In the government sector we've seen many business development operations where it is someone's job to read the Commerce Business Daily (CBD) for notices of pending procurements, even though, by the time a notice appears in the CBD, the opportunity has long been under development and the customer is in very late middle game. Commercial companies that wait for the RFP put themselves in the same position. They are solidly behind the eight ball and are very likely to lose those bids.

Some companies that have more on the ball may get started in mid-to-late middle game. Are they better off? Yes, certainly, but they are still giving away significant amounts of win probability by starting even that late. By that time, the customer has:

➤ *Recognized a business problem and thus an emerging need*. Late starters aren't aware of those problems and aren't able to influence the customer's growing awareness of their needs or definition of the problem.

➤ *Thought about potential solutions*. Late starters aren't able to help customers think through those potential solutions, so they can't build trust by acting as thought partners, can't introduce their own technologies or approaches, can't show how they've solved such problems in the past, can't act as consultants in helping the customer generate solutions, can't introduce their value-added differentiators, and so on.

➤ *Surveyed the market and thought about who could best help them*. Late starters can't establish themselves as the preferred suppliers or help customers think about the qualities, breadth, scope, expertise, people, and products or services that the solution provider should have.

➤ *Contacted consultants, friends, and others who can help them think about and investigate potential suppliers or providers*. Late starters aren't able to influence this process and may be shut out if the people providing advice prefer a competitor.

➤ *Collaborated on the need internally and sought and received approval for funding* (read: The budget is now set). Late starters aren't able to influence the budget, which may be set unrealistically low. If your customer hasn't conducted a procurement of this type in several years, their pricing data may be woefully outdated.

➤ *Found the money in their budget for this purchase*. This means they've developed at least a rough order of magnitude of the scope of work involved and a cost estimate for it. Late starters can't influence the scope of work or help customers think through all of their options.

The customer may have already met with some potential providers. If so, those providers have been trying to build relationships with the key people, to present their team, to build trust and confidence in their ability to do the work, to learn more about the customer's needs and business, to position themselves with the customer, to establish a dialogue, possibly to open doors with some senior customers, possibly to present their solutions and technologies, and potentially to begin to build bias in their favor. *Late starters who miss the boat here are well behind the power curve because their smarter competitors have been working to build their position with the customer and create preference.*

What you lose when you start late is illustrated in Figure 7-1. Be-

Figure 7-1. **Your degree of influence in a typical opportunity.** By starting late on your customer relationship building and opportunity pursuit, you not only lose what those efforts contribute to a winning middle game, you also lose the real prize: entering endgame perceived by the customer as their preferred provider.

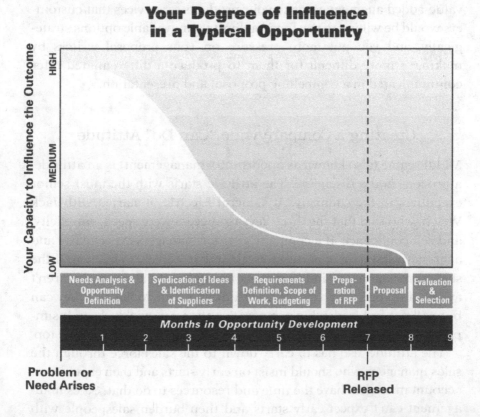

yond the loss of influence potential, you also lose the capacity to build stronger, trust-based relationships with the customer's key people, especially the decision maker and key influencers. Starting late limits the time you have to build relationships with the key people you don't already know. Moreover, it sends the signal that you care less about getting the business than do your competitors who have started earlier—and who have thus demonstrated a stronger commitment to the customer and the work through their behavior.

You lose some more obvious things as well, such as the ability to influence the definition of the requirements, the customer's understanding of their needs, their sense of what's possible—and, often more to the point, what's not. You severely reduce your understanding of the customer's needs because you have less time to probe, and you've devoted less time to building trust, so the customer may not be as candid and forthcoming with you. If you don't already have good connections between your senior executives and the customers, you restrict your ability to establish them. You limit your ability to discover or build good, positive differentiators; hence, you force yourself to compete on price, which means it's more difficult for you to offer value-added augmentations to your products or services that customers would be willing to pay for. You limit your available options strategically, and you put more pressure on your proposal writers by making it more difficult for them to produce a differentiated offer communicated in a compelling proposal and presentation.

Creating a Companywide "Can-Do" Attitude

Middle game (also known as opportunity management) is an attitude, a process, and a discipline. The attitude starts with the most senior executives in the company. At General Electric, it started with Jack Welch, who said that the three keys to success were speed, simplicity, and self-confidence. If a company's senior managers expect early and aggressive starts on opportunities, then that is likely to happen. If the senior managers are indifferent to it, don't care about it, or aren't aware of it, then the people on the front lines will do the best they can but will not feel leadership's imperative to move quickly, keep it simple, and act boldly and confidently. The attitude has to start at the top.

The attitude also has to carry down to the sales force through the sales managers, who should insist on early starts and then ensure that account managers have the time and resources to do that. Sales management can't expect early starts and then burden salespeople with too many accounts, too many administrative requirements, and too many other responsibilities.

Starting early must be built into the company's sales process. It should be part of "how we do things around here." This means that bid decisions must be made early.

Horror stories abound on this issue. We've seen companies, for example, with bid processes that included irrational stipulations such as only making formal bid decisions on the second and fourth Tuesdays of the month. We've also heard of RFPs languishing for days or even a couple of weeks in somebody's in box because the person was out of town or on vacation.

To get bid decisions made early, salespeople must know how to bring opportunities to the table and how to present them so everyone else involved in the bid decision knows what they need to know to make an intelligent decision. Finally, the process should allow for salespeople to hand off the opportunities at the right moment so others can follow through with the proposal. We're not suggesting that salespeople shouldn't be involved in the proposal. Quite the contrary, they must provide the strategic direction and customer details necessary for others to create compelling proposals. When you ask your salespeople to write proposals or manage the proposal efforts, you bog them down in a morass of details that prohibits them from scouting new opportunities and starting early on them. (See Chapter 8 for additional discussion of how salespeople, business developers, and account managers should contribute to proposals as members of the core team.)

Former baseball manager Casey Stengel once observed, "When you're losing, everyone commences to play stupid." His comment reflects an interesting phenomenon in opportunities that start late in middle game: As the pressure builds, everything starts unraveling. People get nervous. They start rushing to get done the things they know they should be doing. Management gets involved too late and dictates changes that should have happened weeks earlier. One senior manager we spoke to described himself in these circumstances as a pig from outer space. "I was too busy to get involved earlier," he said. "When I finally came to the team room and saw what was happening, I panicked, barked a bunch of orders, and then left. I heard later that all hell broke loose once I was gone. It took them three days to recover. It was like I was a pig from outer space—I flew in, landed with a big splat in the middle of the table, scared the hell out of everybody, and then vanished."

This is why you will lose if you wait. As Mae West said, "He who hesitates is last."

Challenges for Readers

➤ If you are as convinced as we are that a powerful middle game is essential to winning, what hard and soft metrics could you establish to help you measure your company's middle game prowess?

➤ Do you see a huge energy surge when an RFP arrives? Could that energy be better applied pre-RFP? If so, how would you see such a change manifested in middle game?

➤ If it really is true that the early bird gets the worm (and we think it is), and your organization isn't exactly populated with early birds, which of the symptoms in Table 7-1 define the problem for you and your company? Are the prescriptions to remedy the problems relevant? Practical? If not, what will it take to start earlier and win middle game in your world?

Note

1. Terry R. Bacon and David G. Pugh, *The Behavioral Advantage: What the Smartest, Most Successful Companies Do Differently to Win in the B2B Arena* (New York: AMACOM, 2004).

Chapter 8

PROPOSAL MANAGEMENT

The Art of Containing Chaos

GOLDEN RULE:

A proposal is a custom-designed product in its own right, one that you will hand to a customer as tangible evidence of your ability to meet requirements, manage a project, and produce quality deliverables on time.

Any proposal manager (or outside consultant, for that matter) who claims to know how to run a major proposal effort free of chaos should be quietly and briskly escorted to the door. Chaos is in the DNA of the proposal beast. The manager who accepts this fact also knows that although the chaos of proposal work cannot be eliminated, it must be controlled, or it will eat alive the manager, the proposal team, and the proposal itself.

Ironically, proposal managers often add chaos to the effort because they either deny or fail to recognize the fundamental philosophy that should drive the proposal process:

Rather than a superior offer in an inferior proposal, give the client a responsive offer in a superior proposal.

In other words, proposal chaos increases when issues related to the offer dominate the time and effort that should be focused on proposal quality. A proposal is a custom product you design and build for a customer. That basic truth means that all those breezy proposal claims about industry leadership, best in class, a relentless commit-

135

ment to quality, we wrote the book (or the boilerplate we call the book), and a passion for excellence have a chilling effect on evaluators if the very proposal making such claims is poorly organized, difficult to evaluate, badly formatted, or simply a physical manifestation of the chaos that produced it. Consider these chilling questions:

- How many companies would want the customer that issues an RFP to be a fly on the wall as the proposal is being created?
- Would that experience create confidence or cause the customer's blood pressure to surge?
- If superb project management capability is a key requirement, what would they see in the proposal area that might make the needle hit the danger zone on the customer's riskometer?

In today's fiercely competitive marketplace, the company that adds more and more elegance to the offer beyond the RFP's scope and specifications (driving up the final price with a "you-get-what-you-pay-for" strategy) and then communicates that offer in an inferior proposal is a company about to snatch defeat from the jaws of victory.

More companies every year recognize that in tight competitions, the proposal that is easy to evaluate and understand can provide the winning edge. Such a proposal can be taken as observable evidence of a company's ability to deliver a quality product under difficult circumstances with careful management and teamwork. In the broadest terms, this type of proposal will have four characteristics:

1. It is 100 percent compliant with the RFP.
2. It is fully responsive to the client's needs, concerns, key issues, values, and goals.
3. It sells by providing substantive answers to "Why us?" "Why not them?" "So what?" and "How so?"
4. It communicates a clear and compelling message.

These four items form the basis for the red team review of the completed proposal draft. (For a full discussion of the red team review process, see Chapter 10.) What a proposal manager needs to produce this type of superior proposal is a simple, repeatable process that drives these four milestone events on the proposal schedule:

1. Front-loading the effort
2. Freezing the offer
3. Planning for and conducting a superior kickoff meeting
4. Revising for quality

With these steps of the process in place, the proposal manager can realistically pursue a responsive design in a superior proposal by minimizing crisis management. Without them, the proposal manager can expect to age prematurely.

Front-Loading the Effort: Plan and Design

The whole concept of *front-loading* begins with a process that allows for planning and designing the proposal before "building" it. That process is shown in Figure 8-1.

Front-loading allows a proposal manager and the proposal team to control the effort rather than let the effort control them, or, as the saying goes, to manage the outputs by managing the inputs. Basically, it's just common sense to plan and design something before building it. Whether we're talking about a house or a proposal, the quality of the finished product will largely be determined by how well we plan the effort to create it and design what it will become.

The manager who understands front-loading also understands that no two opportunities are alike, some being strategically more important than others, some representing larger or smaller revenue potential. So for major, must-win contracts, the first 25 percent of the response period dedicated to planning and designing the proposal should be extended to the left, back into middle game. (The Introduction provides a brief discussion of the chess game of business development. For an expanded discussion of business development and the game of chess, see "Checkmate! How Business Development Is Like Chess" in our earlier book *The Behavioral Advantage*.[1])

With so much at stake and the competition as intense as it has ever been, the old chestnut "He who hesitates is lost" has never been truer. Furthermore, the length of the response period is getting shorter and shorter over time because:

Figure 8-1. **The 25-50-25 proposal process.** Devote the critical first 25 percent of the response period to planning and designing the proposal. If you're going to put in sixteen-hour days, do it on the front end. If you do it on the back end, you're more than likely conducting a salvage operation.

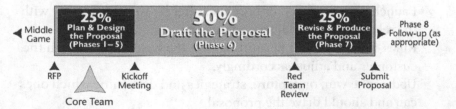

➤ Customers are looking for ways to reduce cost, including procurement overhead.
➤ Customers are learning the value of the pre-RFP information
they derive from the potential providers in articulating their
needs and the specifications of the solution to meet those needs.
➤ Procurement processes have refined the buying process to the
point that providing lengthy proposal response periods is a waste
of time and other resources such as supply chain management
become increasingly sophisticated and professional. (For a fuller
discussion of the advances in supply chain management and
how they have impacted the buyer-provider dynamic, see "The
Changing World of Buying and Selling" in *The Behavioral Advantage*.[2])

If you don't address key issues, anticipate and solve problems, and
identify key elements of the offer early enough, you will convert the
last 25 percent of your proposal period into a salvage operation. Quality revision and production become impossible. The goal is no longer
superior communication but merely getting the proposal into binders
and out the door. (Chapter 7 provides an extensive discussion of the
wait-until-the-RFP syndrome and what it can cost the company that
succumbs to it.)

A superior proposal—like any other complex product a company
would design and produce—cannot be created in the eleventh hour
under ever-increasing pressure from upper management. A smart proposal manager (or account manager) uses the critical days, weeks, or
even months before the RFP to accomplish as much as possible as
early as possible. Here are a few potential objectives for a pre-RFP
jump-start of the proposal:

➤ Gather and assess information on the client, the opportunity,
and the competition.
➤ Identify the proposal team.
➤ Muster high-level support for the effort.
➤ Line up support personnel.
➤ Develop a draft proposal project plan.
➤ Launch a preliminary, or baseline, offer by working closely with
the relevant functional area managers.
➤ Rules of engagement permitting, test the baseline offer with the
customer and adjust accordingly.
➤ Update the win, or capture, strategies and determine which ones
can and should drive the proposal.

➤ Reserve the physical proposal space you'll need so it's available when you need it.

➤ Assemble the boilerplate you'll need and begin the process of customizing it for this customer.

➤ Create a draft executive summary to set down your latest knowledge of the customer's key issues in selecting a provider, your win strategies, your most compelling message or themes, and your strongest visuals.

Everything we do to win work should be scaled to the significance of the opportunity, so for the non–must-win, good-to-have opportunities, front-loading really means using that first 25 percent of the response period to plan and design the proposal. But whether we front-load by initiating critical planning and designing in middle game, or immediately after receiving the RFP, the concept remains the same: Don't start building a proposal until everyone knows and agrees on how it's to be done and what it will be when it's completed.

Later, during the drafting and revising phases of endgame, when the clock is ticking like a hyperactive metronome, the manager, along with the entire proposal team, will be grateful that the proposal is coming together as designed, according to plan.

Freezing the Offer

One of the deep ironies of proposal work is that a company will hire the very best talent, technical and otherwise, to design its products and services, yet when it comes to designing and writing a proposal to sell what it has to offer, the company assembles an ad hoc team with no training whatsoever and tells them, in a voice charged with conviction, "The company's fate rides on your broad shoulders. This is a must-win opportunity!"

The offer—not the proposal—is the star, the hope for the future. And why not? The company hires and pays great minds to design great products and services, not to write great proposals. Yet great minds of every stripe end up writing proposals precisely because they are experts on what needs to be proposed and sold. Thus, the proposal manager knows that an important part of front-loading the effort involves an early start on the technical offer, approach, and solution as well as the preparation of the proposal.

Working primarily from information gathered and validated during middle game, the proposal core team (e.g., account manager, proposal manager, and solution managers) initiates a baseline design *prior* to receipt of the RFP. Once the solicitation arrives, the solution experts can make the necessary adjustments as quickly as possible before freezing the design for the duration of the response period. As Figure 8-2 illustrates, the design freeze allows substantial time that can then be devoted to designing and producing a superior proposal even as the pricing is refined in parallel track to the proposal draft.

The failure to freeze the offer means danger may well lie ahead. One of business development's simplest facts is that if an engineer or a project manager must design part or all of the solution and simultaneously write about it, there is no doubt which task will receive maximum attention and effort. This problem is only the first of many if dwelling on the offer and approach—reviewing them, adjusting them, then reviewing them again—is allowed to cycle throughout the proposal response period. Other potential problems associated with a failure to freeze the offer are:

➤ You beat *yourself* on price by obsessively overdesigning the offer. Your offer is superior, goldplated, assuredly elegant but unacceptably expensive given what the client really needs and can afford to spend. After losing, you debrief with the client and are told that you lost on price. Literally true, perhaps, but so is the proposition that you didn't lose on price at all.

➤ Your pricing effort is chaotic because the offer cannot be clearly defined. This is a sure sign that your presubmittal confusion regarding price will eventually be shared with the client.

➤ Burned-out proposal contributors, in desperation and frustration, provide unfocused "dumps" on their parts of the proposal, proving that even a superior offer badly communicated is a surefire way to lose on price.

Figure 8-2. **The design freeze milestone.** Freeze the offer as early in middle game as possible to get your pricing initiative under way and to avoid massive revisions of the draft proposal in the waning days of the response period.

➤ A muddled, reader-unfriendly, overly "boilerplated" proposal states that, among other things, "no one designs better solutions and manages projects better than we do."

➤ Upper management's red team review declares the proposal, not the offer, a bona fide disaster.

➤ There is a frantic search for additional people and money to carry out the salvage operation.

Savvy account and proposal managers learn many lessons through bitter experience, not the least of which is that superior proposals do not necessarily require working harder, just working smarter. And a major part of working smarter involves knowing when to develop the offer, when to write about it, and where to draw the line between these two tasks.

Planning for and Conducting a Superior Kickoff Meeting

Of all the milestones in the proposal process, none may be more important than the kickoff meeting. It is critically important for the company; for the proposal core team; for each contributor; and, ultimately, for your customer, who rightfully expects a clear, coherent, compelling proposal that communicates your offer in alignment with their needs.

Too often, however, the core team hesitates to plan for and schedule the official kickoff until the RFP appears. Then, because the clock is ticking toward the submission date, they hold the kickoff meeting as quickly as possible so that contributors can get to work, dramatically increasing the likelihood of chaos throughout the entire response period, culminating in the frantic final days.

Properly conceived, the kickoff meeting is not just a symbolic gesture or dark ritual. The benefits of an effective kickoff meeting extend far beyond the meeting itself. In fact, a direct correlation exists between the quality of the proposal kickoff and the actual finished proposal because what the core team does to prepare for the kickoff meeting drives what the team does to create the finished document.

Keep in mind that the people who walk into a kickoff meeting have at least three questions:

1. *What* am I supposed to do?
2. *How* am I supposed to do it?
3. *When* do I have to have it done?

It is the core team's responsibility to provide definitive answers to these questions, plus a host of others, as part of the kickoff meeting. It is the moment of truth for the people who must plan and execute the proposal effort because it allows them to implement three principles fundamental to effective proposal management: teamwork, proposal planning, and process.

Solidify the Team

The key for proposal managers is to recognize that (1) the team consists of many specialists needing focus and direction; and (2) in a very real sense, the full team often includes people other than those officially tapped as contributors, who should, of course, attend the kickoff meeting. Others might be invited to the meeting as well, and they would therefore become invaluable proposal "contributors" simply because they have been recognized by proposal management:

> *VIPs:* One or more executives representing the significance of the upcoming effort speak in specific terms about the importance of the proposal to the company's long-term business plan and strategic goals.

> *Functional Area Managers:* These day-to-day managers of the team members, once they feel included and understand the details and the importance of the proposal, can support their people on the team. They can encourage them rather than pressure them to return to their "real" jobs as quickly as possible, which can lead to cutting corners on their ad hoc proposal assignments.

> *Support Staff:* The keyboarders, administrative assistants, database managers, file clerks, editors, artists, and production people too often are viewed as "grunts," when in fact they are critical contributors, especially in the eleventh hour when the proposal must somehow squeeze through the system and head out the door to the client.

> *Spouses/Partners:* They are the invisible but very real other half of many proposal contributors. Spouses/partners need to be recognized for the support and sacrifices that a proposal effort usually requires, including lost weekends, canceled plans, and many evenings when families must fend for themselves.

> *Field Representatives:* These human sensors are out there picking up signals from the client and the competition. They need to be

brought in from the field, debriefed, and made to feel a part of the company in general and the proposal team in particular. Remember: Everything done on a proposal begins and ends with information.

➤ *Review Teams:* The members of the pink and red teams too often are not even assigned until just before their reviews commence. (The term "pink team" review refers to a formal review of the draft proposal's organization, themes, visuals, and compliance with the RFP before all the text is added. A "red team" review refers to a formal review of the draft proposal in a form as close as possible to what the customer will receive. Chapter 10 discusses in detail both the pink team and red team review process.) Once identified and made a part of the team (even though they should not participate in the actual creation of the draft proposal), the review teams can begin meeting early in the response period to establish their methods for reviewing the drafts. If, as is often the case, the reviewers don't prepare, come review time they end up imposing their own separate biases and preferences on the proposal. This only leads to resentment and chaos in the final days of the proposal period.

A team is not just a collection of people; it is a state of mind. Proposal managers who understand this can use the kickoff meeting to generate among *all* team members the energy and camaraderie that will carry them through the inevitably difficult days that lie ahead. The alternative is trying to get a proposal contributor excited about the work while his or her VP and functional area manager don't know what's going on. Furthermore, the graphics, editing, and production people have declared open season on the next person to dump a proposal section on them.

Lay the Foundation: Proposal Planning

Probably no document a company creates is more complex and more stressful on people and systems than a proposal. It requires:

➤ *Management of a project but also management of a hybrid document* that is both a finished product and a combination of sales and technical information on future unfinished products or yet-to-be-delivered services
➤ *Management of experts in various disciplines doing what they were trained and hired to do but also management of those same people*

doing what they were not trained and hired to do: write parts of a proposal

Given the challenge of managing writing and writers under difficult circumstances, the proposal core team needs to follow this basic principle:

A plan does not exist until it is written. Plans communicated orally do not exist, and they provide the most blatant example of virtual planning. And remember, *virtual planning is virtually useless.*

Applied to a proposal effort with all its attendant complexities, it means that a proposal project plan must be developed and distributed no later than the kickoff meeting. (It's actually better to distribute the plan a few days prior to the kickoff meeting so that every team member has a chance to review it and formulate questions that can then be addressed during the meeting.) Furthermore, this plan establishes the core team's credibility because it is tangible proof of the substantive work they have done to prepare for the proposal effort. Figure 8-3 shows the elements of a comprehensive proposal project plan as a deliverable to the kickoff meeting:

Instead of distributing photocopies of an unanalyzed RFP at kickoff, the core team distributes a plan of action, including full RFP analysis. With a precise and comprehensive proposal project plan, the

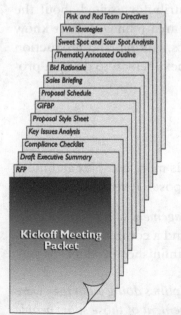

Figure 8-3. **The kickoff meeting packet.** A comprehensive kickoff meeting packet provides tangible evidence that the proposal core team has been working hard to ensure that others won't have to work so hard to create a superior proposal. The packet also allows everyone to work in an information-rich environment.

kickoff meeting will shape a team working on focused assignments and recognizing clear lines of direction. Without the plan, the kickoff meeting will inspire people to do little more than daydream about last weekend's walk in the park.

Establish Credibility: The Process

One of the main reasons proposal work is so frustrating is that contributors—highly trained professionals who need specific physical and intellectual tools to do their jobs—are tossed into their proposal assignments without the proper tools and a process for using them. For this reason, much of a kickoff meeting should be devoted to introducing, explaining, and demonstrating the process and the tools that will be used on the proposal. The critical factor is the core team's willingness not only to talk the system but also to show—via its own pre-kickoff designing and planning—how it works.

If, for example, the core team front-loads the proposal effort by drafting the executive summary prior to kickoff, it lends credence to the process-related issue of designing a proposal top-down. This approach would also show the specific tools that are used to plan, design, and draft the executive summary: full-page mock-ups integrating the visuals, themes, and text; and the hardware and software generating the draft. The point here is as simple as it is important:

Contributors must never leave a kickoff meeting with unanswered questions or serious doubts about the system (the process and tools) they will be expected to use quickly and skillfully.

The following checklist provides some of the key system-related issues (subject to modification within a given company and on a given proposal effort) that a core team might consider as they prepare for a kickoff meeting:

- ❑ Top-down proposal design: from executive summary to the volumes to the sections
- ❑ Limitations on pages and visuals for each contributor
- ❑ Format requirements with the electronic style sheet prepared and distributed in advance of the meeting, then demonstrated via a computer and LCD projector during the meeting
- ❑ Mock-ups of all sections to determine effective design, developing the themes and visuals on the page mock-ups before generating the text

❑ Sources, uses, and tailoring of boilerplate
❑ Sources and uses of templates
❑ Review and revision cycles
❑ Hardware and software commonality
❑ Master copies of the volumes
❑ Dedicated proposal rooms as layout areas
❑ Style and voice in the text

A Failed Kickoff: Danger Ahead

One of the surest signs that chaos is alive, well, and about to enjoy unrestrained growth is a kickoff meeting in which the proposal manager makes some opening remarks over a cup of cold coffee while an assistant at the back of the room begins distributing toasty-warm photocopies of an RFP. Then, with feigned enthusiasm, the manager says, "OK, folks, let's all read this RFP and meet again day after tomorrow to see what we've got." Other signs of proposal doom:

➤ A kickoff meeting attended by some but not all of the proposal team members

➤ A kickoff meeting attended by all the proposal team members but no one else (e.g., red team reviewers, executive sponsors, support personnel)

➤ A kickoff meeting in which Rock Stone, VP of Everything, says nothing more than, "This one is a must win! And remember, I care!"

➤ A kickoff meeting dominated by negative messages expressed in positive tones:

- No one will be expected to work after midnight or before 6:00 A.M. You need your rest.

- If everyone produces, the number of working weekends will be held to four, maybe five, six at the most. Tops. Really. Tops. Max.

- Cancellation of vacations has already been taken care of, so you don't even have to think about that detail. No one can say we don't take care of our people!

- Lunches will be provided every day . . . by automatic payroll deduction, so you don't have to mess with the paperwork or leave your desk.

- To keep things simple, the schedule has only one milestone: the submittal date.

Producing a superior proposal at a reasonable cost means that those in charge must hear the clock ticking before the RFP arrives and must prepare for a kickoff meeting that will control the chaos of the response period. After all, chaos costs money, both short term (an eleventh-hour salvage operation) and long term (proposals that fail to move the company toward contracts). Chaos also mercilessly chews up people and other resources, and the result is often mental mutiny among team members who try to amuse themselves by taking daily, even hourly, readings on how many os there are in *doom*.

A quality kickoff meeting provides proposal management with its major stay against chaos, a means of demonstrating pre-RFP commitment and leadership, and a way of creating a team that can function smoothly because it has identity, direction, focus, and the proper system for success.

Revising for Quality: The Final Touches

The final, comprehensive review of a draft proposal (most often referred to as a *red team review* and discussed in Chapter 10) focuses on such issues as price; 100 percent compliance with the RFP; and full responsiveness to the client's needs, concerns, hot buttons, key issues, values, and goals—all of which contribute to the difference between a good (compliant) proposal and a superior (responsive) one. In other words, final revisions to the proposal itself (i.e., not to the messages per se but to how effectively they are expressed) must be made once it has been assembled and the core team can see, perhaps for the first time, a whole document as the client will see it.

The core team drives the final, substantive changes that will ensure the three characteristics of a superior proposal: It is compliant and fully responsive, it sells, and it communicates. They could, of course, try to rally the original contributors to bend to the task of one more revision, but this approach has two immediate drawbacks:

1. Time is too precious at this point to break apart the proposal and loop all the sections back to their authors for additional reworking.
2. Most, if not all, of the contributors have given the proposal their best effort already, so asking them to rework their sections would invite massive redundancy, perfunctory efforts, and even rubber stamping.

What the core team needs now are not the technical, project management, and other types of experts associated with the complexities of the offer. Rather, the core team needs communication experts (often located in marketing, publications, or graphics departments) who know how to revise because they understand what a proposal—as a stand-alone product—must give evaluators. These experts conduct three major "sweeps" through the proposal to enhance the quality of its three communication elements: themes, visuals, and text:

1. The *themes expert or experts* work across the proposal, checking each theme statement (both at the top of sections and embedded within them) for accuracy, specificity, differentiating features, bottom-line benefits of those features, and implementation of the must-win strategies with the greatest impact. They ignore visuals and text except as they relate to the themes.
2. The *visuals expert or experts* work across the proposal, checking each visual for completeness, clarity, focus, layout, aesthetics, detail, logic, and the effectiveness of the feature-benefit captions in interpreting and selling the visual. They ignore themes and text except as they relate to visuals.
3. The *text expert or experts* work down each column or page, recasting the prose as needed (e.g., moving discussions of benefits to the top of sections and the top of paragraphs, breaking dense paragraphs into smaller units, and "aerating" the text with white space with bulleted lists and single-sentence paragraphs in boldface type to emphasize key points). They ignore the visuals and themes except as they relate to text. Note also that they don't get bogged down in grammar, punctuation, and the like. That work should be left for final editing and proofing.

The time comes when even the best manager can no longer see the proposal for the trees, and that's when tapping other experts can pay huge dividends. These are the people who, in the eleventh hour, turn the proposal itself into a superior product. The issue now is not the offer per se but how effectively it is communicated to the client in this other product called a proposal.

Managing the proposal effort is a complex task requiring careful planning and a proactive application of energy and resources. Fundamental to this approach is a management philosophy recognizing the importance not just of *what* is being discussed in the proposal but also *how well* the proposal discusses it. Keep in mind that a superior offer poorly communicated is a surefire way to lose on price. The issue is not glitz, sparkle, or Madison Avenue slick. Rather, the issue is designing and developing a superior communication product called a proposal.

Beyond the proposal, the issue becomes business development itself and how to be successful at it in the proposal, or endgame, phase.

Many companies (and therefore their proposal managers) insist that the only superior proposal is the one that garners a contract. But in today's marketplace, that sort of short-term view is risky because a company can quickly find itself living hand to mouth with no long-term strategic thinking to ensure its prosperity.

Thus, to manage each proposal effort effectively, a company must recognize the difference between a proposal that moves them toward a contract and a winning, or superior, proposal. The former defines itself by the victory. The latter defines itself not necessarily by winning the immediate deal but always by positioning the company with the client long term, win or lose. If they're not going to award you the work, they'll have to find reasons outside the proposal.

Your proposal should be so good as a proposal—as a product itself— that it establishes a new baseline for excellence during and after evaluation. Then, even if the client cannot award the contract accordingly, the evaluators push back from the table and say, "This is the finest proposal we've ever seen." When this happens, the proposal has made it tough for them to say "no" today, and it will be even tougher for them to say "no" the next time. Furthermore, your superior proposal raises your customer's expectations and their desire that all future proposals match yours in quality. When that happens, you've raised the bar on your competitors while remaining focused on your customer. That's a far better way to compete than standing toe-to-toe with them to see who blinks first on price.

One of the ways companies have to compete today is by rethinking how they differentiate themselves in their highly competitive markets. And what they're discovering—sometimes through the bitter experience of losing important opportunities—is that it's almost impossible to establish and maintain differentiation based on product or service superiority alone. There's just too much available in the marketplace, and unless someone breaks from the pack in new and compelling ways, the client will probably go with low price as the only substantive differentiator available for choosing a winner.

GOLDEN RULE:
When capability becomes commodity,
competition becomes communication.

To put it another way, when you and your first-tier competitors have great messages, the competition isn't about who has the great message but who communicates it most effectively. And if your message doesn't get through, what is suddenly an unacceptably high price most likely will.

Challenges for Readers

➤ Under the best of circumstances, proposal work is stressful work. If you could measure the stress levels among your colleagues trying to finish a major proposal on time, when would the readings be highest? In the early days of the response period (immediately after receipt of the RFP) or downstream toward the end of that period? With few exceptions, we have observed significant spikes in stress at the end rather than the beginning. What could you and your organization do to mitigate the problem of end loading the proposal effort? Front-load it with planning, proposal design, a firm freeze date on the offer, and an excellent kickoff meeting? When proposals require eighteen-hour days—and they will—you're far better off working that hard on the front end of the response period, not the back end when much of the activity is a salvage operation and the only goal is to get the proposal bound and delivered on time. When that happens, quality is just a distant ideal, and mistakes remain in the proposal for the customer to see, then draw conclusions based on them.

➤ For major opportunities, drafting your executive summary prior to the development of the proposal (even doing so in late middle game) is a major differentiator for your proposal process. We recommend that you develop proficiency in this technique as a first important step toward more effective kickoff meetings. Doing the executive summary first drives strategy development, understanding of the customer's key issues in selecting a provider, and crafting of your most compelling messages and graphics. (See Chapter 6 for a full discussion of what powerful executive summaries can do for your company and how to create them.)

➤ Does your company have a proposal process? Is it flexible enough to accommodate small, medium, large, and must-win proposals? Do you have proposal professionals in your organization? If so, are they provided educational opportunities to hone their skills? Have you put in place a commonly shared methodology for designing and creating compelling proposals? Or do your proposal professionals just inherit what older colleagues give them and learn as they go along?

➤ Engineers, business developers, marketers, accountants, and other business professionals typical belong to one or more professional societies. These are learning organizations, and their regional and national meetings offer multiple opportunities for members to network, discuss the issues of the day, and generally recharge their business thinking. Do your colleagues working on proposals belong to such an organization? Does your company encourage their professional development by supporting membership for them in an organization such as the Association of Proposal Management Professionals? Doing so provides tangible evidence that the proposal phase of business development and the people who work there are critical success factors for getting and keeping customers.

Notes

1. Terry R. Bacon and David G. Pugh, *The Behavioral Advantage: What the Smartest, Most Successful Companies Do Differently to Win in the B2B Arena* (New York: AMACOM, 2004).
2. Ibid.

Chapter 9

GETTING IT WRITTEN, GETTING IT RIGHT

Guide to Creating Compelling Proposals

GOLDEN RULE:

When writing a proposal, writing is the last thing you should do.

The RFP has been analyzed. The offer has been determined. The proposal that will respond to the RFP and define the offer has been planned, designed, and strategies have been devised. A draft executive summary is in place. All these are challenging steps in the proposal process, but now the really tough work begins: creating the proposal, the parts and pieces that, once assembled, will go to a customer as your best effort to win their hearts, their minds, and their money.

Perhaps someday in a world far different from this one, we will actually work with a proposal team whose members fairly chirp their way through each proposal day, producing prose so brilliant it illuminates the night sky, asking for additional writing assignments because the fun should never end, and singing snappy show tunes at 2 A.M. in front of the computer. Until then, alas, we have to say that there's no doubt about it, writing a proposal is hard work. Every proposal we've worked on has, at some point, entered the infamous "grind" phase. Talking stops. Heads are down. People are trying to draft the section content for the proposal, and it is typically a grueling, slow process of one paragraph and a cloud of dust.

The Seven-Step Section Development Process

Writing proposals may never be pain free, but it can certainly be less painful and more satisfying if you follow a few simple rules illustrated in Figure 9-1.

First and foremost, the actual writing is the very last step in this process. Once adopted, this process creates a high probability that when you finally reach the moment of truth and begin to write in Step 7, three wonderful things will happen:

1. You will write faster.
2. You will write better.
3. You will write less, which is a win for both the writer who doesn't like to write and the reader who doesn't want to process any more text than necessary to get the messages.

Step 1: Determine the Content

Address the customer's particular concerns as reflected in the RFP, other customer instructions, and any additional key issues, concerns, and/or goals you have learned about during pre-RFP interactions with the customer. Your ability and willingness to do this sort of customizing creates a powerful differentiator, yet many section writers fail to do this. They know that the section is about safety, for example, and so they pull out the standard write-up on safety. But each customer usually has specific questions, requirements, or issues to be addressed, so each safety section may be quite different.

If the customer has asked that particular questions be answered and certain requirements addressed, be sure to respond to all of them. A fundamental mistake that proposal writers make is neglecting to respond to every question or requirement in an RFP. This is a fatal error called noncompliance, and is the fastest way to be eliminated from the competition.

GOLDEN RULE:
In the early phases of evaluation, they aren't looking
for the winner. They're looking for losers.

Step 2: Organize the Content

Now that you know what information will go into your section, you can organize it. Most proposal sections should follow the classic struc-

Figure 9-1. **The section development process.** By postponing the writing until everything else shown in the process has been done, you heighten your probability of creating better proposal sections in less time and with far less painful revisions.

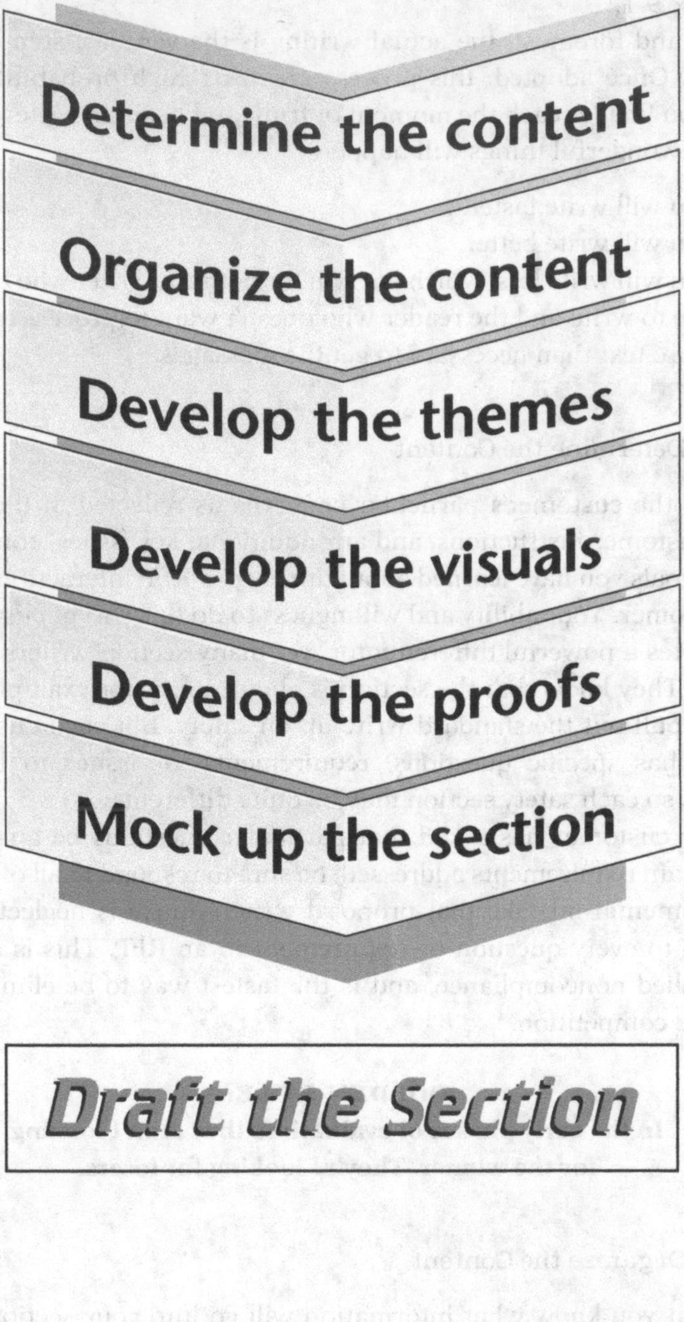

Determine the content

Organize the content

Develop the themes

Develop the visuals

Develop the proofs

Mock up the section

Draft the Section

ture: Tell them what you're going to tell them, tell them, and then tell them what you told them. Organized this way, your sections would follow this structure:

- > *Section Number (if appropriate) and Title.*
- > *Section Theme Statement* (primary message—issues linked to goals, and linked to features linked to benefits): This amounts to an opening summary of the main ideas in the section. You may mention technical content here, as long as you link issues to goals, features, and benefits.
- > *Opening:* Write an introductory paragraph indicating an awareness of the customer's key issues regarding the content of this section and your response to those issues. If the section is long, provide a roadmap—a list of upcoming subheadings or topics you plan to discuss, in the order you plan to discuss them.
- > *Middle Paragraphs:* These provide step-by-step coverage of the customer's requirements. Each paragraph covers one key idea.
- > *Closing Paragraph:* This is a summary of the key themes of the section. In longer sections, the closing can also review key content.
- > *Sidebars* (optional): If you're using a message-column format, you need to write sidebar messages. You can write them first, but it's often best to wait until the section is drafted to see where and how to write them.

Step 3: Develop the Themes

Once you know the content and have it organized, turn your attention to the themes or messages of the section. Know what you are selling in each section and make your messages clear. To give each section strong messages that explain why your offer is uniquely advantageous to the customer, section writers generally create theme statements linking goals, issues, features, benefits, and proofs.

One way to approach this is to view the section topic as the issue that must be linked to the relevant customer goal for that section. In essence, you are creating a GIFBP Matrix, such as the one shown in Figure 6-1, for the section. You link the issue to the customer's goal and then link the features, benefits, and proofs to the issue.

You may also find guidance in your kickoff packet, most likely on the proposal style sheet, about how "deep" you should theme your section (e.g., first- and second-level sections but not third-level sections and lower). If you have a thematic outline, then you already know what the key messages in your section should be. If not, then you need to generate your themes by asking some questions:

> What am I selling in this section? Does that align with what this customer needs to buy?
> How can I use the content of this section to sell my organization and its solution or approach?
> What are the customer's issues or concerns regarding this content?
> What am I proposing in response to those issues or concerns? In other words, what are my features?
> How do those features benefit the customer?
> How is what I'm proposing or describing uniquely advantageous to the customer? Do I have positive differentiators for my section? If so, what are my strategies for powerfully communicating to the customer? If not, what are my strategies for overcoming a lack of differentiation?

Theme statements "drive" proposal sections. Each section leads off with a high-level theme statement that is broken down and made more specific at the lower levels. Theme statements are a key method for promoting your features and benefits to the customer. Ideally, you'll want to locate them throughout each section of your proposal.

Your theme statements must communicate the benefits in a convincing manner, which means they must communicate the linkage of GIFBPs. Here, again, is that linkage:

> *Goal:* What the customer needs to achieve in making the investment
> *Issues:* The customer's concerns with regard to the section topic
> *Features:* What you propose to do or provide
> *Benefits:* What it will do for the customer
> *Proofs:* Validation and substantiation that you can deliver the benefits

In addition to communicating GIFBPs, effective theme statements—like effective strategies—do four things:

1. *Highlight your strengths:*
   "Our lean management team structure, with 173 years of collective experience, promotes efficient communication and heightens confidence in our ability to deliver your equipment on time."

2. *Mitigate your weaknesses:*

"We provide metrics, not rhetoric, for ensuring quality with a detailed TQM plan that sets definitive standards for all outputs. Our diligence reduces your risk."

3. *Neutralize your competitors' strengths:*

"Our solar backup power generation station provides a reasonably priced redundant system, thus helping to avoid even costlier downtime while the main station is being repaired."

4. *Ghost your competitors' weaknesses:*

"We mitigate risk and contain costs on the front end by providing seasoned project managers with proven risk and cost management skills."

Effective theme statements answer the questions "Why us?" "Why not them?" and—at least in a preliminary way—"So what?" They also typically create the question "How so?" in the reader's mind, and that's what the section addresses. Here are some guidelines for writing your theme statements:

➤ Follow the GIFBP formula—except that proofs can follow a theme statement and be elaborated on in the body of the section. Always link features and benefits in your theme statements.

➤ Write complete sentences and make them as concise as possible. Avoid using more than two sentences for theme statements, one sentence for sidebar messages.

➤ Don't make sweeping statements you can't substantiate later. Don't claim to be uniquely qualified, for example, without including enough proofs in the body of the section to make your claims in the theme statement believable. And keep in mind that "state of the art" does not equal "unique."

➤ Be as specific as possible and quantify the benefits if you can (e.g., "Our fast-track approach will bring your plant on line at least two months early").

➤ Write in the active voice. Don't say, "Real-world accuracy can be achieved through complex calculational modeling." Instead, write, "Complex calculational modeling achieves real-world accuracy."

➤ Use "we" and "our," even "you" and "your," instead of continually referring to your and the customer's organizations with full company names. A proposal is people communicating with people, and the occasional use of these pronouns gives your proposal a human voice.

Once you have drafted your themes, your proposal design should include a style sheet that specifies how all themes will be displayed in the sections. Here are some ideas for displaying your theme statements in a proposal:

➤ Prominently display theme statements at the top of each section.
➤ Choose one or two typographical options to emphasize and set them off
➤ Use type that is one or two points larger than the text.

• Boldface or italicize them.
• Box them.
• Place rules (lines) above and/or below them.
• Place screens (shading) behind them.
• Extend section themes across both columns on double-column pages.

➤ Embed them in the text and typographically highlight them.
➤ Place them at the tops of paragraphs and boldface them.
➤ Make them separate, single-sentence paragraphs.
➤ Build them into sidebar messages when using the message-column layout. Sidebar messages have several advantages:

• You can place the key messages apart from the text and surround them with white space, which makes them visually emphatic and highly noticeable.
• Unlike a single theme statement at the top of a section, sidebar messages can be strategically located throughout the section to cover secondary, but still important, points.
• They can deliver a message embedded in the text, either by repeating or paraphrasing the message, when it wouldn't be appropriate or attractive to highlight it in the text.
• They can differentiate your proposal from those of the many organizations that have adopted the double-column layout with boxed theme statements as a standard.

➤ Align sidebar messages with related text or visuals.

Figures 9-2 and 9-3 show both theme statements (for the overall section and first-level subsections) and sidebar messages, which are really mini-themes located throughout the section.

Step 4. Develop the Visuals

GOLDEN RULE:
Visualize first; then write.

Figure 9-2. **Model section page—double column.** For any proposal of more than eight to ten pages, consider using the double-column format for maximum reader friendliness, comprehension, and retention. If an RFP imposes page limitations on your proposal, the decision to use double columns should be automatic.

▌GeoFiber Inc.

3.2 Project Execution Approach

MacFarland's proposed approach to project execution features merit shop construction management, a single-source design/build contractor, and a fast-track schedule. This approach will allow GeoFiber, Inc. to simplify the management of the project, reduce the project schedule, reduce construction costs, and realize earlier operational revenues, as demonstrated successfully on numerous previous projects.

As one of North America's leading EPC contractors, MacFarland E&C has considerable experience in projects of this kind. In this section, we will address the three key elements of our proposed project approach:

- Merit shop construction management
- Single-source design/build contracting
- Fast-track scheduling

Merit Shop Construction Management

Our merit shop approach will give you access to a broader range of local subcontractors, and it will help you reduce construction costs through the competitive bidding process.

MacFarland recommends performing the construction of this project using a merit shop construction management approach. Under this approach, the execution contractor will act as construction manager, contracting all work on a lump-sum competitive basis to either local union or open-shop subcontractors.

To ensure that you benefit from lower costs and on-time project completion, MacFarland uses a proprietary competitive bidding process called MacSub and a subcontractor management system that we have perfected through forty years of subcontractor management. MacSub uses a proprietary set of specification standards and a quantified bid analysis format to ensure that subcontractor bids are comprehensive, complete, and accurate. By ensuring accurate comparisons of competing bids, we are confident of receiving the lowest costs for subcontracted services. Our subcontractor management system receives input from the MacSub

process and allows us to produce highly accurate schedules for phased work and materials and equipment deliveries.

Together, our proprietary competitive bidding process and subcontractor management system enable us to take full advantage of local union or open-shop contractors and provide you with efficient construction management services.

Single-source Design/Build Contractor

We offer a single-source design/build approach in which the engineer/designer and construction manager function as a team, enabling you to meet your aggressive schedule and cost goals.

GeoFiber, Inc. could use separate firms for engineering/design and construction management. However, in light of the aggressive schedule, we recommend the single-source design/build approach.

Our preliminary project schedule (section 3.4) shows construction activities beginning only two and one-half months after the start of engineering. Consequently, the engineering/design team will be under significant pressure to produce construction drawings quickly. This will require the engineering/design team and the construction manager to work very closely and to coordinate constructability, procurement, and construction management issues. Of particular concern are the contract bid packages for subcontractors. The engineering/design team will have to issue bid packages before the design is complete. Or they will have to issue many smaller bid packages, which increases costs and makes coordination more difficult.

Figure 9-3. **Model section page—message column.** The message-column format is very effective for skimmers, who will use the message column on the left, and for scanners, who will immerse themselves in the right-column detail. It would not be the format of choice whenever an RFP imposes severe page limitations on your proposal.

General Aerospace
Corporation

Technical Approach

What is AccessNet?

AccessNet is an easy-to-use and cost-effective, yet extremely capable, international messaging network solution. AccessNet will provide General Aerospace users with all the capabilities they need using their existing equipment, at a cost lower than some systems offering internal e-mail only.

Our AccessNet service—which integrates **electronic mail, fax, file transfer, and application sharing** through Integrated Hub Office Processing (IHOP) and Inverted Network Interconnection (INI) technologies—will greatly extend the communications reach of General Aerospace Corporation. IHOP is a host-based application that enables your users to exchange text, image, and data files via electronic mail and central filing. INI provides a bridge from your host to AccessNet's processing resources. Host-to-host applications available through INI include bulk data transfer, distributed transaction processing, distributed database applications, and protocol conversion.

Your investment in hardware, software, and communication equipment is protected.

We provide a cost-effective approach to meeting your processing needs today and in the future.

Our solution will enable you to:

• Open electronic communications with remote personnel

• Establish an international network standard

• Communicate with a variety of platforms, including:

— IBM 3090
— AS/400
— DEC VAX All-in-One
— LANs
— Standalone PCs (IBM DOS or Windows, Macintosh)
— Fax machines
— Telex

GAC users can easily navigate the Access network using our seamless, intuitive interface. (See Figure A-1 on the following page.)

Our seamless, intuitive interface allows GAC users to communicate easily with your internal e-mail system.

AccessNet's menus provide both mouse and keyboard options for: (1) checking the user directory; (2) dialing other users; (3) sending a message; (4) scheduling messages, reminders, etc.; (5) creating reminders and other notes; (6) retrieving news items; (7) creating messages via Access' or your host e-mail system; (8) checking the mailbox and viewing messages; and (9) filing saved messages. Section 2 contains detailed illustrations and descriptions of AccessNet's menus and options.

9

Access
Information Services

At this point, you know your section's content and primary messages. The next issue is your visuals. Whenever possible and practical, a section should have at least one visual illustrating its theme. The preferred ratio of text to visuals differs depending on to whom you talk, but most people agree that proposal sections should be about one-third visual in terms of space allocation. When designing visuals, ask these questions:

➤ What is the main point or key message of the section?
➤ If I could communicate one thing that would result in a win, what would it be? How can I make it visual?
➤ What are the supporting ideas in the section and which of them would best be conveyed visually?
➤ What is the technical content?
➤ What are the selling points?
➤ Where in my section will I need to communicate dimensions, configurations, spatial concepts, relationships (e.g., a team or organization), and/or a process or flow? How could I communicate them visually rather than explain them in words?

Every visual should have a simple and clear message, so it's often best to start by asking yourself which messages are simple and then finding effective ways to translate those messages visually.

It's probably best at this point to actually sketch the visuals, to play with visual concepts until you find those that do a good job of conveying the message. You might even write a sentence or two indicating what the message is. These rough ideas will become your section visuals and interpretive captions.

For most readers, visual communication has a much greater impact than straight text. Visuals draw attention to themselves, and readers tend to retain concepts presented visually better than those presented in words alone. Consider these guidelines as you develop ways to convey the information in your proposal:

➤ Try to have at least one visual in every section.
➤ If at all possible, picture any key strengths to give them a dramatic impact and a precision that words alone may not be able to achieve.
➤ Keep the visuals simple and uncluttered. A visual should focus the reader on a particular idea or concept that should be clear without additional explanation external to the visual. Effective visuals stand alone.

➤ Introduce the visuals in the text. The introduction should supply a transition to the visual and explain its significance (e.g., "Figure 12-1 shows the correlation between experience and reliability").

➤ Integrate visuals and text. Don't stick the visuals in an appendix.

➤ Align visuals vertically rather than horizontally (portrait). If you need more horizontal space, consider a foldout before flipping a visual on its side (landscape).

➤ Write full-sentence, interpretive captions for all visuals. A visual without a caption is more interesting than a block of text; without a caption, however, the interpretation of the visual is left to the reader.

➤ Do not confuse titles with captions. A *title* is merely a heading (e.g., "Figure 16-3. Project Organization"). A *caption* is more informative than a heading. An interpretive caption actually interprets the visual for the reader. It tells the reader what to look for, what to see in the visual. Here's an interpretive caption:

"Our project team is organized for both internal reporting efficiency and external communication with other suppliers."

➤ Interpretive captions work best when they link features and benefits to the customer's issues:

"Our project team is organized for internal reporting efficiency, which minimizes administrative costs, and for external communication with other suppliers, thereby enhancing collaboration."

In this caption the issues are cost and collaboration. The feature is the team structure; the benefits are minimal costs and enhanced collaboration.

Given all that we've said regarding visual communication, you might easily conclude that visuals—charts, graphs, photographs, maps, flow diagrams, and so on—are the most powerful form of printed communication, but that's not quite true. The most powerful form of printed communication is neither visual nor verbal. It is a combination of the two. Consider, for instance, a full-page, color photograph of a volcano in a prestigious periodical such as *National Geographic*. Below this image is its caption: "Volcano." That would border on the absurd because the reader would quickly think, "I'm not stupid. I can see that it's a volcano. What I don't know is why I'm looking at it. What's the significance of this volcano? What makes it different from other volcanoes, and why would I possibly care?"

Yet we have seen visuals in which the proposal equivalent of "Volcano" is the norm for the captions (e.g., a project organization chart with the caption "Project Organization Chart," or a process flow diagram with the heady caption "Process Flow Diagram"). Together, the visual and its caption deliver the complete message, and that's what your proposal visuals should do as well. Here, then, are some additional guidelines for writing interpretive captions:

- ➤ Write a single, complete sentence that tells readers what you want them to see.
- ➤ Link issues, features, and benefits. The visual should give the proof and elaborate on the claims in the caption.
- ➤ If you can't devise an interpretive caption, consider redesigning or rejecting the visual.
- ➤ Differentiate visual titles and captions from text by using a different typeface or an emphatic device such as boldfacing or italics.
- ➤ Place the caption below the visual. The figure number and title can either go above the visual or run into the caption. Either way, be consistent throughout the proposal, not just in a given section.

Figure 9-4 displays a proposal's visual and accompanying interpretive caption.

Step 5: Develop the Proofs

Next you should search for proofs of the benefits you are going to cite. What tangible or intangible evidence can you provide that proves that you can achieve the benefits you're going to state in this section? The proofs will be embedded in the section, but it's a good idea to discover them now so you know what you're going to write about and how you're going to support it. Make sure to look at the GIFBP Matrix (see Figures 2-3 and 6-1 for examples) to see whether proofs have already been identified. Proofs may include:

➤ *Facts, Figures, or Published Information on Your Product, Service, or Company:*

- • History
- • Experience
- • Size
- • Revenues
- • Product features/test results

Figure 9-4. **Proposal visual and caption.** The complete message to the customer includes the visual and its interpretive caption. The caption sells; the visual proves/ shows.

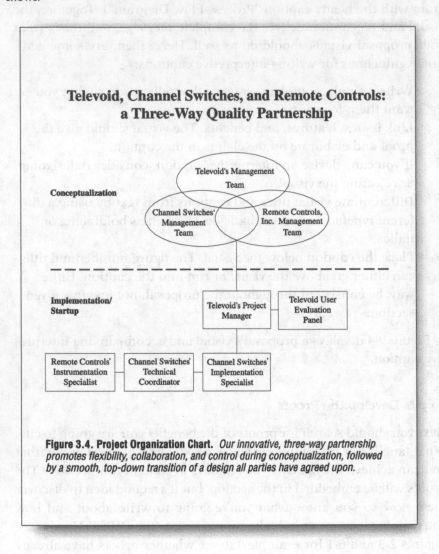

Televoid, Channel Switches, and Remote Controls: a Three-Way Quality Partnership

Conceptualization

Televoid's Management Team

Channel Switches' Management Team

Remote Controls, Inc. Management Team

Implementation/ Startup

Televoid's Project Manager

Televoid User Evaluation Panel

Remote Controls' Instrumentation Specialist

Channel Switches' Technical Coordinator

Channel Switches' Implementation Specialist

Figure 3.4. Project Organization Chart. *Our innovative, three-way partnership promotes flexibility, collaboration, and control during conceptualization, followed by a smooth, top-down transition of a design all parties have agreed upon.*

- Customer base
- Product comparisons
- Service areas/locations

➤ *Hard Data and Other Verifiable Information:*

- Photographs and written details of past projects
- Cost/schedule savings of different approaches or designs
- Quality or performance statistics (e.g., mean time between failure [MTBF] on different parts, designs)

- Third-party test data
- Site testing, verifications by government regulators
- Service data
- Written warranties or guarantees

➤ *Customer References and Testimonials:*

- Letters of reference
- Verifiable quotations
- Customer internal documents, such as newsletters

Remember that you should offer proofs of the benefits, not the features. You are not proving that the features exist; you are proving that the benefits you promise will actually happen for the customer.

Step 6: Create a Mock-Up

A mock-up is basically a visual outline. Where the outline gives structure to the verbal content, the mock-up reveals the structure of both the verbal and the visual content. It will help you create the best-looking, most effective proposal because you are able to see it *before* you begin writing. If you don't like the flow or layout, you can adjust it at the outset. In this regard, the mock-up is a time and money saver.

As shown in Figure 9-5, begin with (1) a basic page—blank, except for running headers and footers. Next, add (2) main headings and theme statements, (3) visuals, (4) captions, (5) introductory text and subheadings, and (6) text.

The number of mock-up iterations depends on the complexity of the task. For a large, team-written proposal, the leader might insist on half a dozen iterations. For a smaller document created by one or two individuals, fewer iterations are necessary. In either case, the fundamental principle here is that you are, in a very real sense, building something: a section of a proposal. Therefore, it makes sense to design it first, then build it. That is what a mock-up helps you to do.

Step 7: Draft the Section

Every proposal has, or should have, three communication elements—themes, visuals, and text—and we cite them in order of communication power and also in order of preparation. Your most compelling messages should be expressed in your themes and visuals, not just in the text. Use the text to prove, elaborate upon, and reinforce those

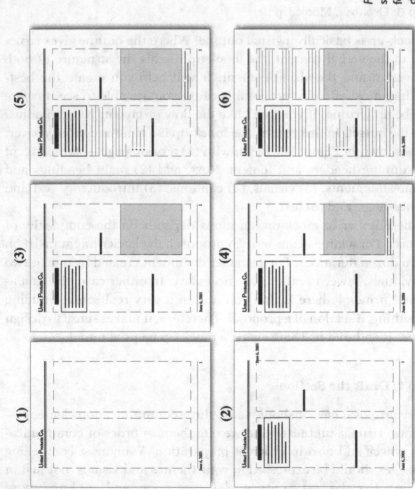

Figure 9-5. **A section mock-up.** Mocking up your section allows you to "manage" space and content for maximum effect and efficiency. It makes sense to design something before you build it.

messages, not as your primary medium—or, worse yet, only medium—for getting those messages through to your readers.

So now you're ready to write the text, to put some flesh on the bones of your section. It may seem as if it has taken a long time to get to this point, but unless you are an exceptional verbal communicator who can generate quality proposal text at high speed, this process can be one of your most powerful communication tools. Our experience tells us that by postponing the writing until you've done everything else to prepare the way, you will actually use significantly less total time to complete your draft proposal section.

If you had started by writing the words, you would most likely still be doing just that, with no organization, themes, visuals, captions, proofs, or mock-ups. But all of that is completed when you follow the rules, and you leave the writing for last. By that time, you have a much clearer sense of what you need to write about because you have already communicated a great deal with the themes and visuals. In addition, doing so usually means writing faster, writing better, and writing less.

Every proposal has a deadline that must be met. Therefore, to get the writing process under way and meet the deadline, we recommend that you:

➤ Work from an outline. Begin where you feel most confident and write one piece at a time.
➤ Write quickly, without editing. You can edit later. Don't try to get it right the first time. It almost always takes longer that way.
➤ If you're planning to use boilerplate be sure to follow these simple guidelines:
  • Locate and review applicable passages before you begin.
  • Make sure any passages you use are tailored to the customer and the opportunity.
  • Replace your terminology with customer terminology wherever appropriate.
  • Don't use long passages that you've used before with the same customer.
  • Make sure all the facts and figures are up-to-date.
  • Make sure the details in boilerplate passages agree with those in other passages in your section.
  • Create transitions between boilerplate and newly written paragraphs.

➤ Review these items when you are finished to make certain you have covered everything and adequately addressed the customer's issues.

In addition to writing efficiently, it's critically important that your section's text be as clear as possible. We've learned over and again, sometimes the hard way, that clarity is a major contributor to a reader-friendly proposal. Given the limited time that evaluators have for understanding and assessing proposals, anything you can do to help them see a clear path to success is value added.

GOLDEN RULE:
Ease of evaluation is a very real factor of success.

Here are some of the lessons we've learned in the field about writing clearly:

➤ Stay focused on giving the customer reasons to choose you and your solution. Remember, they buy benefits, not features.

➤ Write a brief introduction that previews the content and provides a roadmap for your section (a list of upcoming subheadings or topics you plan to discuss, in the order you plan to discuss them).

➤ State the main ideas first, followed by details, explanations, examples, and so on. Write in descending order of importance.

➤ Keep your paragraphs short.

➤ Develop one key idea per paragraph: (1) State the idea; (2) explain it, using transitional or key words to link sentences; and (3) move on to the next idea.

➤ Think about your readers, and then write as if you are having a conversation with them. Use simple, everyday language. Valid technical terms that readers will understand are fine, of course—but avoid inflated terminology, obscure abbreviations, and jargon.

➤ Just as we recommended for theme statements, use "we," "you," "us," "our," and "your" throughout the section. Doing so personalizes your writing.

➤ Minimize your use of acronyms and abbreviations or provide a list or glossary for reference.

➤ Use the customer's words and terms wherever possible.

➤ Write a closing paragraph that restates the key benefits and features discussed in the section. Often a simple paraphrase of the theme at the top of the section is an effective conclusion.

Figure 9-6. **Model section page.** The process for creating proposal sections produces finished pages with an effective blend of the three communication elements of every proposal: themes, visuals, and text.

United Nations Environmental Oversight Council
Worldwide Environmental Remediation Project (WERP)

TECHNICAL APPROACH

2.2 Turnkey Environmental Remediation Operation

Worldwide will provide timely, cost-conscious responses to remedial action assignments at UNEOC sites, using experienced environmental engineers and support personnel employing the latest, most cost-effective, and environmentally friendly remediation technologies

Worldwide Environmental Services has been working with the U.S. Government on environmental remediation projects for over 20 years. Several large-scale remediation programs are in progress or have been completed successfully. Treatments range from simple removal or incineration to sophisticated techniques such as ultraviolet, bioremediation, and jet grouting. All work will be overseen by Professional Engineers registered in the country and state or province where the work is to be done, supported by other properly licensed environmental remediation specialists as necessary.

This section presents our capabilities in the following areas:

- Treatment Facilities at Priority Sites
- Soil Excavation, Treatment, and Disposal

2.2.1 Treatment Facilities at Priority WERP Sites

Worldwide Environmental Services uses the experience gained in the construction, deployment, and operation of our treatment facilities to evaluate and to utilize proven and commercially available treatment technologies.

At the five UNEOC priority sites already identified, we propose to employ the technologies shown in Figure 2.2.1.1 (right). All five technologies are either WES developed or licensed.

Contaminated soil can be treated by our Oblivionator system or our licensed Bleeznerov Organic Blasting Incendiary Treatment System (BOBITS). The Oblivionator is for block stabilization and slurry wall

construction projects up to 60 feet deep. BOBITS is a transportable counter-rotating arm-based system.

Contaminated soil and groundwater can be treated simultaneously by our licensed Microbial Soil or Groundwater Remediation (MSOGR) system. Our Ultrahydrozone process can be used to treat groundwater. Our Jetwall barrier system can be used to create slurry walls in support of treatment and containment projects. State-of-the-art continuous air monitoring systems and air pollution control systems are used to monitor and control our excavation, ventilation, and treatment operations.

MSOGR use air injection and extraction wells to strip organics and accelerate bioremediation. Ultrahydrozone uses UVB rays, hydrogenated vegetable oil, and alozone

Figure 2.2.1.1. Worldwide Environmental Services will use its own or licensed technologies to address the specific environmental challenges of the five priority sites identified in UNEOC's Site Characterization document.

orldwide
Environmental Services

112

Figure 9-6 on the preceding page (along with Figures 9-2 and 9-3) is an example of finished proposal pages prepared according to our seven-step process.

We all learned to write essays, book reviews, and term papers in school, but not proposals. So we learn as we go, and we go as we learn. Furthermore, whether you work on proposals full time, part time, or only occasionally, it's tough work done under the pressure of time, the confusion of an often chaotic/obtuse/contradictory RFP, and the angst of needing to win. These are reasons for us to embrace process at every level of proposal management and preparation. A simple, repeatable process—applied consistently over time and many proposals—for creating the sections can provide your company a powerful differentiator in the marketplace.

When you debrief with your customer after the award has been announced, and they say as if with a single voice, "Yours is the finest proposal we've ever seen and evaluated," they are also saying that they hope all future proposals from all providers will achieve the level of excellence yours just established. In short, you and your proposal have once again raised the bar on the competition by raising your customer's expectations. To be sure, any process that helps us achieve that goal is a process worth considering.

Challenges for Readers

➤ Revisit one of your company's recent proposals to a customer. How do the sections measure up to what you have just read? Do each section and at least the first-level subsections start with a benefits-rich theme statement? Is roughly one-third of the space devoted to visuals of various kinds? Do all visuals have interpretive captions? Is the writing clear and crisp, and are the sentences and paragraphs relatively brief? Draw some conclusions from your analysis. With whom should you share them? What could your next steps be?

➤ What are the standards for proposal quality, not just in your company but in your industry? Are they high enough? Do they represent best practices? Wherever your answer is "No," you are confronted with opportunity. We urge you to identify the benchmarks in your industry. Then you can break from the pack and establish new standards of proposal excellence, which the competition will then have to try to figure out how to imitate.

➤ If you have contributed one or more sections to a recent proposal, examine one of your efforts. Now that it's finished and you know as much as you are going to know about it, what could you have done differently in preparing your section? Redo it if only in your head, following the seven-step process. What would have been different in terms of time, effort, and quality of the finished product if you had prepared your themes and visuals before you prepared the text?

Chapter 10

THE REVIEW PROCESS

Making Sure the Power Is in the Proposal

GOLDEN RULE:

Properly understood and conducted, proposal reviews are not driven by Attila's First Law—pillage and plunder first, then burn.

Red Team is an odd term for a formal review of a draft proposal. Although no one knows for certain where the name comes from, speculations include a military origin (i.e., a strike force); Roman mythology (Mars, the red planet and the god of war); or, somewhat less dramatic, the color the proposal team sees once the red team has finished its review. Regardless, the mere mention of a red team review seems to foster highly charged reactions in response to the destructive forces bearing down on a proposal that the team has labored long and hard to create.

With rare exceptions, proposal reviews all seem to have certain traits in common:

➤ The red team members are identified within a few days, if not hours, of the review. This approach falls very close to a standard business practice, the only more negative practice being no review process whatsoever. We have seen both practices many times across industries and around the world.

➤ The red team has no opportunity to review the RFP, the basic proposal design, and the win strategies early in the writing period, or to recommend adjustments before all the content is developed.

(This important milestone is typically called the "pink team" review, i.e., a lighter shade of red, discussed in detail below.)

➤ The reviewers aren't given adequate time to prepare, so they default to their own biases and preferences regarding what a proposal should and should not be.

➤ No one has developed a review methodology the red team can use to ensure thoroughness and consistency while also representing, as closely as possible, the customer's reactions to the proposal. If all of a company's proposals were red teamed according to the same standards of excellence, those who prepare them would know in advance how they and their work would be judged, and they could design their proposals accordingly. Indeed, a rising tide lifts all boats, and a simple repeatable review process would do just that.

➤ Red team critiques are often vague and negative and offer little in the way of constructive suggestions for improvement. Typical comments are "Not clear" or "Make better" or "Needs work" or, the grand-prize winner, "Flogging is too good for you" (which we actually found on a feedback sheet). We can only hope there was considerable tongue in cheek behind that imperial edict.

➤ By the time the red team convenes, does its work, and reports that the proposal needs a major, inside-out overhaul, the final days before submission find the proposal team scrambling madly just to get the proposal in good enough shape for a sprint to the airport and a breathless delivery to the customer. (Horror stories abound regarding proposal delivery, including a proposal to United Parcel Service delivered by Federal Express because that was the only service available when the proposal team finally got their volumes printed, assembled, and packaged. They lost.)

Learning how to conduct powerful red team reviews will directly contribute to a higher-quality proposal (as distinct from the quality of the offer) that will, in turn, contribute to the evaluators' overall favorable impression of your organization and your proposed solution. One of the key qualities of a superior proposal is that it's easier to evaluate, and we have learned over the years that this factor alone can mean the difference between winning and losing in a tight competition.

By following the process and using the tools and techniques we discuss below, you'll discover what we did after far too many negative review efforts: Excellent proposal reviews don't have to be complicated, just rigorously and consistently applied. What is needed is a simple, disciplined process; specific review tools and the skills for using them; plus a way to implement the reviewers' findings quickly, efficiently, and positively along with both the support and active participation of managers and executives with a business stake in the proposal.

The Role of Reviews in the Proposal Process

Basically, four teams are directly or indirectly involved in the red team review process:

1. Core Team
2. Pink Team
3. Red Team
4. Writing Team

Formal proposal reviews are milestone events in the process of creating a proposal, and as such need to be planned and executed at the right time, by the right people, and with the right tools. Therefore, all people directly or indirectly associated with preparing the proposal need to know exactly when the pink and red team reviews will occur; how to prepare for them; and what to expect before, during, and after they occur. No one likes surprises or sudden deviations from the charted course, so understanding proposal reviews as subprocesses of a larger process really helps.

A macrolevel view of the proposal process reveals one of its most important messages: Don't start writing the proposal until it has been carefully planned, even when the RFP has arrived and the clock is ticking. Why? Because postponing the writing to analyze the RFP, assess the opportunity, develop/adjust a strategy, identify win themes, create an outline and a style sheet, and draft an executive summary will pay huge dividends on the back end of the response period.

GOLDEN RULE:
Virtual planning is virtually useless.

The 25-50-25 approach to proposal management gives us the opportunity to plan the proposal and schedule the formal reviews. These reviews, as Figure 10-1 shows, occur during the 50 percent drafting period, the pink team fairly early and the red team at the end. (Chapter 8 provides a detailed discussion of the 25-50-25 approach to proposal management, focusing on the importance of the planning phase in the first 25 percent of the response period and preparing for the kickoff meeting. Here we shift to the 50 percent writing phase and the two

Figure 10-1. **The formal review process.** The pink team verifies the basic design and direction of the sections early so that critical adjustments can be made *before* writing the text and reviewing the completed draft via the red team.

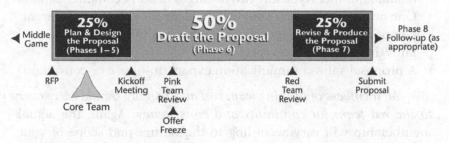

formal proposal reviews, both of which need to be planned by the core team during the initial 25 percent phase as set forth in Chapter 9.)

Given the sense of urgency about getting started on writing the proposal, the kickoff typically occurs within hours or a couple of days of receiving the RFP, which means that writers are generating raw content without knowing (1) the final definition of the offering, (2) what it will take to win in each section, and (3) the design of the proposal. When this happens, problems accumulate at the end of the response period, where time is precious and changes can wreak havoc.

For this reason, we advocate a pre–red team review—often called the "pink team" review—before the sections are actually written. This early review alleviates many of the problems associated with waiting until the entire proposal has been drafted before launching the major, final review. When that happens, trying to "back out" the problems and reengineer the fully written version is a nightmare. It is important, therefore, for the core team to form the review teams and complete the Pink Team and Red Team Directives by the kickoff meeting. To do this, the core team needs answers to three essential questions:

1. Who is needed for the pink and red teams?
2. What do they need to get started?
3. What review methodologies and tools will they use?

➤ *Who is needed for the pink and red teams?* The answer to this question will vary depending on the nature and scope of your proposal, but, in general, the following slots should be filled for the pink team:

- The tactical manager, such as a project manager, who "owns" the proposal (i.e., the person who will get the work and be responsible for successfully providing the contracted deliverables)

- Relevant account manager/salesperson/business development manager
- A small number (typically two or three) of subject matter experts
- One or two nonexperts who will, by definition, bring a different perspective to the proposal draft, a perspective that often simulates the customer's perspective
- A proposal/sales communication expert (in-house or consultant)

All members of the pink team can and usually should carry over to the red team for continuity and consistency. Again, the actual membership will vary according to the nature and scope of your proposal, but, in general, the following slots should be added for the red team:

- An upper manager/executive for sales/business development
- Upper managers/executives representing the functional areas that will get the work and be responsible for contracted deliverables to the customer
- An executive (e.g., the CEO and/or CFO) representing the business issues surrounding the proposal, such as revenue, margin, market share, and strategic impacts
- Additional subject matter experts (in-house or consultants), as needed, to cover the specifics of the offer, such as project/ program management, technical design, schedule, risk, legal, finance, contracting and subcontracting, procurement, and pricing issues

➤ *What do they need to get started?* The answer lies in the kickoff meeting packet generated by the proposal core team during the initial 25 percent planning phase discussed in Chapter 9. In brief, the proposal reviewers need what the proposal team needs plus some specific methodologies and tools for contributions to the proposal effort.

➤ *What review methodologies and tools will they use?* The answers to this question are the heart of the process. You can have all the right people with all the right information from the core team's planning, but if you don't know how to proceed and how to use the proper tools designed specifically for the job, the formal reviews will flounder or even fail.

Themes and Visuals: The Contributions of the Pink Team

A compelling proposal consists of three communication elements— *themes, visuals,* and *text*—and we list them here in declining order of communication power and in chronological order of preparation. Therefore, although a proposal typically includes a substantial amount of technical, managerial, and price-related detail in the text to comply with the solicitation, the essential nature of the proposal is that it is a sales document written for a customer who is prepared to spend a large sum of money as a business investment.

Because the proposal must sell the offer, not simply describe it, and because selling is fundamentally a communication issue, the pink team will determine the quality of the two most important communication elements in the proposal: the themes and visuals. These are your primary vehicles for getting your best selling messages to the customer. They can be reinforced in the text for some additional impact, and lesser messages may be only stated in the text, but you should plant your most differentiating answers to the four major questions of selling—"Why us?" "Why not them?" "So what?" "How so?"—in your proposal's themes and visuals. That's where the pink team will focus its review.

The pink team review, as Figure 10-2 shows, should be conducted after the sections have been designed (i.e., outlined and the themes and visuals drafted) but before the text has been generated. Why? Because if the reviewers discover organizational or structural problems, noncompliance issues, and/or flaws in the primary selling messages (e.g., strategies) conveyed through the themes and visuals, it is much more efficient and far less discouraging to make the needed adjustments before the text is embedded in the sections. Furthermore, once the outline, themes, and visuals are in place for a given section, the text will more naturally flow out of them rather than just be "dumped" on the pages, later requiring massive rewriting and editing.

Pink Team Objectives

Having studied the contents of the entire kickoff packet (see Chapter 9), the pink team focuses on the *Pink Team Directive*, which describes their objectives as well as the process and tools for achieving them.

The pink team has two objectives. First, without the benefit of the proposal's text, determine to what extent the proposal measures up—via the outline, the themes, and the visuals—to these four critical questions:

1. Is the proposal compliant?
2. Is the proposal responsive?

Figure 10-2. **Pink team review tool.** The pink team reviews the outline, themes, and visuals to determine if the draft proposal is compliant, responsive, selling, and communicating before adding all the text. Discovering deep structural problems after the text has been completed creates a major revision effort that pink team reviews can avert.

Pink Team Review

Instructions: Put an x or a check mark in the box that represents your answer—yes (Y), partially (P), or no (N)—to each question. Then explain your answer in specific, constructive terms and assign a score of 0–5 for each question. Total the scores for each group of questions. Add the four totals at the bottom of the form. Recommended scoring: no = 0–1; partially = 2–3; yes = 4–5.

Company:

Proposal:

Section(s):

Reviewer:

Criteria	Y	P	N	Comments	Score
A. Will it be compliant?					
1. Does the outline, as represented by headings and subheadings, follow all customer instructions for organizing the proposal or section?					
2. Does the outline suggest the proposal or section will meet all the customer's requirements regarding the offer or solution?					
3. Does the draft adhere to all customer instructions regarding page limitations, graphics, type, foldouts, appearance, etc.?					
				Total: Will it be compliant?	
B. Will it be responsive?					

I. Does the draft indicate the proposal or section will address the customer's key issues, concerns, hot buttons, needs, and values in addition to the stated requirements?		
Total: Will it be responsive?		
C. Will it sell throughout?		
I. Does the draft indicate the proposal or section will echo, reinforce, and expand on the executive summary themes? If there is no executive summary, does the draft suggest a compelling value proposition or an essential piece of one?		
2. Does every section down to a predetermined or appropriate level begin with a draft theme statement linking features and benefits to a customer issue or goal? Are the features and benefits specific and quantified wherever possible?		
3. Do the draft themes, visuals, and text at all levels differentiate us from the competition by highlighting our strengths, mitigating our weaknesses, neutralizing competitors' strengths, and ghosting their weaknesses? Will the proposal or section answer "Why us?" and "Why not them?"?		

(continues)

Figure 10-2. '(Continued).

Pink Team Review
Page 2 of 2

4. Does the draft associate substantive, bottom-line benefits with all key features?			
5. Does each major section include an appropriate number of visuals or figures in support of important sales messages? Will the first one reinforce or amplify the section theme?			
6. Does each draft visual or figure include a full-sentence, interpretive caption linking features and benefits?			
Total: Will it sell throughout?			

D. Will it communicate?		
1. Are draft theme statements, captions, and text written in active voice and free of excessive jargon and wordiness with at least occasional use of personal pronouns?		
2. Do the draft visuals appear likely to communicate their main messages in 8 seconds or less?		
3. Does the draft indicate the proposal or section will employ ample white space and effectively use emphatic devices (e.g., headings, italics, boldface type, bullet lists, boxes) to call attention to important content?		
Total: Will it communicate?		
Grand Total		

Best Possible Score: 65

Additional Comments and Recommendations

▲

3. Does the proposal sell throughout?
4. Does the proposal communicate?

Second, the reviewers assist the proposal contributors by providing specific feedback, both pro and con, along with concrete recommendations on what should be done to improve their sections' structure, themes, and visuals before adding the text.

Pink Team Process

The pink team's methodology consists of a series of "passes" through the proposal outline and the draft section themes and visuals to answer the four questions. They do this by addressing more specific subquestions, which we call pink team criteria, of each question. As Figure 10-2 shows, each of the four major questions and their corresponding criteria constitutes a simple but effective pink team review tool, including an overall assessment of "yes," "partial," or "no"; narrative commentary for each criterion to elaborate on the overall assessment; a numerical scoring system; and additional summary comments and recommendations.

Much of the art of pink team reviewing is driven by the fact that the criteria questions are cast in the future tense (e.g., "Will the visuals communicate their main messages in 8 seconds or less?"). In addition to reviewing the printed draft, the reviewers must judge whether what they see will translate into what the red team reviewers, and ultimately the customer, will see. That's not always an easy task, but it is a critically important one because the key communication and selling elements of a proposal—its themes and visuals—ultimately determine its impact on those who will evaluate it. This review determines if the proposal (as revealed in the outline, themes, and visuals) has what it takes to sell and to communicate the right messages to the right people in the customer's decision-making process.

With your people, information, process, and review tool in place, you are almost ready to pink team the proposal. Depending on its size and complexity, the length of the response period, the experience of the review team members, and your company's facilities, if you haven't already covered them in the Pink Team Directive, you should also address these issues:

> Time
> Colocation
> Rehearsal
> Equipment
> Debrief
> Budget and charge number

Time. There are five keys to managing time on a pink team review.

1. *Ensure that upper management is committed to a quality review.* The appropriate executive(s) must either participate directly in the review or at least support all who do by providing necessary resources, deflecting all efforts to distract the reviewers, keeping calendars clear during the review period, and personally reviewing the pink team's findings.

2. *Ensure that all reviewers are dedicated.* Each reviewer must make an emotional and intellectual commitment both to doing a good job and to spending the necessary time. Like any team effort on a tight schedule, a proposal review will never stay on schedule, and the quality of the results will diminish dramatically unless every reviewer stays on task and focused 100 percent of the time.

   If a prospective reviewer cannot commit to these simple terms, the pink team leader should find an equivalent person who can so that quality is managed going in and not found lacking on the back end after the damage is done.

3. *Manage efficiency and productivity.* Ensure that all necessary resources—such as equipment (discussed below), facilities, meals and refreshments, and support staff—are close by or readily available. Chunks of time and effort go by the wayside when reviewers have to hunt for what they need.

4. *Monitor the individual reviews.* Ensure that they are on or close to schedule. The pink team leader should do this, informing individuals as well as the whole team about their progress on the schedule.

5. *Never forget Parkinson's Law, which says that work expands to fill the available time.* In practical terms, this means that the official schedule may show the review being completed in an eight-hour day, but reality usually intrudes to make the day much longer. So in addition to gaining commitment from each reviewer to serve on the pink team, the leader needs to ensure that that commitment extends as late into the day as necessary to get the job done right. Such is life for anyone associated with proposals, as the members of the actual proposal team know only too well.

Colocation. If at all possible, the review team should work together, if not in the same room then in very close proximity to one another. This not only helps keep the entire review on schedule (because everyone is where they're supposed to be and doing what they're supposed to be doing); it also facilitates communication, clarification, and any cross-checking that needs to be done.

If adequate space for colocation is not available inside your company's facilities, consider taking the pink team review off-site. For what that costs, you can get a very positive ROI by enabling the team to work comfortably, efficiently, and without distraction.

Rehearsal. The pink team leader should consider conducting a pre-review rehearsal for any rookie reviewers or others who feel unsure about the approach and tools to be used. This session might include an overview, with models, of the basic proposal elements they'll be examining (e.g., outline, themes, and visuals) along with the criteria and review sheets they'll use to critique them.

It is also a good idea during this rehearsal to conduct a "dry run" of the review by creating some sample pre-text sections (perhaps taken from a recent company proposal and modified) and having the reviewers practice on them, making both narrative and numerical assessments in the process.

Equipment. Most professionals today prefer to work on computers rather than in longhand, so if this is the case, the team leader should ensure that computers are in place and ready to go with the appropriate electronic templates, such as the review sheets, loaded. (Note: Be sure that each person is literate in the software to avoid bogging down. If not, a quick tutorial is in order as part of the rehearsal.)

In addition, everything from paper clips to a photocopier and one or more printers (all close by) should be in place when the review begins, along with sufficient work space, tables, and comfortable chairs.

Debrief. As quickly as possible after completing the review, the entire proposal team should meet for a debrief from the pink team, whose members should also be present.

To save time and because much of the details will be covered during feedback meetings between authors and reviewers, the pink team leader should provide a brief (one hour or less) overview of the approach taken and the team's findings. This overview should address strengths and weaknesses according to the criteria, with representative examples of what was done well and what needs to be improved, including why and how. For multiple-volume proposals, the review team's volume leaders should then provide similar overviews for each of the volumes, again indicating strengths and weaknesses along with recommended corrective steps.

Figure 10-3 provides an example of an actual completed pink team review tool that formed the basis for the debrief between the reviewer and the author. (While the critiques, recommendations, and scores are real, we have changed the names of people and the proposing company to maintain confidentiality.) Note not only what is being communicated but the tone of the comments: as positive as possible, helpful, proactive, and benign. This can make all the difference in the collaborative effort required to produce a superior proposal communicating a highly competitive offer. Lacking the former, the latter would be severely handicapped during evaluation.

Finally, the appropriate executive should close the debrief by pointing out the critical importance of the feedback meetings and offering encouraging comments about the work remaining to be done and what a successful proposal effort can mean for the organization and its people.

If circumstances require or permit, the pink team leader should also debrief any executives who haven't attended the meeting. This keeps them linked to the proposal effort and affords them an opportunity to ask questions and provide input. It also helps avoid last-minute objections to anything they've suddenly discovered in the proposal either as part of the red team review or, even worse, just before it is supposed to go to the client. When that happens, an entire proposal effort can unravel in world-record time. After all, one of the primary reasons for an early proposal review is to identify and solve problems before they can occur, so debriefing not only the proposal team but the relevant executives just makes good risk-management, quality-assurance sense.

Budget and Charge Number. How proposals are financially accounted for varies widely from company to company, but in general any costs associated with the formal reviews should be projected by the core team as part of the bid/no-bid decision. In other words, one factor in deciding to bid via a proposal includes knowing that the bid process can be successfully completed while maintaining whatever margins the company requires. Unless you are involved in a strategic

Figure 10-3. **Completed pink team review tool.** The pink team's use of the review tool gives writers guidance, reinforcement, and ways to improve the section early rather than late.

Pink Team Review

Page 1 of 2

Company:	ABC, Inc.
Proposal:	Northwest Regional Hospital System Engineering and Construction Support Services
Section(s):	Management Volume
Reviewer:	Stanley Dutton

Instructions: Put an x or a check mark in the box that represents your answer—yes (Y), partially (P), or no (N)—to each question. Then explain your answer in specific, constructive terms and assign a score of 0–5 for each question. Total the scores for each group of questions. Add the four totals at the bottom of the form. Recommended scoring: no = 0–1; partially = 2–3; yes = 4–5.

Criteria	Y	P	N	Comments	Score
A. Will it be compliant?					
1. Does the outline, as represented by headings and subheadings, follow all customer instructions for organizing the proposal or section?	x			Yes, down to the second level (A.1, A.2, and so on). Below that I can't tell.	4
2. Does the outline suggest the proposal or section will meet all the customer's requirements regarding the offer or solution?	x			Headings at the third level (A.1.a, A.1.b) would make it easier to follow.	4
3. Does the draft adhere to all customer instructions regarding page limitations, graphics, type, foldouts, appearance, etc.?	x				5
				Total: Will it be compliant?	13

B. Will it be responsive?

1. Does the draft indicate the proposal or section will address the customer's key issues, concerns, hot buttons, needs, and values in addition to the stated requirements?	X	Nice job of addressing the evaluation factors in the Introduction. Subsequent sections rarely get more specific than meeting the budget or schedule or providing a safe workplace. Be more specific about goals and problems. Need to show NRHS we understand the challenges of building and maintaining a network of hospitals, on a level of detail below that of the RFP. Let's show them what we can envision beyond the sample tasks.	2
		Total: Will it be responsive?	2

C. Will it sell throughout?

1. Does the draft indicate the proposal or section will echo, reinforce, and expand on the executive summary themes? If there is no executive summary, does the draft suggest a compelling value proposition or an essential piece of one?	X	Don't see public sector experience or ability to manage complexity being driven down to the section level in this volume.	3
2. Does every section down to a predetermined or appropriate level begin with a draft theme statement linking features and benefits to a customer issue or goal? Are the features and benefits specific and quantified wherever possible?	X	Theme statements are all present at the second level, but very few exist at the third level. Need to fill in the holes and strengthen weak themes at A.3, A.4, B.1, B.2, C.1, and C.4.	3

(continues)

Figure 10-3. (Continued).

Pink Team Review

Item			Comment	Score
3. Do the draft themes, visuals, and text at all levels differentiate us from the competition by highlighting our strengths, mitigating our weaknesses, neutralizing competitors' strengths, and ghosting their weaknesses? Will the proposal or section answer "Why us?" and "Why not them?"?		x	Good ghost of XYZ's financial situation on p. 57. Otherwise, you'd never guess we have competitors. Need to mitigate our shortage of private hospital experience in the Experience section. Again I don't see our public sector experience or ability to manage complexity.	1
4. Does the draft associate substantive, bottom-line benefits with all key features?	x		Benefits tend to be vague and are frequently only implied; need to be more specific and quantify where possible: e.g., a 2-week schedule reduction instead of a significant schedule reduction.	3
5. Does each major section include an appropriate number of visuals or figures in support of important sales messages? Will the first one reinforce or amplify the section theme?		x	No visuals other than team org chart, schedule, and résumé photos.	0
6. Does each draft visual or figure include a full-sentence, interpretive caption linking features and benefits?		x	No visuals, no captions.	0
			Total: Will it sell throughout?	10

D. Will it communicate?					
1. Are draft theme statements, captions, and text written in active voice and free of excessive jargon and wordiness with at least occasional use of personal pronouns?	x				5
2. Do the draft visuals appear likely to communicate their main messages in 8 seconds or less?			x	No visuals.	0
3. Does the draft indicate the proposal or section will employ ample white space and effectively use emphatic devices (e.g., headings, italics, boldface type, bullet lists, boxes) to call attention to important content?			x	Nice page design.	5
Total: Will it communicate?					10
Grand Total					35

Best Possible Score: 65

Additional Comments and Recommendations

▲ Create a visual for every major section.

▲▲ Someone should go through all the theme statements to (a) strengthen the weak ones and (b) make sure our weaknesses and competitor strengths are addressed.

bid, it makes no sense to spend more to get a contract than the contract is ultimately worth in profitability. Thus, the cost to produce a proposal, typically referred to as the bid and proposal (B&P) budget, needs to include any costs to be incurred as part of the pink team review (e.g., reviewers' time, equipment, supplies, food, support staff time).

Having addressed the six issues discussed above, use the following checklist to ensure that you're ready to pink team your proposal:

- ❑ The kickoff packet (see Chapter 9) has been distributed to all pink team reviewers.
- ❑ The pink team objectives are clearly understood.
- ❑ Reviewers understand the pink team process.
- ❑ Reviewers understand the criteria to be used in answering the four critical questions for pink team review.
- ❑ Primary and secondary reviewers have been assigned to each section.
- ❑ The Pink Team Directive has been thoroughly reviewed and all questions have been answered.
- ❑ All reviewers understand how to use the review sheets for both narrative and numerical assessments.
- ❑ Any necessary rehearsals have been completed.
- ❑ All people, facilities, equipment, and other logistics are in place.
- ❑ Reviewers have their assigned proposal sections.

Applying the Pink Team Review to the Final Draft

If the answer to all these items is "yes," it is time to conduct the pink team review. Once those reviewers have accomplished the objectives and debriefed the proposal team, the members of that team will take their pink team assessments and recommendations back to the proposal and begin the arduous task of producing a completed draft of the proposal that adheres to the schedule and is ready for the single most critical review in the entire proposal process: the red team review. Ideally, the improvements made in the proposal based on the pink team review will ensure that this next review is more a matter of fine-tuning the proposal than a major overhaul when every tick of the clock moves them closer to proposal submission.

Does It Have What It Takes: The Red Team Review

Keeping in mind that a proposal consists of three communication elements (themes, visuals, and text) and that it must sell the offer, not just describe it, a well-conceived proposal review provides a consistent, repeatable process from start to finish. That process continually examines those three communication elements to judge the quality of the proposal, including whether the sales messages are getting through to the evaluators.

The pink team has already assessed the outline, themes, and visuals to address these very issues. The red team's charge is to review them again to verify that any changes based on pink team comments or other factors have actually improved proposal quality. The red team will then review the text as well to verify that the meat has been put on the bones, so to speak, in complete, effective, and compelling ways. They also want to know that the entire proposal is logical and coherent, doesn't contradict itself, and reads as though it were written by a single hand, a single mind calmly responding to a customer's call for help.

Moreover, a fundamental reason for designing the proposal review *as a process rather than an isolated event* is that the pink team review, coming as it does early in the writing phase, encourages management of outputs via management of inputs. Better to find out early that a section is headed for noncompliance rather than to discover that fact only days before submittal. Thus, the pink team critiques the draft inputs to shape and determine what the proposal must become; the red team examines those final draft outputs to determine whether the proposal has become what it will take to win.

The added value, therefore, of a well-devised pink team review is that it provides the foundation and the rehearsal for a full red team review. That is, the red team simply becomes a more extensive and higher-level version of the pink team, carrying forward the basic methodology and expanding its application to critique the proposal's text as well as the visuals and themes. The pink team makes early adjustments and course corrections to ensure that the proposal heads in the right direction.

The red team then determines whether the proposal has "arrived" (i.e., is it a compelling, responsive offer set forth in a selling proposal answering the Big Four: "Why us?" "Why not them?" "So what?" "How so?"). If these things are not being done or done well, the red team must also determine what it will take to make the necessary course corrections and produce a superior proposal.

Who Is Needed: Selecting Team Members

The precise number and types of people who make up a given red team vary widely, depending on the size, nature, scope, and business/

strategic significance of a particular proposal. In general, however, the following guidelines (subject to modification by any or all of the above factors) provide a baseline for staffing a red team:

- All members of the pink team.
- An upper manager/executive for sales/business development.
- Additional subject matter experts (in-house or consultant) to cover the offer, project/program management, terms and conditions, contracting and subcontracting, and pricing.
- A person knowledgeable in how the customer evaluates competitive proposals. This is often the relevant account manager/salesperson/business development manager, but it could be either an internal or external consultant.

Red Team Objectives

The pink team's first objective was to project the proposal's future, finished condition based on a skeletal draft (e.g., "Will it be compliant?"). The red team's first objective is to determine whether the proposal has, in fact, achieved affirmative answers to the four critical questions:

1. Is the proposal compliant?
2. Is the proposal responsive?
3. Does the proposal sell throughout?
4. Does the proposal communicate?

Like the pink team before them, the red team's second objective is to provide specific feedback to the authors, pro and con, including what must be done to thoroughly and effectively address these four questions, and what should be done to further improve their sections in other ways, time and other resources permitting.

If possible, the red team should also pursue a third objective of reviewing the final draft through the customer's eyes: How will they evaluate it? What will matter most to them? How can we communicate in ways that they will appreciate and understand? The most effective red team review provides a simulation of evaluation, and to this end, the evaluation tools we provide here can and should be modified to match your customer's whenever that information is available.

Red Team Process

Before commencing their formal review, the red team needs to do two more things:

1. Clarify responsibilities.
2. Assign the sections.

Clarifying responsibilities basically involves the red team leader (usually the manager or executive who "owns" the proposal) gaining consensus among all the team members that they understand and accept their charter:

➤ Adhere to the red team schedule, whatever it takes.
➤ Be thorough and specific.
➤ Avoid vague comments and sweeping generalities (e.g., "Not clear" or "Huh?").
➤ Indicate weaknesses or deficiencies wherever necessary but always include specific suggestions for improvement.
➤ Make positive comments to recognize quality work.
➤ Assume "benign intent." That is, assume that the section being reviewed has been created by a colleague who is trying to do his or her very best, even if this person doesn't know as much about the subject and/or proposals as you do.

Assigning the sections depends, of course, on the makeup of the red team in relation to the proposed offer. However, here's a basic approach you can follow:

First, match reviewers to specific sections according to each person's primary area of expertise. Thus, for example, practicing engineers would review section on design, configuration, technical approach, and so on. Similarly, the manager or executive who "owns" the proposal might review the executive summary, and a project manager could start with the sections on project management, scope, schedule, and personnel. The key point is that this initial set of assignments constitutes the *primary review*, and it is critical, especially in the technical disciplines, to ensure that technical accuracy, risk, and costs are all acceptable.

Second, rotate the reviewers' assignments so that everyone reviews certain sections for which they are not the subject matter experts. These assignments constitute the *secondary review*. In its own way, this review holds equal importance with the primary review because it simulates reactions to the two most noticeable parts of the proposal—the themes and the visuals—by customer evaluators who aren't subject matter experts but who must make critical decisions about the proposals they're evaluating.

All reviewers address the same four questions the pink team addressed earlier. There are also additional criteria questions because the proposal is now a completed draft, not just an outline, themes, and visuals. Figure 10-4 beginning on p. 196 shows the red team review tool containing the additional criteria not part of the pink team review. Note, too, that the criteria questions for the pink team tool were cast in the future tense but the red team questions are in the present tense. In the here and now, the proposal is either ready according to each criterion or it isn't. That's what the red team must determine, and time is running out.

The concept of secondary, nonexpert reviewers is particularly important for the technical proposal because nonexperts will read those sections differently from the way experts will. Nonexperts ask different questions and expect a proposal to communicate the technical messages and concepts in ways that can be understood and appreciated by people who, nonexperts though they may be, function as customers who typically start identifying losers long before selecting the winner.

The narrative comments provide detail, discussion, insight, suggestions, and a human voice speaking to the writer. Conversely, the numerical assessments provide a fairly clinical summary judgment. It gives authors a sense of how evaluators—who often judge quickly and in absolute terms—will score the sections.

For instance, a reviewer may conclude that a score of 1 (on an ascending scale of 1 to 5) is the proper score for whether a section meets a particular red team criterion (i.e., the section is clearly and fully unacceptable as measured by the criterion). The narrative comments then help the author to understand why the section is flawed and what needs to be done to move it from that 1 to at least a 3 or, one hopes, a 4 or 5.

Having addressed these issues, you are almost ready to conduct the red team review. Depending on the proposal's size and complexity, the length of the response period, the experience of the review team members, and your company's facilities, you should also, just like the pink team, address the issues of time, colocation, rehearsal, equipment, debrief, and budget and charge number.

Once you have accounted for these issues as part of your red team planning, use the following checklist to ensure that you're ready to red team your proposal:

❑ The kickoff packet (again, see Chapter 9) has been distributed and thoroughly reviewed.

❏ The red team objectives are clearly understood.
❏ Reviewers understand the red team process.
❏ Reviewers understand the criteria to be used in answering the four critical questions for red team review.
❏ Primary and secondary reviewers have been assigned to each section.
❏ The Red Team Directive has been thoroughly reviewed and all questions have been answered.
❏ All reviewers understand how to use the review sheets for both narrative and numerical assessments.
❏ Any necessary rehearsals have been completed.
❏ Reviewers have their assigned proposal sections.

If the answer is "yes" to all these items, it's time to conduct the red team review. Figure 10-5 beginning on page 200 provides a completed version of the red team review tool, one we actually completed while working with a client on their proposal. (While the critiques, recommendations, and scores are real, we have changed the names of people and the proposing company to maintain confidentiality.)

Long-Term Benefits

Although a quality red team review produces positive short-term results for any given proposal, a commitment to proposal reviews and excellent processes and tools for conducting them also provides a significant long-term ROI. When an organization's people know ahead of time that certain criteria will be applied to their proposal to determine how well it has answered a consistent set of four questions, then they can write to those questions and criteria from the outset. They don't have to wait until the review to find out how the reviewers will judge the drafts. They know what they must do and how they must do it, and invariably the quality of their answers will be better than if they had no clue about the questions until they were distributed on exam day.

As the saying goes, a rising tide lifts all boats, and if simple, repeatable processes are put in place for conducting proposal reviews, the quality of all your company's proposals will be raised over time. That's a win for you, your company, and your customers. Alas, the only losers will be your competition, but we assume that is an acceptable outcome.

Figure 10-4. **Red team review tool.** The red team review should take place once you have your proposal draft as close to what the customer will see as possible. Then you can review it with the Red Team Big Four and their criteria.

Red Team Review
Page 1 of 2

Instructions: Put an x or a check mark in the box that represents your answer—yes (Y), partially (P), or no (N)—to each question. Then explain your answer in specific, constructive terms and assign a score of 0–5 for each question. Total the scores for each group of questions. Add the four totals at the bottom of the form. Recommended scoring: no = 0–1; partially = 2–3; yes = 4–5.

Company:					
Proposal:					
Section(s):					
Reviewer:					
Criteria	**Y**	**P**	**N**	**Comments**	**Score**
A. Is it compliant?					
1. Does the outline, as represented by headings and subheadings, follow all customer instructions for organizing the proposal or section?					
2. Does the proposal or section meet all the customer's requirements regarding the offer or solution?					
3. Does it adhere to all customer instructions regarding page limitations, graphics, type, foldouts, appearance, etc.?					
				Total: Is it compliant?	

B. Is it responsive?

1. Does it address the customer's key issues, concerns, hot buttons, needs, and values in addition to the stated requirements?			
2. Does it demonstrate customer focus rather than self-focus, by regularly acknowledging the customer's concern and mentioning the customer first wherever possible? Is it respectful and confident without sounding arrogant or demanding unwarranted trust?			
Total: Is it responsive?			

C. Does it sell throughout?

1. Does the proposal or section echo, reinforce, and expand on the executive summary themes? If there is no executive summary, does it supply a compelling value proposition or an essential piece of one?			
2. Does every section down to a predetermined or appropriate level begin with an effective theme statement linking features and benefits to a customer issue or goal? Are the features and benefits specific and quantified wherever possible?			

(continues)

Figure 10-4. (Continued).

Red Team Review

Question					
3. Do the themes, visuals, and text at all levels differentiate us from the competition by highlighting our strengths, mitigating our weaknesses, neutralizing competitors' strengths, and ghosting their weaknesses? Does it answer "Why us?" and "Why not them?"?					
4. Does it associate substantive, bottom-line benefits with all key features?					
5. Does each major section include an appropriate number of visuals or figures in support of important sales messages? Does the first one reinforce or amplify the section theme?					
6. Do all visuals or figures include full-sentence, interpretive captions linking features and benefits?					
Total: Does it sell throughout?					

D. Does it communicate?

1. Is it organized deductively with the main idea first, followed by supporting detail and proofs? Does it have a natural, believable ending?				
2. Is it written in active voice and free of excessive jargon and wordiness with at least occasional use of personal pronouns?				
3. Do the visuals communicate their main messages in 8 seconds or less?				
4. Has boilerplate or other preexisting content been effectively tailored to this customer and procurement and seamlessly integrated with original content?				
5. Does it employ ample white space and effectively use emphatic devices (e.g., headings, italics, boldface type, bullet lists, boxes) to call attention to important content?				
Total: Does it communicate?				
Grand Total				

Best Possible Score: 80

Additional Comments and Recommendations

Figure 10-5. **Completed red team review tool.** The red team's use of the review tool will drive the final critical revisions of the draft before editing and production.

Red Team Review

Page 1 of 2

Company:	ABC, Inc.
Proposal:	Northwest Regional Hospital System Engineering and Construction Support Services
Section(s):	Management Volume
Reviewer:	Stanley Dutton

Instructions: Put an x or a check mark in the box that represents your answer—yes (Y), partially (P), or no (N)—to each question. Then explain your answer in specific, constructive terms and assign a score of 0–5 for each question. Total the scores for each group of questions. Add the four totals at the bottom of the form. Recommended scoring: no = 0–1; partially = 2–3; yes = 4–5.

Criteria	Y	P	N	Comments	Score
A. Is it compliant?					
1. Does the outline, as represented by headings and subheadings, follow all customer instructions for organizing the proposal or section?	x			Appears fully compliant.	5
2. Does the proposal or section meet all the customer's requirements regarding the offer or solution?	x			The lack of subheadings in some sections (e.g., Project Management and Safety) makes responses difficult to locate. Need to insert a subhead for every requirement.	4
3. Does it adhere to all customer instructions regarding page limitations, graphics, type, foldouts, appearance, etc.?			x	Too many foldouts (limit is three); résumés are in two different formats.	3
				Total: Is it compliant?	12

B. Is it responsive?

1. Does it address the customer's key issues, concerns, hot buttons, needs, and values in addition to the stated requirements?	X	Safety and Quality sections are too standard; need more customer-specific issues, problems, and goals.	3
2. Does it demonstrate customer focus rather than self-focus, by regularly acknowledging the customer's concern and mentioning the customer first wherever possible? Is it respectful and confident without sounding arrogant or demanding unwarranted trust?	X	Too many sentences begin with "we" or "our" throughout this volume. Statements like "Our management team members strongly advocate the joint success of *both* NRHS and ABC" (p. 13) sound self-serving. Why not just say, "Our management team members strongly advocate the success of NRHS"? p. 74: "It will all work because our people are the best" sounds like "trust us." In the third paragraph on that page, it says we will draw on people from one area to contribute in another when it is the right thing to do. Do we need to give an example, or will they know and trust us to do it properly?	3
		Total: Is it responsive?	6

C. Does it sell throughout?

1. Does the proposal or section echo, reinforce, and expand on the executive summary themes? If there is no executive summary, does it supply a compelling value proposition or an essential piece of one?	X	The introduction to the technical volume actually repeats the executive summary in places. Please rewrite to eliminate redundancies and pick up relevant executive summary themes in tailoring the Safety and Quality sections.	3

(continues)

Figure 10-5. (Continued).

Red Team Review

Page 2 of 2

2. Does every section down to a predetermined or appropriate level begin with an effective theme statement linking features and benefits to a customer issue or goal? Are the features and benefits specific and quantified wherever possible?	x	Safety and Quality sections lack theme statements. Benefits need to be more specific and quantified, especially in the Management Approach and Key Personnel sections.	3
3. Do the themes, visuals, and text at all levels differentiate us from the competition by highlighting our strengths, mitigating our weaknesses, neutralizing competitors' strengths, and ghosting their weaknesses? Does it answer "Why us?" and "Why not them?"?	x	This volume is greatly improved in terms of addressing our weakness in private hospital experience. Need key visuals in Safety and Quality, better key visual in Management Approach. Suggestion: Visualize full EPCM plus M&O capabilities under a single "roof."	3
4. Does it associate substantive, bottom-line benefits with all key features?	x	Yes, with greater specificity and quantification as noted in C.2.	4
5. Does each major section include an appropriate number of visuals or figures in support of important sales messages? Does the first one reinforce or amplify the section theme?	x	Yes, except as noted in C.3.	4
6. Do all visuals or figures include full-sentence, interpretive captions linking features and benefits?	x	Org charts, schedule, project photos, and sample task staffing tables need captions.	3
		Total: Does it sell throughout?	20

D. Does it communicate?

1. Is it organized deductively with the main idea first, followed by supporting detail and proofs? Does it have a natural, believable ending?	x		This volume is very well written but needs proofreading to eliminate typos.	4
2. Is it written in active voice and free of excessive jargon and wordiness with at least occasional use of personal pronouns?	x		Too much third person in some sections; sounds too formal. Need more "you/your" and "we/us/our."	3
3. Do the visuals communicate their main messages in 8 seconds or less?	x		Key visuals for Management Approach and Schedule are too detailed. Simplify these to better support our message of managing complexity.	3
4. Has boilerplate or other preexisting content been effectively tailored to this customer and procurement and seamlessly integrated with original content?		x	Safety and Quality sections contain obvious boilerplate.	2
5. Does it employ ample white space and effectively use emphatic devices (e.g., headings, italics, boldface type, bullet lists, boxes) to call attention to important content?	x		Yes, but some sections are inconsistent in the use of boldfacing vs. italics and numbered vs. bulleted lists.	4
			Total: Does it communicate?	**16**
			Grand Total	**54**

Best Possible Score: 80

Additional Comments and Recommendations

➤➤ Tailor the Safety and Quality sections so boilerplate is unrecognizable.

➤➤ Have someone go through the entire volume to work the theme statements and visuals and make sure the executive summary themes are driven down at every opportunity.

➤➤ Then have someone edit for personal pronouns and typographic consistency.

➤➤ Proofread!

Challenges for Readers

➤ Familiarize yourself with the red team tool we have provided. Then randomly select a recent proposal you submitted to a customer and conduct a red team review of it. You may discover that had you done so before submission, you could have significantly improved that proposal.

➤ As you conduct red team reviews of proposals in the future, monitor the pink and red team scores you assign to them. This practice provides a metric of how much you are improving via the formal proposal review processes. For example, if, over a two-year period, your average red team review score moves from 38 to 59, you are definitely doing a better job of creating the drafts. That's an important thing to know.

➤ Try to link the impact of your proposal reviews to customer feedback regarding the proposals you give them. Is there a correlation between improving scores from the reviews and more positive customer comments on the proposals?

➤ As part of the review debriefs when proposal contributors are mentally and physically tired, consider some lighthearted awards the reviewers can bestow upon their proposal colleagues. The "Purple Prose Award" might get a chuckle, along with the "Verbal Black Hole Prose Award," or the "Graphic from Hell Award." Think of awards that would fit your company's culture and people, and do so because you know that a moment of levity and the smiles it produces can go a long way during the tough times proposals invariably create.

Chapter 11

LEARNING FORWARD

Win or Lose Protocols for
Continuous Improvement

GOLDEN RULE:

Whether you win or lose, always debrief with the customer and your own organization.

As often as we claim with unfettered certainty that proposals are not isolated events, we admit that it's hard not to think of them as such. The actual response period from receipt of the RFP to proposal submission is precisely defined, and during that time people work in ways that they don't at any other time. The proposal project seems self-contained, the work itself a hybrid set of tasks and activities, and many of the people who work on proposals have "real" jobs elsewhere in the company. They weren't hired to contribute to proposals, and we've found that, almost without exception, supporting proposal initiatives is not included in the job descriptions of people who are the in-and-out, ad hoc proposal contributors (e.g., from engineering; contracts; operations; or, odd as it may seem, business development/sales). Their work on proposals is not included in their annual performance reviews, either, confirming that proposal duty is an aberrant assignment with a clear beginning and a defined ending— and, for many, the sooner that ending happens, the better.

Despite this, we know that proposals are not isolated events but part of a business development continuum. The process itself is not linear so much as it is circular. A company no sooner puts one proposal out the door than the business development effort that drove it loops back to middle game and begins anew, heading toward another RFP and proposal. What is more, the circles often overlap because at any given time, a company has several proposals in the works and in varying stages of completion.

Our point here is simple: If you are going to work through a process in essentially the same way, many times each year over many years, you ought to do it better each time. And if you do it better each time, you should see tangible business impact in the form of greater efficiencies; enhanced productivity; increased effectiveness in pre-RFP business development; higher-quality proposals that differentiate you in the marketplace; and, most important, an increased probability of improving your win rate and revenues. These bottom-line business results begin with a simple, repeatable post-award process consistently applied over time, a process that will yield trend analysis on what the critical drivers of winning and losing are in your market(s).

Given that premise, we began asking ourselves some questions to see where they would lead us:

- Is the business development effort with a customer concluded when the customer announces the award?
- After the customer announces the award, if we were to debrief with them, what would we ask beyond "Why did we win?" or "Why did we lose?" as the case may be?
- What could we ask ourselves once we know who won and who lost?
- Could we develop a methodology—a simple, repeatable process—that, applied consistently over time, would provide trend analysis in our markets and metrics indicating improvement or lack of improvement in our business development process? That process would certainly include proposals, but a lot more as well.

Based on these questions and others, we created and field-tested a process model and a standard set of questions within this model, which we call "Post-Award Protocols for Continuous Business Development Improvement." Figure 11-1 shows the process model, and Figure 11-2 provides the eighty-two questions within the model. In most cases, you will need to customize some of the questions for your business environment.

Administering the Protocols

This process model and the questions within it can systematically measure and continuously improve the effectiveness of your business

Figure 11-1. **Post-award protocols for continuous business development improvement.** A simple process model, consistently applied, enables you to conduct trend analysis on what really drives wins and losses in your markets.

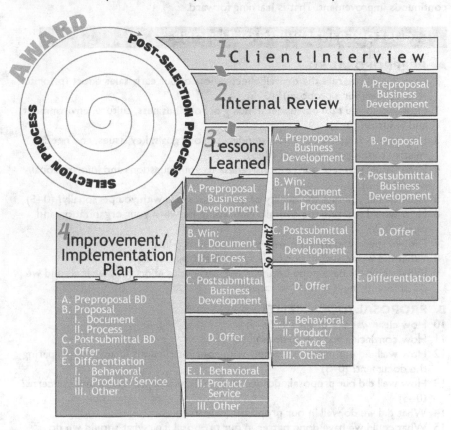

development efforts. It is most effective to do this in four distinct phases:

1. Client interview
2. Internal review
3. Lessons learned
4. Improvement/implementation plan

The protocol can be administered in person, by telephone, on paper, or even online if you have IT support. It consists of questions for the customer with corresponding questions for internal team members. Most questions ask for ratings on a scale of 0 to 5, with a few narrative and yes-or-no responses. The questions cover five areas:

1. Preproposal business development
2. The proposal (both the document and the process of preparing it)

Figure 11-2. **Questions within the process model.** After every major award has been announced, a consistent set of protocols allows you to debrief internally and with the customer, determine lessons learned, and implement next steps for continuous improvement. That is learning forward.

I. CUSTOMER INTERVIEW QUESTIONS

A. PREPROPOSAL BD
1 How would you rate the overall effectiveness of our early sales effort (prior to your request for a proposal)? (0–5)
2 How would you rate our understanding of your business, culture, environment, and industry? (0–5)
3 How would you rate our understanding of your goals, key issues, and needs relative to this procurement? (0–5)
4 How would you rate our responsiveness to your questions and informational needs? (0–5)
5 How would you rate the quality of our relationship with you personally? (0–5)
6 How would you rate the overall relationship between your organization and ours? (0–5)
7 Did we spend enough time with you in person? (y/n)
8 What did we do well in our early sales effort? (narrative)
9 What could we have done better in our early sales effort (i.e., what should we do differently next time)? (narrative)

B. PROPOSAL (DOCUMENT)
10 How clear was our proposal? (0–5)
11 How convincing was our proposal? (0–5)
12 How well did our proposal comply with your instructions (if any) for preparing the document? (0–5)
13 How well did our proposal address your goals, problems, issues, and concerns? (0–5)
14 What did we do well in our proposal? (narrative)
15 What could we have done better in our proposal (i.e., what should we do differently next time)? (narrative)

C. POSTSUBMITTAL BD
16 How would you rate the overall effectiveness of our postproposal activities? (0–5)
17 What did we do well after submitting our proposal? (narrative)
18 What could we have done better after submitting our proposal (i.e., what should we do differently next time)? (narrative)

D. OFFER
19 How well did our offering comply with your stated needs and requirements? (0–5)
20 How would you rate the value of our offering relative to its price? (0–5)
21 What were the strengths of our offering? (narrative)
22 What were the weaknesses of our offering? (narrative)

E. DIFFERENTIATION
23 How well did we differentiate from the competition before you asked for a proposal? (0–5)
24 How well did we differentiate from the competition in our proposal? (0–5)

25 How well did we differentiate from the competition after submitting our proposal? (0–5)

26 What differentiated our organization or offering from the competition in a positive way? (narrative)

27 What differentiated our organization or offering from the competition in a negative way? (narrative)

28 What behaviors, positive or negative, do you see as being characteristic of our organization? (narrative)

GENERAL QUESTIONS

29 Why did we win or lose? (narrative)

30 Please rank the following in terms of the degree to which they influenced your decision: (forced ranking)
Preproposal activities
The proposal (document)
The offering
Postproposal activities
Individual or organizational behavior

2. INTERNAL REVIEW QUESTIONS

A. PREPROPOSAL BD

1 How would you rate the overall effectiveness of our early sales effort (prior to the customer's request for a proposal)? (0–5)

2 How would you rate our understanding of the customer's business, culture, environment, and industry? (0–5)

3 How would you rate our understanding of the customer's goals, key issues, and needs relative to this procurement? (0–5)

4 How would you rate our responsiveness to the customer's questions and informational needs? (0–5)

5 How would you rate the quality of our relationship with the customer personally? (0–5)

6 How would you rate the overall relationship between the customer's organization and ours? (0–5)

7 How much time did you spend with the customer in person prior to delivering the proposal? (numeric or pulldown selection)

8 What did we do well in our early sales effort? (narrative)

9 What could we have done better in our early sales effort (i.e., what should we do differently next time)? (narrative)

B. PROPOSAL (DOCUMENT)

10 How clear was our proposal? (0–5)

11 How convincing was our proposal? (0–5)

12 How well did our proposal comply with the customer's instructions (if any) for preparing the document? (0–5)

13 How well did our proposal address the customer's goals, problems, issues, and concerns? (0–5)

14 What did we do well in our proposal? (narrative)

15 What could we have done better in our proposal (i.e., what should we do differently next time)? (narrative)

(continues)

Figure 11-2. (Continued).

C. POSTSUBMITTAL BD
16 How would you rate the overall effectiveness of our postproposal activities? (0–5)
17 What did we do well after submitting our proposal? (narrative)
18 What could we have done better after submitting our proposal (i.e., what should we do differently next time)? (narrative)

D. OFFER
19 How well did our offer comply with the customer's stated needs and requirements? (0–5)
20 How would you rate the value of our offer relative to its price? (0–5)
21 What were the strengths of our offer? (narrative)
22 What were the weaknesses of our offer? (narrative)

3. LESSONS LEARNED

A. PREPROPOSAL BD
1 What could we do to improve the effectiveness of our early sales effort (prior to the customer's request for a proposal)?
2 What could we do to improve our understanding of the customer's business, culture, environment, and industry?
3 What could we do to improve our understanding of the customer's goals, key issues, and needs?
4 How could we be more responsive to the customer's questions and informational needs?
5 How can we build a better relationship with our key contact?
6 How can we build a better relationship between our organization and theirs?
7 Do we need to spend more time with our key contact?
8 What adjustments do we need to make, based on what the customer said about our early sales effort?
9 What other adjustments do we want to make to our early sales effort?

B. PROPOSAL (DOCUMENT)
10 What can we do to make our proposals clearer?
11 What can we do to make our proposals more convincing?
12 What can we do to ensure 100% compliance with proposal instructions?
13 How can we do a better job of addressing customer goals, problems, issues, and concerns in our proposals?
14 What adjustments do we need to make, based on what the customer said about our proposal?
15 What other adjustments do we want to make to our proposals?

C. POSTSUBMITTAL BD
16 What can we do to increase the effectiveness of our postproposal activities?
17 What, if any, adjustments should we make based on what the customer said we did well after submitting our proposal?
18 What adjustments should we make based on what the customer said we could do better after submitting our proposal?

D. OFFER

19 What can we do to make our offerings more compliant with customer needs and requirements?
20 What can we do to increase the perceived value in our offerings?
21 What adjustments do we need to make, based on what the customer said about our offering?
22 What other adjustments do we want to make to our offerings?

E. DIFFERENTIATION

23 What can we do to better differentiate from the competition before the customer asks for a proposal?
    a Behaviorally
    b With regard to our products or services
    c With regard to other domains of differentiation
24 What can we do to better differentiate from the competition in our proposals?
    a Behaviorally
    b With regard to our products or services
    c With regard to other domains of differentiation
25 What can we do to better differentiate from the competition after submitting a proposal?
    a Behaviorally
    b With regard to our products or services
    c With regard to other domains of differentiation
26 What actions do we need to take, based on what the customer said about our positive differentiation?
    a Behavioral
    b Product- or service-related
    c Other
27 What actions do we need to take, based on what the customer said about our negative differentiation?
    a Behavioral
    b Product- or service-related
    c Other
28 What adjustments do we need to make, based on the reported characteristic behaviors?

GENERAL QUESTIONS

29 If we won: Do we want more wins like this one (i.e., for the same reason)? If so, what should we do to ensure similar wins in the future? If not, what should we change? If we lost: What do we need to do to avoid similar losses in the future?
30 What do the customer's rankings suggest we need to do in each of the following areas?
    Preproposal activities
    The proposal (document)
    The offering
    Postproposal activities
    Individual or organizational behavior

3. Postsubmittal business development
4. The offer (what you proposed)
5. The degree to which you created positive behavioral, product/ service, and other differentiation in the customer's mind

Differentiation is a separate category because it crosses the other four categories and is so critical we feel it warrants a focused effort.

Client Interview

The customer interview is an indispensable and driving element of this process. Before conducting the customer interview, we recommend you ask the customer's preference on the format. The online format has advantages for both parties, but only if the customer completes the questionnaire. Don't just send them a link and expect a response. Someone—preferably the person with primary responsibility for the relationship, such as an account or a project manager—should have a conversation with the customer, emphasizing the importance of their feedback and conveying a commitment to act on it. The account or project manager may also interview the customer in person or on the phone and then enter the responses online.

If the customer completes the online questionnaire, don't let that be the last transaction. You should follow up soon afterward to thank that person and to clarify responses as needed. For example, if the customer rated the quality of the relationship lower than expected and didn't explain or provide any clues in the narratives, you should call and ask about that. This not only creates a chance to fix things but it is also a behavioral differentiator demonstrating that you cared enough to ask and gain deeper understanding.

Internal Review

An internal review will help you check your perspective against that of the customer. This review consists of the questions that correspond to the customer interview, and up to thirty-two additional yes-or-no questions for the account manager and proposal manager. These yes-or-no questions are designed to suggest critical success factors in the management of the customer relationship and proposal development effort and to identify trends over time.

In addition to the account and proposal managers, anyone whose participation in the pre-RFP pursuit or proposal development effort was substantial (e.g., the project team leader, the executive sponsor, or a technical writer) should complete the questionnaire. The point, again, is to check the internal perspective against the customer's, with the customer's judgment taking precedence.

Lessons Learned

Once you've asked the questions and compared the responses, the next step is to determine the implications and the need for action, by asking "So what?" What are the implications of what you have learned? What do you need to do or what needs to change?

For example, if you thought you had clearly superior capabilities but the customer didn't see much difference between you and your competitors, it might mean you need better competitor intelligence. Or you didn't put enough thought into the win strategy. Or the business developer could have been more skillful in probing for the customer's key issues and priorities. Or the information gathered in the pre-RFP effort didn't make it into the proposal. Or it just might mean the customer's assessment is accurate, in which case you need to develop specific strategies for creating capabilities differentiation.

Asking a series of structured questions helps shorten the list of possible problems and identify the actions most likely to improve your results the next time. The post-award protocol includes a set of questions to guide your thinking in developing lessons learned.

Improvement/Implementation Plan

The final step is to develop an action plan to correct deficiencies and fine-tune your business development process. This, too, is organized around the five areas addressed in the protocol: preproposal, proposal, postsubmittal, offer, and differentiation. The plan must be implemented, obviously, and subsequent post-award debriefs measure progress and effectiveness. The 0–5 scoring system will help in measuring progress over time by averaging multiple scored answers for each question to see if the average rises, stays steady, or declines. You can also track the average total score for each of the five areas in the protocol for a broader view of improvement or the lack of it.

A final thought: Let's say that you deploy the Post-Award Protocols for Continuous Business Development Improvement after your next twenty-five wins, and you get essentially the same customer answer to a particular question (e.g., "What did we do well in our early sales effort?") twenty-three times. You may have just defined a major driver of wins in that market. The same would be true regarding a major driver of losses should you get a consistent answer to a particular question after multiple unsuccessful pursuits. In either case, using this debrief process gives you a method for conducting trend analysis, which, in turn, can contribute to the critically important improvement in your overall business development, your proposals, and ultimately your business. And at the end of every day, month, and year, isn't that what it's all about?

Challenges for Readers

➤ Consider the internal questions in the post-award debrief model. What do they tell you that you might do differently and/or better prior to the RFP and after receiving it?

➤ Consider the differentiation questions in the post-award debrief model. Would a plan for creating differentiation, including strategies for implementing the plan, move your people and your business development initiatives forward? Do your markets attempt to commoditize your products and/or services, then tell you that you lost on price? Would differentiation help you to avoid that trap? To sell your price?

➤ Put a plan in place for your next proposal that, win or lose, will enable you to debrief with the customer. At the end of the debrief, ask the customer two additional questions: "Do you see value in this process?" and "Would you like to see all bidders debrief with you using this or a similar systematic process?"

Appendix A

THE ULTIMATE WEAPON

*Maximize Proposal Effectiveness
with Techies Who Can Sell*

GOLDEN RULE:
Nothing happens until somebody sells something.

Question: How do you know if an engineer is an extrovert?
Answer: He looks at *your* shoes when he's talking to you.

And so it goes. We've probably heard more engineer jokes over the years than any other kind, simply because we've worked with so many engineering, construction, aerospace, telecommunications, and high-tech organizations where this brand of humor thrives. With the occasional exception of the touchy engineer, the young one still puffed up with being an engineer, or the outright sorehead, we've found that

Figure A-1.

Dilbert

DILBERT reprinted by permission of United Feature Syndicate, Inc.

engineers and other technical professionals have a marvelous sense of detached humor about themselves and their professions.

Moreover, they readily admit that the engineer stereotype—nerd, dweeb, techno weenie, geek, data dumpster, wonk, gearhead, and so on—is only too appropriate. And although they typically process information, concepts, and ideas differently from the way nontechnical people do, they almost never wear propeller beanies (in public), white socks with a dark suit, or the same socks for more than a couple of days. Indeed, engineers who move into upper management and executive positions often become sharp dressers, not necessarily because they enjoy it but because it's a logical aspect of their career metamorphosis.

We can safely say that most of the engineers we've worked with are at once highly adaptive and almost religiously task-focused professionals who love one thing above all else in their work: solving problems, either as a practicing engineer or as one who has moved up to other, nontechnical business challenges. (For an extended look at how the technical mind prefers to process incoming information and transmit outgoing information, see Chapter 3.)

An engineer is a professional problem solver. There is nothing a good engineer enjoys more than a good problem followed by a great solution, and that's not only the best definition we've ever devised, it's a trait smart companies are learning to capitalize on to grow their businesses. These firms understand that their engineering world is actually populated with Dilberts, and the comic strip showing our introverted, analytical hero begging to be transferred out of sales and back into engineering represents a significant reality they can exploit for positive differentiation in the marketplace. Before we explore that notion further, we should point out that Dilbert reflects a set of perceptions about sales, selling, business development, and marketing widely held in engineering circles:

> While salespeople are out wining and dining prospects and customers, the engineers are back at the company doing the real work and delivering what customers pay for. Nobody ever spent money to be sold to and nobody ever will.

> Engineers solve problems that many salespeople can't even understand, let alone attack.

> People who work in sales do so because they can't work in engineering (or probably anywhere else, either).

> Selling means embracing a lower class of corporate citizenship because it requires groveling for and schmoozing with custom-

ers for the base reason of getting their money. Anyone who has ever come face-to-face with a car salesperson knows what selling really involves.

➤ Any engineer who willingly migrates into business development (sales or marketing) is either simply someone being lured to the dark side or someone who couldn't cut the technical mustard but needs to remain employed.

➤ Any engineer worth his or her calculator will avoid proposal duty, the least glamorous and most pressurized part of sales, as though it were a heat-seeking missile.

The work is chaotic, unsophisticated, sales driven, and unconnected to an engineer's performance review. If you could read the thought balloon over many engineers' heads when the topic of selling comes up, you'd see "If we engineer it, they will come" ("they" being an endless stream of customers dazzled by the sheer wizardry of what those engineers have done).

Thus, there's really no need for sales. Technical superiority sells itself. Arrogance? Maybe. Maybe not. These attitudes may be held by your company's technical professionals (and we hope that's not true), but over the years we've heard these Dilbertesque expressions countless times, and often in reference to proposals. To their credit, these engineers almost always couch their chagrin at being involved in some aspect of sales in dry humor or mock sarcasm. They're out of their element, undervalued, underutilized, and not playing to their strengths. However, it may also be true that they're between projects; it's just their turn; or as Dilbert's boss might put it, "You eat what you gather" (i.e., if you want to be a project engineer, you have to contribute to winning the project).

There is, however, another reason certain engineers end up in sales, and today many successful companies are figuring out how to create powerful differentiation by not endorsing the notion that all engineers are basically the same. Generally speaking, engineers may share certain characteristics—an introverted operating style, inductive logic, reliance on empirical data, a religious commitment to measurement, a nonintuitive and nonemotional approach to decision making, an abiding devotion to process flow, and a Herculean ability to remain task focused.

Yet among them are the rare, exceptional engineers, who aren't necessarily better engineers than their colleagues, but who are, without a doubt, different from them because they enjoy sales and selling.

They enjoy building relationships with prospects and customers. They are energized by competition and winning. They find professional satisfaction not just in solving problems in the project phase but in helping prospective customers define and understand the problems in the pre-award phase. They are professional problem solvers in a much broader sense. They can create the need for exploring draft solutions that will ultimately impact the specifications in the RFP and the selection of one company over all the others. And because they can do that, they serve as invaluable and enthusiastic members of proposal teams:

> They bring to bear technical and project-related strategies including technical ghosting to provide the customer with compelling reasons not to choose a competitor. (We discuss "ghosting"—what it is and how to do it—in Chapter 2.)
> They offer insights into what customers are really thinking and needing technically that no RFP will ever reveal. We concluded long ago that an RFP has never been written that would disclose everything you need to know to win these days, and the doer-seller is a prime resource for the additional insight needed to gain a competitive edge in the proposal. It can make the critical difference between giving the customer a compliant proposal and giving them a fully responsive proposal.

(Chapter 10 articulates the differences between a compliant proposal and a fully responsive one. In brief, if a customer were to award letter grades to competing proposals, a compliant one would receive a C, which is insufficient to win today. You need to get an A, and the customer will award that grade only if your proposal is not only compliant but fully responsive. Also see Chapter 1, which concludes with definitions for the full spectrum of letter grades.)

For these hybrid engineers—those who have an extra chromosome labeled "sales capability" in their DNA—it's not a matter of ceasing to be engineers, it's a matter of being one thing while becoming another.

When companies recognize and grow their doer-sellers, everyone (except the competition) wins. Most of a company's technical staff does fine technical work, and they should be compensated and recognized accordingly. The doer-seller, on the other hand, can still perform well technically but is also engaged in winning the work that sustains the company and all who work there, engineers and nonengineers alike. This rare breed should be compensated and recognized on a different level, their career track pointing sharply upward.

One of our clients, a global engineering firm, has in place a long-standing policy stating that although they are a technical organization through and through, anyone—including their engineers—who aspires to upper management/executive positions will spend a minimum of two years (more likely up to five) in business development. Moreover, that journey to the top typically begins with an arduous stint in the proposal department analyzing RFPs, developing win strategies or recasting pre-RFP versions of them, writing theme statements, developing visuals, generating text, doing production work, establishing and supporting review teams, drafting cover letters, assembling and shipping finished proposals, and so on. And when the right people (i.e., the Dilberts with that extra chromosome) are selected, their performance and execution in the sales process, not just on proposals, often is astonishing.

When companies invest in knowledge, skills, tools, and coaching for their doer-sellers, they are investing in differentiation their current and prospective customers will value. Doer-sellers provide their companies and their customers with many advantages:

➤ While becoming an exceptional engineer requires years of formal education followed by more years of experience, becoming an effective salesperson requires a far shorter learning curve if the will to succeed is strong. The prospective doer-seller needs to obtain the knowledge, skills, and tools necessary to win contracts, (e.g., account management, relationship management, supply chain management, behavioral differentiation, opportunity management, positioning to win, proposal management, presentations, and negotiations)—all of which are readily available and can be learned in a fairly short amount of time. (In Chapter 2, we explore the elegant simplicity of selling versus the complexity of achieving and applying technical expertise. The key differentiator here is recognizing and acting upon the concept that prospective customers need clear and relevant answers to only four basic questions. The provider who gives them those answers gains a tremendous advantage.)

➤ In a complex world, customers are faced with complex problems requiring complex solutions. The last thing customers need from providers is more complexity. Instead, they seek clarity, simplicity, and a clear path to success. More than anyone else, the doer-seller has the ability to design and articulate that path. The pure salesperson has to call in technical reinforcements and then attempt to communicate an approach that's largely a mystery to all parties, including the salesperson. The doer-seller possesses expertise in both the substance of the message and how to communicate it in ways that will be understood by the customers' technical and non-technical personnel.

➤ Thus, the doer-seller eliminates the need for the middle person brokering the customer relationship. The pure salesperson turns to the technical expert in an attempt to gain trust, credibility, and compatibility with the prospect. The doer-seller, having subject matter expertise plus the appropriate selling skills, proceeds to create the relationship firsthand. (If we've learned anything in our work, it's that at some point fairly early in the relationship, prospective customers crave direct and sustained contact with experts rather than with a "gofer" who has to find the expertise and relay it to the customer.)

➤ The motivated doer-seller is an invaluable resource in the proposal phase; someone who can add value at practically every turn by scrutinizing the offer, correlating it to the pricing, and providing numerous litmus tests on the proposal to ensure that what is being proposed is meeting the customer's needs and that the messages are getting through loud and clear. The doer-seller also contributes by understanding better than anyone else in the sales group what the competition is offering, how formidable it will be, and what technical strategies can best neutralize it.

➤ The doer-seller is an invaluable resource in the presentation phase of the process. The last thing the customer wants from a presentation is the classic sales pitch: breezy, overly rehearsed patter, slick slide shows, and a string of executive platitudes. The antidote (and differentiator) for this approach is putting your best doer-sellers in front of the customer to walk the talk, thereby giving them compelling, substantive reasons to choose you and not someone else (which is a good definition of what selling in the best sense of the word is all about).

Never forget that the presentation is basically a chemistry test. There is no absence of engineering talent in the marketplace today. If that's all you bring to the customer, you'd better have the lowest price. On the other hand if, in addition to technical capability, you successfully pass the chemistry test by providing the right answers to one all-important question—"Do we want to work with you?"—then you are breaking from the pack and positioning your company for the win. By definition, the doer-seller is the best weapon in your arsenal for achieving this end.

GOLDEN RULE:
If you've gotten to the shortlist presentation, you've successfully answered the customer's first question: "Can they do the work?" Now you must answer the second question: "Do we want to work with them?" If the customer thinks you can do the work but they don't want to work with you, your likelihood of winning plummets to almost zero.

When working with technology clients to improve their business development effectiveness, we consistently ask a series of analytical questions including, "What are your critical weaknesses, not as you see them but as they are perceived by your current and prospective customers?" The answer we hear far more than any other is "Arrogance." Ironically, this answer (clearly a negative in any company's efforts to get and keep customers) is often accompanied by a slight grin, at once acknowledging that the answer is true but also that it's both inevitable and justified. Interestingly, we've heard almost every first-tier engineering firm in the world claim arrogance as a weakness with that same grin, and this chorus has driven us to a quirky conclusion: Arrogance runs so wide and deep that it's time to declare it a commodity weakness! Everyone's got it, appears willing to live with it, and actually seeks ways to promote it.

In proposals, presentations, and brochures, we find the *rhetoric of arrogance*, the language of "us": *We're* state of the art. *We* wrote the book. *We're* on the cutting edge. *We're* a recognized industry leader. *We're* best of class. And please never forget that *we're* uniquely qualified.

That conclusion leads us to a few others:

➤ If you want to fail the chemistry test and receive a resounding "No!" to the question, "Do we want to work with you?" allow unrestrained arrogance to permeate all your interactions with the customer pre-RFP as well as in the proposal and presentation.

➤ Companies that square off against arrogance among their technical staff realize that arrogance is not a behavior, it is an attitude that drives behaviors. Therefore, they work to change the attitude. This profound shift in thinking is easier to define than to do, of course, but some of the best, industry-leading companies we've worked with have launched cultural change initiatives under such banners as Customer First, Customer Focus, Customer Intimacy (a wording we might want to reconsider but the intent is right-minded), Service First, and so on. Whatever the label, the motive includes establishing new ways of seeing and serving customers rather than oneself. (For an in-depth discussion of behavioral strategy, see "Creating a Behavioral Differentiation Strategy" in our earlier book *The Behavioral Advantage*.[1])

➤ Over and over we've seen the engineer doer-sellers become the leaders of their organizations' efforts to break from the pack of commodity arrogance, first to understand how their industry—not just their own firms—is perceived in the marketplace, and then to determine what it will take to be different and better than everyone else. Doer-sellers are the first to recognize what customers have long understood: Technical capability is largely available from a host of providers, each claiming to be the best but in reality having about the same engineering prowess as all the other companies. Furthermore, doer-sellers know about the impact arrogance has on customers and are well suited to mitigate that weakness with a fine blend of technical knowledge communicated in the context of a customer's needs and goals.

A client recently quipped over lunch, "Engineers. Can't live with 'em. Can't live without 'em." Then he chuckled into his soup. He was, of course, an engineer with a permanent kink in his tie, and had he been more outgoing, he would have stared at *our* soup while he made his comment on the profession. So, although it may be true that engineers make the world go 'round, it's the process itself and the fact that it works that's so compelling. It's elegant. It's robust. It's great engineering. It's the solving of the problem. It's what Dilbert loves to do and will always do unless his boss sends him to sales.

Challenges for Readers

➤ How does your work in an engineering or other technical company shape your organization's culture? How would you characterize an engineering culture as opposed to a nonengineering culture? What impact, positive or negative, does such a culture have on how your customers perceive your company and the people who represent it in the marketplace? If your company is engineering focused, what would be required to shift it to a market-driven, customer-focused organization without losing that engineering passion?

➤ Brainstorm with colleagues possible answers to these questions: If we were to look among our engineers for that rare one with the extra chromosome in his or her DNA (i.e., the person who is not only a fine engineer but who genuinely loves business development and all that it involves), what would we look for? What outward signs could we seek that one or more of our technical staff is a strong candidate for becoming a doer-seller?

➤ If you were to create a model of the engineer as doer-seller, what would it be? What capabilities beyond the strictly technical would this person possess? What would this doer-seller do and do differently from the pure engineer? What could this person contribute to your company's business success?

Note

1. Terry R. Bacon and David G. Pugh, *The Behavioral Advantage: What the Smartest, Most Successful Companies Do Differently to Win in the B2B Arena* (New York: AMACOM, 2004).

Appendix B

MODELS OF ISSUE-DRIVEN AND AD-STYLE EXECUTIVE SUMMARIES

Figure B-1. **Model issues-driven, brochure-style executive summary.** By using the customer's key issues in selecting a provider as the basis for you executive summary, you are demonstrating customer focus and a deep understanding of their needs.

Why Howard Rose Financial Services?

Telecomp wants a flexible plan that will meet the needs of more employees. Flexibility and employee satisfaction are hallmarks of our innovative, award-winning, cafeteria-style employee benefit plan, HR Café. HR Café features the largest selection of benefits available locally, including high-yield, no-load mutual funds and Flexible Spending Accounts (FSAs) for employees; plus low-cost, low-maintenance administration for employers; and world-class customer service for both. Here's what's on the menu:

Return on Investment

- No-load mutual funds with the highest average yields in the industry motivate long-term investing and provide high returns on individual and company dollars.
- Low administrative burden reduces your overhead costs.

Selection and Quality of Benefits

- More choices in type and cost of benefits encourage employee participation.
- Individual employee benefit statements help employees appreciate the company's investment in them.

Cost/Ease of Administration

- Not having to deal with multiple vendors reduces administrative time and cost.
- A single, integrated statement simplifies the accounting task.
- Reporting options give you the information you need, in the format you want, further reducing the administrative burden.
- We ensure compliance and provide continuing education so you are always in compliance with state and federal laws—no hassles, no fines.

Customer Service

- Our dedicated consultants provide complete support, including on-site training, further reducing your administrative burden.
- World-class customer service, available 24/7, means questions are answered and problems solved quickly.

Vendor Experience and Track Record

- Being one of the world's oldest and most respected investment firms, with more Fortune 100 and 500 clients than any other firm, means you can be confident in your benefit provider.
- Local offices with dedicated benefit consultants in every state enable us to respond rapidly to your needs as you grow.

Return on Investment

Industry-leading fund performance and reduced administrative burden mean both you and your employees get the highest possible return on your investment in the company benefit plan.

HR Café performs well in terms of both the return on employee investment dollars and the return on the company's investment of time and money in maintaining an employee benefit plan. Instead of focusing solely on short-term gains, we recognize that long-term participation guarantees the most lucrative results for the company and its employees. Our no-load mutual funds allow maximum reinvestment and reduce fees. Our Flexible Spending Accounts (FSAs) save employee tax dollars, with significant tax deductions for the employer as well.

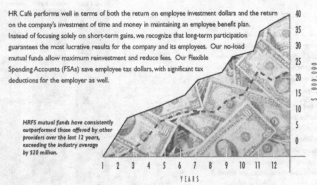

HRFS mutual funds have consistently outperformed those offered by other providers over the last 12 years, exceeding the industry average by $20 million.

Other Companies

37% 33%
30%

HR Participation

28% 27%
45%

HR Café allows employees to customize benefits to their unique circumstances and desires. Employees assess their own needs and make their own investment decisions, promoting "ownership" of the benefit plan and increasing satisfaction by eliminating fees for benefits of little value to the employee. On-site seminars and free first-time benefit consulting sessions help employees assess their risk tolerance, understand where their dollars go, and help them feel more confident in their decisions.

HRFS clients (many of whom are large, multi-state firms with more than one benefit plan) report that their employees, on average, are more highly satisfied—not just with the plan, but with their employers—and are willing to invest more in HR Café than other plans.

■ Participated in Full Benefits Package
□ Did not participate in a Flexible Spending Plan
■ Did not participate in a Health Plan

HR Café Plan increases employee participation over other benefit plans.

Selection and Quality of Benefits

HR Café offers the widest array of benefits available through a single vendor, maximizing employee participation and satisfaction with their employer as well as their benefit plan.

HR Café provides all the benefit options a diverse group of employees could need or want, all available through a single provider who assumes the administrative burden for you. No other single-provider plan offers as many options.

More employees are inclined to invest when they can choose the ideal package for their age, family status, and risk tolerance. The HR Café plan offers Telecomp employees a side variety of benefit options ranging from popular conventional investments to comprehensive insurance coverage to unique and individual choices that appeal to diverse lifestyles.

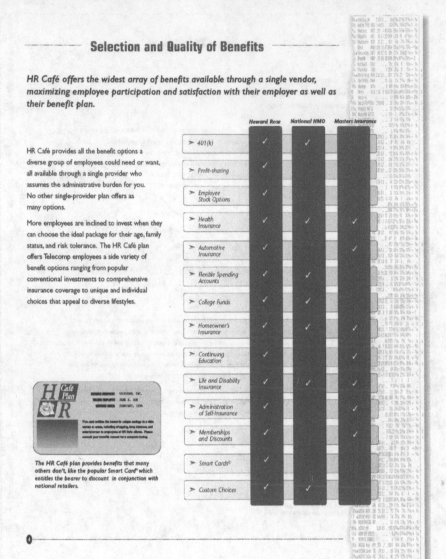

	Howard Rose	National HMO	Masters Insurance
401(k)	✓	✓	
Profit-sharing	✓		
Employee Stock Options	✓		
Health Insurance	✓	✓	✓
Automotive Insurance	✓		✓
Flexible Spending Accounts	✓	✓	
College Funds	✓	✓	
Homeowner's Insurance	✓		✓
Continuing Education	✓		✓
Life and Disability Insurance	✓	✓	✓
Administration of Self-Insurance	✓		✓
Memberships and Discounts	✓		✓
Smart Cards©	✓		
Custom Choices	✓	✓	

The HR Café plan provides benefits that many others don't, like the popular Smart Card® which entitles the bearer to discount in conjunction with national retailers.

Cost and Ease of Administration

HR Café is designed to simplify and reduce the time your employees have to spend on every task associated with the company benefit plan, from implementation to accounting and reporting. The compliance task is eliminated, which not only reduces overhead but also minimizes your risk.

The HR Café plan will cut Telecomp's administrative costs dramatically when compared to using a variety of different service providers. HR Café offers all the benefits of an HMO, retirement plan, life insurance company, and a variety of other providers under a single service fee, with a single monthly statement.

HRFS assumes the entire administrative burden for your comprehensive benefit plan. Instead of having to go to multiple vendors with different paperwork and procedures, your human resources staff can get everything they need through a single phone call. Like all your employees, your HR professionals will be happier because they will be free to manage individual employee challenges, without additional headaches and hassles.

As an employer, you are required by law to provide continuing education for your staff to ensure compliance with the many laws, rules, and regulations applicable to your employee benefit plan. We assume your compliance burden and provide continuing education at no cost, removing your worries about paperwork, fines, and lawsuits. Our specialists understand changing employee benefit laws, and our research ensures that we are always on the leading edge of employee benefits management and human resources trends.

Federal Laws

Paperwork

Continuing Education

Our compliance specialists are experienced in dealing with multi-state companies like Telecomp and will help you navigate the maze of federal and state compliance.

State Laws

Customer Service

Whether they need to talk to a person or just want to check their accounts online, Howard Rose provides your benefit plan managers and employees the help and information they need, around the clock.

Studies show HRFS has a reputation for world-class customer service, the best in the industry. Our dedicated local benefit consultants visit each site in their area at least once a month to meet with employees. In addition, our friendly customer service operators are available 24 hours a day, 7 days a week, toll-free. Excellence in service means your employees will love their benefit plan.

We will send a member of our Customer Advocate Team (CAT) to your headquarters to learn about your culture, your employees' concerns, and your business operations and tailor our plan to your specifications. Our full-time account representatives will deliver thorough on-site training to your administrators with consistent, continuous ongoing support.

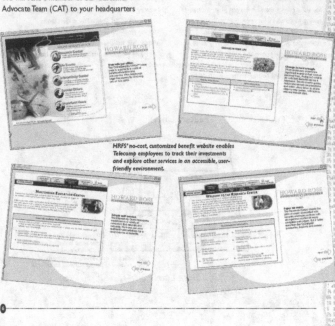

HRFS' no-cost, customized benefit website enables Telecomp employees to track their investments and explore other services in an accessible, user-friendly environment.

Vendor Experience and Track Record

Howard Rose is small enough to be flexible and responsive to your local offices, yet large and capable enough to support your multi-state plan as you grow.

HRFS has more experience, more top companies as clients, and more local offices with employee benefit consultants who understand the culture and economy of the area. We aggressively recruit the most experienced and innovative investment managers, account managers, and other specialists for our client benefit management teams, particularly those who are capable of addressing the unique needs of high-tech companies like Telecomp.

HRFS is small enough to be fast and flexible, with the resources to support you as you grow and the innovations to keep the cost of your plan below and the quality of benefits above those of our competitors. Offices in all 50 U.S. states and a client base totalling over 15 million employees provide assurance that we will be around and able to support your future expansion.

Benefit specialists at HRFS offices in all 50 states understand local economies and employee cultures, helping us effectively manage your multi-state plan.

Telecomp's Customer Advocate Team

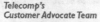

Patrice McCormick
Account Manager
15 years experience

Denise Kowal
Continuing Education
18 years experience

Charles Flavins
Customer Service Manager
16 years experience

Robert Tis
Investment Advisor
20 years experience

Ben Kennedy
Insurance Plans
28 years experience

Telecomp's Customer Advocate Team is comprised of the very best of the HRFS team. With over 97 years of combined experience in successful employee benefit programs, these executives and administrators will help you create and maintain the ideal plan for each and every Telecomp employee. The CAT team and support for Telecomp's benefit plan will be located in our San Francisco office, just a 10-minute drive from Telecomp headquarters.

Why HRFS?

▶ *Industry-leading returns on employee and company investment dollars = company and employees make more money*

▶ *A customized benefit plan for virtually every employee means greater participation = more satisfied employees*

▶ *Affordable plan with dramatically reduced administrative burden and fewer compliance headaches = cost savings, low risk*

▶ *Friendly 24/7 customer service plus online tracking = information and help when you need it*

▶ *Experience, resources, and reputation = a provider you won't outgrow*

Figure B-2. **Model ad-style executive summary.** The ad-style executive summary is still focusing on the customer's key issues but is addressing them with a highly graphic and more "outside-the-box" communication design.

The challenge of sharing Alta Vista with the world··········

Pinnacle Structures, LLC, and SkyTram Corporation

have the *expertise* to *transform*

Altaguaya's precious national landmark

into a *world-class* tourist attraction that is both

profitable and *environmentally sound.*

Working in partnership with the Altaguayan Department

of the Interior and using local resources, we will build

beautiful, low-profile ground facilities

with *fast, safe* transportation to

the trailhead on La Noche Peak, providing

easy access to the Alta Vista ruins

without degrading the ruins

or the surrounding site.

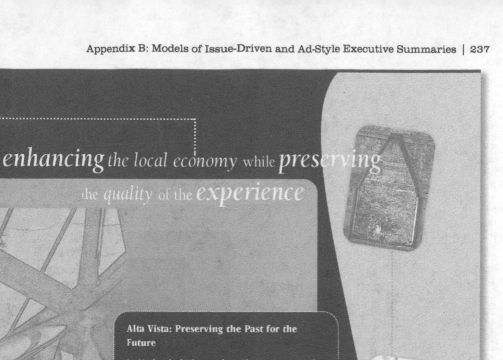

enhancing the local economy while *preserving* the *quality* of the *experience*

Alta Vista: Preserving the Past for the Future

La Noche, the highest peak in Altaguaya, is topped by the famous Alta Vista ruins. Each year, thousands make the difficult and dangerous ascent up the mountain to view the most remarkably preserved and architecturally significant ruins in the southern hemisphere.

Pinnacle Structures has the expertise to make this national treasure accessible to the world. With the unparalleled design and construction capabilities of the Pinnacle/SkyTram partnership, the proposed improvements—ground-level visitors' center and lodge, paved roadways, a new parking facility, a ground-to-top tramway, and a mid-mountain restaurant—will transform the La Noche region into a sought-after travel destination. Pinnacle Structures' SkyTram to Alta Vista will provide the first, crucial step in the commercial development of this location.

Experience meets expert project management ·················

Pinnacle Structures and SkyTram have *worked together* on several large-scale international projects, bringing them in *on time* and *under budget*. Among these are Olympic facilities and ski resorts in the U.S. and Europe, and the *recently completed* *Valparaíso al Abismo* project in the Chilean Andes, which includes the *world's longest* ground-to-peak transportation system.

Our *unique* Project Checkpoint system provides *constant collaboration* and *communication* with the project owner. The audit function of the process assures *quality control* and *cost containment*.

Constant collaborati

Conceptual Phase

AD Appp

- Pre-project planning
- Collaborative goal setting
- Detailed bid

- Pre
- Sub pre
- Gua max

Our collaborative Project Checkpoint process p with specific approval checkpoints to ensure yo

Name	Location	Planne
Campo al Abismo Amusement Park	Argentina	June 19
Los Hermanos Gordos Trail Improvements and Facilities	Chile	January
Tortulaga Ski Resort	Peru	August
Navarro Mountain Ski Resort	Chile	Septem
Nuevagrande Dude Ranch	Colombia	Februa

Pinnacle and SkyTram have collaborate countries. All five were completed on o

ntrolling **quality** and **costs** through

constant **collaboration**

ces your cost and risk

| ign | ADOI | **Construction** |
| ase | **Approved** | **Phase** |

ign

- Subcontractor quality control
- Periodic schedule/budget review
- Periodic site/facilities inspections

ontinuous client involvement throughout the process, ith our performance.

| rformance | Budget Performance | |
Actual Completion	Planned	Actual
May 1998	$12.5 million	$12.3 million
January 1999	$6.7 million	$5.5 million
August 1999	$58.9 million	$57.2 million
March 2000	$68.3 million	$68.4 million
February 2001	$22.0 million	$21.1 million

* Pinnacle-Sky Tram partnership All budget figures in U.S. dollars

f five recent successful projects in neighboring chedule and on or under budget.

Mastering the mountain ...

The Pinnacle/SkyTram team is uniquely qualified to tackle the geographic challenges inherent in this project. The terrain and project size are similar in scope to five previous Pinnacle/SkyTram projects. With a permanent South American office in nearby Sao Paulo, Brazil, Pinnacle has the equipment and resources already in place to commence work on the Alta Vista project.

SkyTram is the leading designer of tramway and aerial transportation systems. The top 12 ski resorts world wide use SkyTram chairlifts. In 1991, SkyTram designed and built what is currently the longest tramway in the world in Albuquerque, New Mexico (United States).

Pinnacle has also completed five other large-scale construction projects in neighboring countries to Altaguaya. Reliable supplier networks and familiarity with local operating procedures are already established.

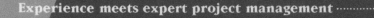

Experience meets expert project management ....

Pinnacle **pre-qualifies** local subcontractors to participate in *large-scale* projects, assessing the skills of the workforce and *training* where necessary. The *local workers* receive *skill development* and experience, along with *attractive compensation*.

Our projects have *consistently exceeded* the *environmental requirements* set forth by the United Nations Environmental Council. IEC "Clean Site" *inspections* ensure *diligence* in preserving the *natural* environment.

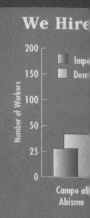

We Hire

Number of Workers

200

150 — Imp

100 — Dom

50

25

0

Campo a
Abísmo

Rewards of partneri
Pinnacle/SkyTram:

A local hiring office will
place for the duration of
pay scale averages 10 pe
government-published st
wage for the region. Tra
will benefit future local
Expenditures for many r
labor will be funneled di
economy.

The publicity generated
struction event and incre
Alta Vista ruins will boo
a vacation destination, b
the region.

livering *economic* and environmental **benefits**

through *local participation*

Train More Local Workers

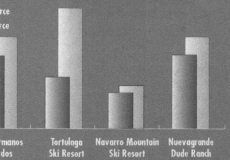

rce
rce

| manos dos | Tortulaga Ski Resort | Navarro Mountain Ski Resort | Nuevagrande Dude Ranch |

nrl remain in
Pinnacle's
than the
struction
al workforce
efforts.
plies, and
nto the local

tious con
bility to the
Altaguaya as
e revenue to

Keeping the area pristine ...

Pinnacle projects always exceed international environmental standards. Because we have completed several projects similar in scope in South America, we are familiar with the unique environmental challenges and concerns of this region. A 1998 project in neighboring Argentina received an International Environmental Commission Award for low-impact environmental friendliness.

Other awards we've received:

2000 - Salt Lake Olympic Committee
Cleanest, Most Responsive Contractor

1999 - Andean Environmental Council
Award of Recognition for work
on ski resorts in Chile and Peru

1998 - South American Green Committee
Awareness in Construction

Why Pinnacle/SkyTram?

▸ *CONFIDENCE* - We have proven expertise in international construction.

▸ *TIMELINESS/COST CONSCIOUSNESS* - Our "project checkpoints" ensure Pinnacle projects are completed on time and on budget. Disciplined, professional project management.

▸ *PROSPERITY* - We guarantee maximum local participation including skill development and job placement.

▸ *PRESERVATION/STEWARDSHIP* - Our environmental standards protect Altaguaya from costly damage and fines.

"The earth is the mother of all things, the Great Mother. She is the guardian who caringly watches over all that exists. She has burba and we live on her."

- Cacique General Enrique Guerrero

Index

About the Authors

David G. Pugh is cofounder and executive vice president of Lore International Institute and an internationally respected authority on business development.

He has worked with clients throughout the United States and in Canada, Brazil, Hong Kong, Japan, United Arab Emirates, New Zealand, Australia, Portugal, France, Germany, England, Scotland, South Africa, the Netherlands, Singapore, Sweden, Switzerland, and Norway. As the architect of Lore's proposal training and consulting services as well as the author of *Proposing to Win*, his knowledge of proposal design and communication techniques has helped generate billions of dollars in signed contracts for Lore clients.

David has worked for more than twenty-five years in both the academic and business worlds. He has conducted hundreds of engagements for more than 10,000 Fortune 500 personnel and has helped thousands of engineers, marketers, sales executives, business development professionals, and managers improve performance by providing practical, down-to-earth techniques that work. An award-winning author and instructional designer, David has been a primary developer of Lore's business development services and a popular keynote speaker at more than twenty regional and national conferences in just the last two years.

Based on his work with Lore clients around the world and across industries, David has coauthored two recent books with Terry Bacon: *Winning Behavior: What the Smartest, Most Successful Companies Do Differently* and *The Behavioral Advantage: What the Smartest, Most Successful Companies Do Differently to Win in the B2B Arena*.

David's education includes a Ph.D. in American Studies, Washington State University; an M.A. in English, Washington State University; and a B.A. in English, Eastern Washington University. He is also a graduate of executive programs at The Wharton School, Stanford Graduate School of Business, and University of Chicago Graduate School of Business.

Terry R. Bacon is cofounder and president of Lore International Institute and a recognized expert in business development.

His client work includes advising business development pursuit teams on major winning opportunities, including the Space Station, the Advanced Tactical Fighter, the T800 nuclear submarine design, and numerous other multibillion-dollar procurements. He is considered an expert on opportunity management, competitive strategy, business development audits, and process redesign. He has delivered addresses to conferences and forums in South Africa, Mexico, Canada, Australia, Japan, Singapore, and throughout Europe on such topics as leadership development, behavioral differentiation, global account leadership, client relationship development, and customer engagement skills.

Terry wrote *Selling to Major Accounts* and has coauthored, with David Pugh, *Winning Behavior: What the Smartest, Most Successful Companies Do Differently* and *The Behavioral Advantage: What the Smartest, Most Successful Companies Do Differently to Win in the B2B Arena*.

He has a B.S. in engineering from the United States Military Academy at West Point and a Ph.D. in literature and theatre from The American University. He has also studied business, marketing, and related disciplines at Roosevelt University, Goddard College, University of Chicago Graduate School of Business, Stanford University Graduate School of Business, Wharton School of Business, and Harvard Business School.

Printed in the USA
CPSIA information can be obtained
at www.ICGtesting.com
JSHW03082731023
50669JS00022B/210